GEORGE LOWE

ANG NYIMA II/M

CHARLES WYLIE

ALFRED GREGORY

GRIFFITH PUGH

JAMES MORRIS

WILFRID NOYCE

MICHAEL WESTMACOTT

DA TENSING

SOUTH COL

LOOKING DOWN THE CWM

SOUTH COL
A Personal Story of the Ascent of Everest

by

WILFRID NOYCE

Foreword by SIR JOHN HUNT

WILLIAM SLOANE ASSOCIATES, INC.
Publishers   New York

Line Drawings and End-Papers by
A. J. VEILHAN
with the cooperation of the Author

First published in Great Britain in 1954.
First published in the United States in 1955.

Second Printing, February, 1955.

To

MY WIFE AND SONS

Contents

List of Maps

List of Coloured Plates

List of Drawings

List of Photographs

xi

Foreword

All of us who climbed Everest have brought back imper-
ishable memories of those momentous months last spring and
summer, memories not only of what we did, but of how we
felt in the doing. But unlike most of his companions, Wilfrid
Noyce was ever recording his thoughts as they came to him,
day by day, almost hour by hour. My most vivid memory of
him was his patient perseverance in the writing of his journal. As we walked towards Everest through the green foreground of Nepal, he was ever at it, in the tent while we chattered, or the shade of some boulder or bush. While Charles
Evans sketched and others photographed the events upon
the stage of our adventure and its great backcloth of mountains, he was storing it up in his notebook; while some chased
butterflies, beetles or grasshoppers, he was capturing some
impression as it flitted through his mind. And he continued
to make his notes in the Icefall, the Western Cwm, on the
Face of Lhotse, upon the South Col itself. *South Col* is the
product of all that labour. In it we can follow again the story
of Everest in 1953, but we see it afresh through the eyes of
one who is not only a great mountaineer, but whose attitude
to mountains is that of a poet.

Most of all, perhaps, there looms in our memories the
great mountain itself and our relationship with it. Before
even we set eyes upon it, while we were studying the problems with which we would be faced, Everest began to fill our
minds almost to the exclusion of everything else. It was an
inspiration, a vision. Later, the mental picture we had sev-
erally conjured up was confirmed, corrected or confounded,
when we first caught sight of that thrusting pyramid from
afar, flaunting its mile-long pennant of snow cloud above its
attendant satellites. And as we approached it, the vision grew
until the mountain became real; Everest, focussing our desires, was thus clothed with personality. To some, Everest
was mighty Nature herself, inimical to Man, out-matching

his puny strength, but a worthy opponent to his spirit; to others, Everest was, as Tenzing put it, "Like a friend."

But to Wilfrid, Everest appeared neither as friend nor foe. The spirit of the mountain seemed to him to be supremely aloof from our struggles, sure in the knowledge that our footsteps would be effaced overnight, indifferent to the brief triumph which left the mountain unscathed. Perhaps he is right: such concepts are playthings of the mind. But I fancy it is in this sphere that the ascent of Everest will endure. Wilfrid Noyce, who contributed greatly to our physical achievement, has now made a further contribution, no less fine, to the story of Everest.

JOHN HUNT.

Camberley,
February 6th, 1954.

Preface

There are many books about Mount Everest. Some might say too many. Each addition, therefore, to the long list requires a larger apology, and I must give briefly my two reasons for entering this crowded field. The first is that among all the books I have read on Himalayan travel, very few give the "inside story," to use an over-worked expression, of a man's life at high altitudes; or make you *see* the scenes that he saw. Of those few I would mention specially Howard Somervell's *After Everest*, Eric Shipton's *Nanda Devi*, and Frank Smythe's *Camp Six*. Usually I am left, however good the book, with a myriad trifling but persistent questions in my head. What does it feel like waking up? Did he ever change his underpants? What did he actually *say* to the Sherpas when they gave up, and could they understand? Just what did he think of when he was trying to get to sleep in that high wind? And at lower levels it is the same story, for their scenes need an equally intimate descriptive treatment if they are to live. The smell of the Sherpas, the sensation of hunger jumbled with the æsthetic joy of peak-gazing, bathes after dusty plods, the talk with the wizened lama; these are all an intensely personal experience and must be described in personal terms, or let us say in terms of personality.

Therefore I was irresistibly tempted to try what may be impossible, and what a leader's expedition book does not from its very nature do. The task of such a book is to describe, in the compass of a few hundred pages, something of everything that was conceived and done by a large number of people for more than a year. John Hunt's book is the magnificent record of what has proved an historic achievement. But there may remain a further interest in what the members of the party, their untidy everyday individual selves, were seeing and feeling and thinking through all those months; in the closer expression of their fears and doubts and delights. My attempt is complementary to *The Ascent*

xvii

of Everest, now a classic of mountaineering literature. I aim to give not the collective, but the personal story, as it cannot be given in lectures, and certainly not in the expedition film. In the former, time is too short; in the latter, however superlative the photography, you are looking at the scene through your own eyes, not those of the climber. The arrangement and commentary, however expert, are necessarily ordered by men who were not on the mountain. The best, and it is a good best, that can be hoped is a series of vignettes of certain incidents that will go to complete the final picture.

I am not Ed Hillary or Tenzing giving their summit chapter. This means that, as the writer of a personal story, I may even have one advantage, that of being able to focus their crowning climb more clearly and with less modesty than they themselves, and to relate it to the struggles of the whole expedition. The views are often better from the sides than the summit of a great mountain; though this truth may have escaped the persons in all countries who seemed at one time to have no idea at all that there was a mountain to be climbed below the summit reached at 11:30 A.M. on May 29th, 1953. If your interest is limited to that summit, read no further. But if you do read on, in the hope of a full and true picture of the adventure, you must accept an apology for the corresponding *dis*advantage from which I suffer. I am only one person, and you will hear the story of only one member of a group. You will receive the impression that I did much more on the mountain than I did, because I can only give you my own experience. To redress the balance you would need eleven such books, with perhaps one by the Sherpas thrown in. This apology is due to my companions even more than to my readers, for it is the relation of myself to them and the mountain that I am recording. Suffice it to say that their parts, if they had written them here, would be as big or bigger than my own.

But there is a second and more urgent reason for writing. Everyone who has been upon a great mountain must feel the need to pay tribute, as it were, by expressing his relation to it in some way. The painter will paint, the photographer will photograph, the scientist will scratch and theorise upon its surface. Each will use the medium that comes naturally to him. My own reaction was to write, in prose and verse, about the experiences I was sharing. Much of the verse written high up was rubbish, and I never dared let on that I was writing it. Some poems I have included at the end of this book. I needed to grind into words something of the emotion that was holding me; not only at the beauty of slope and cliff and cloud and pinnacle, but also at the sense of common endeavour. This last feeling is extremely difficult to put into words. I am afraid that most of the newspaper attempts, received on the march back, to praise the "high valour" and "courage on lonely heights" of the "little band of intrepid mountaineers" caused a good deal of innocent laughter. But although the thing is not quite as simple as that, the feeling of unity in endeavour is at bottom a fine one, which we all try to express in our own way. When we were exploring the country south and west of Everest in April, from every height the huge black pyramid dominated a complete circle of princely peaks, just as it dominated our common thought. It stood there like a presence summoning us, hemming our every view. Now we have trodden upon it in company and climbed it. The desire to record this fact artistically is as natural as would be the urge to describe a Miserere in the Sistine Chapel. In these circumstances, one who, like myself, has been accustomed to turn his experiences and readings into words, has no choice but to put pen to paper. I knew before I went that I must scribble something, even if I were laid low with chilblains at Base Camp.

In writing, I had and have a hope that there is still a gap here in literature which is being gradually filled. A tradition is growing in Himalayan writing of terse and brilliantly exciting narrative like Shipton's. But Everest and the other great peaks have so far been treated mainly from the point of view of the climber. I am a climber too, but I dare to think that there is great hope for future generations of literary and artistic travellers as well. When Mont Blanc was first climbed, in 1786, Alpine literature was in its infancy.

It would be almost impossible to write a book like this about an unhappy party. Either the facts must be slurred and distorted, or the unhappiness increased by references which might breed a whole series of differing and acrimonious accounts. Our party was in its way the happiest I have ever joined. This was greatly due to a leader who united affections; it was quite simply true that all were friends, Sherpas and British alike. We all got on well on the very simple planes. There was not much profound discussion of the Universe at high camps; there was a great deal of discussion of food. There was a wealth of anecdote and a pleasing unwillingness, even among the experts, to be pedantic or heavy-handed about pet subjects. And always, through all the expedition, there was laughter.

To these friends and companions I shall owe this book; I already owe many illustrations, particularly to Alfred Gregory. And I have other debts of gratitude to pay. I must thank the Himalayan Committee, both for giving me the chance to write and for co-operation while I was writing. I must thank those who have read the text, made suggestions and corrected many inaccuracies: particularly Professor A. C. Pigou, John Hunt, Tom Bourdillon and Alan Hill; the authorities of Charterhouse, for kindness, help and patience throughout these months; L. P. Kirwan for many things, and the Map Room of the Royal Geographical Society under E. E. T. Day for generous assistance with the illustrations; The Indian Air Force for three magnificent aerial photographs, taken a few days after the summit had been climbed; the many friends and companions who have given advice and correction on special points; lastly and above all my wife, who, after backing me up stoutly in my absence last year, has been constantly by me as I wrote the book, and typed much of it herself.

SOUTH COL

A.J.VEILHAN.

1

Are You Free to Come to Everest?

October 11th, 1952—February 12th, 1953

1

It was Saturday, October 11th, 1952. My first son was to be christened that afternoon. In the morning I was teaching, as usual; when I arrived home for lunch my wife told me that there had been a trunk call from London, from John Hunt. I shall not forget the afternoon, for the feeling of unreality that lay over it like a cloak. I had a fair guess what the telephone call meant.

It was three days before we finally made contact. I came out of the classroom to do it.

"Please look at the irregular verbs on page ninety-six for a few minutes," I said to the form. Over the long-distance phone I heard John's voice.

"If you *can* come to London, Wilf, there are one or two things about Everest I'd like your opinion on. And secondly, are you free to come yourself?"

So it had happened, as I had suspected, and perhaps it came as more of a shock to me than to any other member of our party. I had planned no such thing. I thought I had seen my last of the high Himalaya, and for the summer I hoped to visit Italy and finish a book about some of the nineteenth-century travellers there. Nor did I know how fit I was. But now—into all plans this utterly new idea had intruded. And I think my wife and I felt that there was something of fate about it. A choice, yes, but how could it be made otherwise than by consent?

◀ *Trying out the oxygen in North Wales.*

3

I told John that I could not think of any other friend who could have persuaded me that I was "free" of commitments to accompany his party to Everest. But when the formal letter from Basil Goodfellow, Secretary of the Himalayan Committee, arrived upon the breakfast-table, we again both felt for the moment that it was an inevitable rather than a joyous occasion, this breaking back to a new life in an unknown. I must go because . . . I must. Just as Everest must be climbed.

Walking about next day, I realised that there come times when a decision turns up, hat in hand and asking to be taken, so out of keeping with the rest of life that the first reaction is to laugh outright. Our way has been charted, our groove peacefully oiled and made easy to run in. Then this thing is before us, marriage or war or even an expedition; we know that a difference has come over our sky, we are different people even, and yet we walk along the street as usual, nodding to our friends. "Good morning," we say, as though nothing had happened. Yet a great deal has happened, something which defies the imagination of everyday. Afterwards, incredible to relate, we shall be walking down this same road once again, books in hand, nodding once again and saying "Good morning" as though even now nothing had happened.

Therefore it felt slightly unreal, when on November 17th I walked into a room in the Royal Geographical Society, to a large table, baize-covered and bordered with agenda and sharpened pencils. Several others were there already. We were introduced to each other (some of the party were already friends from the Cho Oyu Expedition [1]), and took our seats. For two hours peace and tobacco smoke filled the room. For two hours John Hunt led a discussion on organisation, equipment, money, diet, aluminium ladder, wireless, a host of details. We were as business-like as any board meeting.

I pulled myself up from time to time and turned to the photographs of the summit on the wall. It needed that to assure me that we very ordinary people in lounge suits would at some time be out there, where the Swiss might even now

[1] Bourdillon, Evans, Gregory and Pugh. Hillary and Lowe had also been on Cho Oyu, and Bourdillon, Hillary and Ward on the 1951 Reconnaissance Expedition to Everest.

4

be dizzily clinging. And it was faintly uncanny to meet for the first time a number of men with whom I would soon be living for five months at very close quarters under very different conditions. My imagination began to run away with me as I pictured the Swiss, men of iron muscle and nerve, lying crumpled by the buffeting wind, their toes and hands numbed. I looked at my own hands, projecting from my pullover: very ordinary hands, hands that looked cold even with the chill of a London November. I wondered, could a medical test *really* diagnose my fitness for height? For Lord Horder, who examined us, had kindly said to me that he could not "forbid the banns." Or is it merely that the spirit is expected to overcome the undiagnosed medical difficulties? Yes, that must be it. I feel the cold severely, but I *mustn't* feel it, on Everest.

"Will you help with the despatches?"

John Hunt's voice. I frowned knowingly at the agenda. We had arrived at "Appointments: In the field."

"Yes, willingly," I said.

The appointment of a wireless operator caused momentary delay (but perhaps John knew all the time who was to be the victim).

"Who would like to be signals officer?" There was a silence.

"Well, I was in the Signals in the Army," George Band was rashly volunteering.

"That's fine. You're the man. And meteorologist goes with it, of course."

"I was messing officer, actually," George murmured, but it was no good.

"Excellent! You can help Griff with the food as well." That evening he went off to buy the Pelican book on the weather, and doubtless a suitable companion volume on dietetics.

Writing, that was all right. I could do that. But what else? Everybody had at least two jobs. I hastily volunteered to help with packing. Anybody, surely, could have ideas about packing. And would I be in charge of climbing equipment? Alas, I thought, how little they knew. I saw the possible expressions of Tom Bourdillon's face, as he sat in hot sun among the crevasses and discovered that this absent-minded person had left out the glacier cream. We passed into the next room to be measured for boots, oxygen masks and clothes. Then we had tea, dispensed by Joy Hunt, John's wife. Her well-governed province was the cookery box.

2

Of course, at this stage nobody knew whether the Swiss had succeeded in their autumn attempt. The burden of this uncertainty weighed chiefly on John, but all were concerned. However convinced the intellect might be that the Swiss had not camped 150 feet from the summit, it was impossible for the emotions not to be shaken by the many newspaper reports that they had. And what if they should succeed? Some were in favour of making a second attempt, on the theory that our effort should be independent of those of other nations. This course seemed to me as illogical as it would be not to use the Swiss experience when they returned. Others favoured another mountain. But if the expedition went to another mountain, as the Himalayan Committee rightly decided it should, money would be difficult. So magical is the name of Everest. Coming home one evening from a meeting, I saw a headline in an evening paper: "His Ambition—Everest." A boy had been drowned in the Avon, and this one fact about him had been thought worthy of the headline. Kangchenjunga, which the Committee agreed at John's suggestion to attack if the Swiss succeeded on Everest, has not the same magic. Therefore the same funds are not forthcoming, either from newspapers or private sources. It was a very trying wait; all I could think of doing myself was to walk over our home fields with loads of bricks in my rucksack, in preparation for carrying oxygen apparatus.

The week-end of December 6th, John Hunt, Charles Wylie, Gregory and Pugh spent on the Jungfraujoch (11,400 feet) in Switzerland, testing equipment, samples of which were provided by various firms: tents, sleeping-bags, down clothing and boots. The large Sherpa sacks marked "British Mount Everest Expedition, 1953" might have been politely mocked if the news of a Swiss success had come through during the visit. But the Swiss retreat was announced, and all was well. On December 10th the selected firms were asked to go ahead with making equipment, for which they were allowed little more than a month. The boat sailed on February 12th, packing was to begin at Lusk's of Wapping in mid-January.

On December 15th Charles Evans, in charge of stores, and I had our first interview with Stuart Bain, who was in charge of the packing. We sat in the small office on a big upper storey where operations were to take place. Delicious warehouse smells lingered from below. Charles, from experience, found it easier than I to visualise the final crates made up from our improbable-looking lists. Soon these component stores would be pouring in from the various parts of England, from France and Switzerland. They must be sorted and packed in three categories: stores to be unpacked at Kathmandu marked with a black stripe; at Base Camp marked with red and yellow stripes; and at Advance Base Camp (21,200 feet) on the mountain marked with blue stripes. A fourth category was considered, of stores to be unpacked on the South Col. But who could possibly picture what "they" would need for that last man-in-the-moon push? Category Four was abandoned by common agreement.

We then started sorting the other categories into sections, as far as an incomplete and uncertain inventory allowed; mountaineering, clothing, cooking, bridging and structural, tents, wireless, medical, physiological, photographic, food, oxygen and miscellaneous. These were the sections; and there were many queries of detail. How many tents would be needed on the march? How many pairs of gloves below Advance Base? How much rope for fixing? Some questions the Cho Oyu experience and the Swiss on Everest could answer. For the others, it was guess-work. Each of us was working at his special department, and the reserves were working too. Emlyn Jones worked untiringly, both now and when we had gone. Then there were Jack Tucker, John Jackson, Hamish Nicol. Anthony Rawlinson did most of the ordering of climbing equipment on my behalf. Tom Bourdillon was heavily committed with the oxygen, George Band studied wireless, Michael Westmacott ordered tents, Griff Pugh the food—and

7

so on. Each was expected to produce some sort of final list; but the lists were very rough.

On a visit to Wales in early January, Charles Evans and I worked one evening in greater detail, making up the list of stores into packages of the right weight: approximately 60 pounds for stores wanted up to Base, 45 pounds for Advanced Base stores. I should add that it was Charles who did the suggesting; I listened mainly in admiration at his ability and made tentative comments which I hoped would not reek too strongly of inexperience. Take one item from the section "Mountaineering" in which there are thirteen packages. This is how one case was finally made up into a coolie-load:

No. 5:   1 waterproof-lined plywood case containing:

11	tins	Skreen Sunburn Preventive—132 oz.
2	jars	Skreen Sunburn Preventive—4 oz.
Quantity		leaflets regarding application of above.
500 ft.		Nylon string.
14		Glacier Lanterns (with candles).
8		Magnetic Compasses.
2 reels		Sticking Plaster.
61		Candles for Lanterns (2 hours).
2		Binoculars—W.D. pattern.
2		Aneroids in leather cases.
3		Compasses in leather cases.
1 only		Theodolite in leather case.
2		Altimeters.

Gross Weight—69 lb.

There were many anxious flurries of pencil calculation.

Outside Pen y Gwryd, in the calm frosted air of Snowdon, I looked up at those still unrivalled pyramids, snow-covered and dimly shining in the starlight. I thought back to the storms and cold, cold immeasurably greater than that which made me shiver now, that had bent and smoothed those outlines. To compare tiny Snowdon with Everest is absurd; yet not so absurd, if you think of Snowdon as a withered and shrunken ancestor. When the top of Everest floored the sea, Snowdon stood greatly upon pedestals whose fragments remain. And now she lay coiled in dreams of that past, yet watching, as it seemed, the tiny creatures preparing to swarm up her gigantic successor.

The need to start a car recalled me. Next time I met Charles, it was back in the murk of a London January. Together we climbed into the damp little tube to Wapping. We inspected together the stores already assembled on that large third floor. In the office overlooking the river we tried to arrange final details of packing. Again, I played a good deal the part of Greek chorus. There were more queries. How could we be certain what each packing-case would weigh? Did it matter some items, like gloves, being packed in separate cases? Which cases, like the cookery box, needed to be opened and shut, and which could be nailed down? How many sleeping-bags would a man need on the icefall? Should the rifle be carried separately, and what about the two-inch mortar? This fierce weapon, because of the terror which it inspired in British Railways, had been isolated and was now reposing, appropriately, in Woolwich Arsenal. It would have to be conveyed by car to the docks, and we were to pick up the bombs in India, if the Indians could be convinced that they were not for Communist use.

Meanwhile the goods had started to pour in. Many firms generously supplied free, but this created Customs difficulties. Oh to be an organiser! A glance at the list of items, then at the jumbled cases on the floor, filled me with admiration for Stuart Bain, who moved tranquilly about and was clearly confident of rounding all his sheep into their containing walls. To me they seemed destined to lie through eternity scattered over a dusty floor.

3

There came a curious interlude: the oxygen trials in North Wales. We met at Helyg, the Climbers' Club hut, on the morning of January 18th, and spent that and the next day, in glorious weather, trying out types of carrying frames over the hills. Tom Bourdillon and George Band tortured themselves experimenting with the Closed-Circuit apparatus on an unusually hot morning up Snowdon. I do not want to anticipate a description of this. As explained then, to one of an unscientific turn, the general principle seemed to be that with the ordinary Open-Circuit (as used on previous expeditions) the air breathed out is lost; but in Tom's Closed-Circuit you are cut off from the outer world. What you breathe out passes to a canister of soda-lime and there, by one of those miracles special to science, is reconverted and comes back to you as oxygen. As your mask must fit very closely, on a hot day this set can be uncomfortable, to say the least. John tried it, but removed himself, purple and perspiring, at the end of ten minutes. "It's really too hot for Closed-Circuit," Tom said. In the evening Helyg was transformed. Carrying frames cluttered the floor, cylinders, flashlights and bulbs jostled for position with the electric kettles. For we were being filmed, an attentive class listening to Tom expounding oxygen. And next morning, in the blinding sunshine, we were photographed by a collection of pressmen as "Members of the British Mount Everest Expedition, 1953." Well, that was very pleasant for the moment and very kind, though, of course, quite unconnected with the sheer effort of Everest, which hovered demon-like at the back of my mind.

On the 20th we tried on our clothes and marvelled at our muffled-up selves. On the 27th, before a reception at the Royal Geographical Society, many visitors came to inspect the equipment. The neatly arranged boxes and packages seemed remote from hardship. Too elegant, too easy: green eiderdown quilts peeping from half-opened cases, stacks of very light aluminium plates and pots, neat little coloured flags, and the sections of the duralumin ladder resting casually against a wall. That all this—the product of three countries and of thousands of workers—should be provided for us, filled me with a sense of humility.

Now they were photographing the rations, tiers of brown boxes whose contents it was impossible to think of as so many appetising meals going into so many hungry climbers. The first time I climbed to this floor, I had thought we must be going to live entirely on green peas, for a huge consignment of them seemed to occupy the floor. Our own boxes had stood more modestly to the side in one corner. There were the

Army-type Compo rations for the march, the eleven-pound biscuit-boxes, the beverage boxes, and the odd chutney bottle sticking out of the "luxury box." All these our friends prowled around and approved: our friends, who had come this long way to London to see what we were getting and to wish us well. Chris Briggs and his wife had driven 240 miles from Pen y Gwryd in a fog, simply to see this. And unreal as it all seemed—all the good wishes and the handshakes, "Good luck with the weather," and "I'm sure you'll do it this time"—yet the total sum did seem in a strange way to propitiate some particular mountain sprite, or add one comfort to our own anxiety, which is after all the same thing.

For a great contributor to my feeling of unreality was the public limelight upon us. No one, saying "yes" to an Everest expedition, could foresee himself as broadcaster, television artist, even film star. Yet, in a sense, we were all of these. And this *"gloire,"* as the French would term it, goes on, seemingly quite irrelevant to the job of putting one foot before another on those great slopes. Moreover, there is an imp in each of us which is pleased by such hostages to fortune, which whispers: "Bask your short moment while the sun is out, before the storm clouds find you."

Our effort was going on too, all the time, despite these distractions and the frightening prowls of the Press after a story. (Being under a contract to *The Times,* we moved in daily terror of unwittingly forfeiting their generous financial support.) By mid-January each had rounded up his particular department, and the packing at Lusk's was complete in the first days of February. It was a great moment when we saw the last set of objects enter their allotted case or kitbag and come forward to be weighed. Stuart Bain, white-coated and smiling, was still moving among them and still seemed to know where everything was, and what it should weigh. Each item was ready for the S.S. *Stratheden's* departure—except Griff Pugh's rifle, which, however, sneaked its way on to the boat at the last minute and was allowed through an indulgent Indian Customs by the very polish on its barrel.

Apart from physical preparation, there was the planning and thinking. It was not for nothing that John had worked for four years on various planning staffs. His labours as leader, and those of Charles Wylie as organising secretary, were the core of the whole job, and far too complicated to list here. Theirs was the real burden and responsibility of those days. Fortunately, their worries were lightened occasionally by letters of advice like the following from a doctor in Spain:

DEAR SIR,

Having read in the papers something about your preparatives for your next intent of escaling the Everest, I dare explain to you an idea of me, for the case it may be of some use to you.

Noticing the great difficulty of the ascension during the last yards up the hill, I think it should be of great use that the handle of the piolet should be wide or empty, and should be in it (in the handle) a strong spring which might be shot at the manner of the submarine guns used for fishing.

Then an arpoon, or well, a cupping glass or air-hole could be shot at some 80 yards distance, bound to a nylon rod, which may be phosphorescent. That could have the advantage that being shot in the right direction towards the top of the mountain, on a clear weather you could very well:

1st: Go up the hill without losing the right direction, even between the fog.

2nd: The uphill ascension could be helped by the hands.

3rd: The whistling of the wind against the nylon rod, should indicate the best moments to go on in the uphill climbering.

There follow some medical suggestions.

But apart from moments of academic speculation, it was a cold-blooded thinking in ounces of human effort; a studying of photographs of the Lhotse Face, to decide whether two camps are endurable upon it; a reckoning of how many stores, carried by how many porters, would be needed for how many nights on the South Col—a place, as one of last year's Swiss climbers had put it, which has "the smell of death" about it; and, finally, a flying visit by John and Charles Evans to Switzerland itself. At Zürich the Swiss generously allowed their brains to be picked, showed photographs and gave ideas. Because it is true that Everest is climbed over other men's shoulders, John was determined to be as generous with the French, who were planning the next attempt if we failed.

The last days were something of a scramble. By this time we had attacked our personal affairs, and the arrangements for a family needed care. Then came the bad news that John must undergo a minor operation for antrum infection; he would have to fly out and join the main party later. Charles Wylie, Michael Ward, George Band, Michael Westmacott, Tom Stobart (ciné-camera-man) and myself would travel by sea, and I was to be in charge of handling the baggage across India. Charles Evans and Greg were to fly out by Comet as Advance Party; Tom Bourdillon would fly out later, having worked to the last minute on the oxygen; so would John and Griff Pugh (physiologist). Ed Hillary would fly direct from New Zealand, after spending the last days tucking up his bees. George Lowe would join us at Bombay, where his boat arrived a week earlier than ours.

Personal preparations had to be made for the journey. How much toothpaste does one get through in five months? How soon would my family move from Hindhead to Heswall? I had by now ceased teaching; it was a relief no more to be writing on a blackboard symbols which, for the moment, meant nothing to me. Dentist, inoculations, decompression chamber at Farnborough, broadcast, television, friends, even a course of boot-repairing, all with surprising suddenness were over. Somehow I felt very ordinary, almost shorn, when on the afternoon of February 12th we climbed aboard the *Stratheden*, faced the last press and TV batteries, said the last good-byes and turned our eyes towards the high sea.

A.J. VEILHAN.

2
Dramatis Personae

Now that we are sailing away, it is a fit time to introduce ourselves; or rather, for me to act chronicler and present the company converging upon Kathmandu.

I hope to be forgiven for the incompleteness of my portraits. It is a pleasant privilege of the writer of a personal story that he is not expected to give what he, being a person, does not know. He can record only his impressions, and leave the amateur psycho-analyst to unravel his states of mind. The impression made by his companions is the biggest single element in a man's memory of such a party, bigger than the mountain itself. His companions make or mar the journey, just as they make or mar the outcome of the adventure. They should properly appear at the end, for it is after the adventure that they stand out vividly in the mind. I am introducing them here, like characters in a Victorian novel, before the action starts, because the reader may like a clear picture before he fits them into the scene.

It seems to me, reading between the lines of other Himalayan accounts and speaking to members of other parties, that there has not been an expedition happier than ours—which is certainly one reason for its happy outcome. Altitude plays queer tricks with the affections. The friend of sea-level might become the intolerable enemy of the South Col. I am repeating a commonplace in saying that his mannerisms, his tricks of speech, his way of blowing his nose, snivelling or snoring, coughing or crooning, may drive his companions to consider murder. And the truth that the friends of Kathmandu in March were still friends, indeed far firmer friends, in June, is the greatest tribute I can give them. It is a tribute particularly to the man who gathered this company together: John Hunt.

John needs little introduction. Within a few months he has

◄ *John Hunt, leader.*

15

become one of the best known figures in the world. I met him first when I was a young, newly commissioned lieutenant in the K.R.R.C., he a major of dignified standing. He was the sort of man whom, at the first handshake, you know will be a friend. We talked of his photographs. Some time after, when he organised a brigade course in North Wales, I went as an instructor, along with Alf Bridge. We little thought then that the trio would continue; for it was Alf, in the spring of 1953, who held the oxygen arrangements together in so masterly a fashion that the exact consignment went off at exactly the right time, and that there was enough oxygen and a little to spare on the mountain.

The first and most obvious quality of John, in those months before we left, was determination, concentration upon our objective. He was resolved that, if human ingenuity could get us to the top, then nothing human should prevent us. In the course of preparation he was willing to fly at the shortest notice to Switzerland, indeed would have flown to any part of the earth that might produce useful information. These preparations left very few free hours, and those few John used to think out the problems of the assault. One day, just after Christmas, my family and I went over to his house at Brookwood. We discussed the Lhotse Face. On the march and mountain the story was the same. I have never seen any-one spare himself so little, too little as his companions some-times feared. Three days after having to give up on a peak owing to incipient pleurisy (as Mike Ward diagnosed it), he was making the 2,000 feet ascent from Lake Camp to the ice-fall above Camp II, in order to "inspect the conditions." In the same spirit he insisted in being himself on the recon-naissance in early May. Most of the party were going down, at one time or another, for a rest on grass below. John could not be persuaded to leave Base, where there was wireless communication with the higher camps. He only once visited the rest camp—on a flying visit to the sick Tom Stobart. I think it was this resolution that created such admiration for John that no criticism could easily find voice, even when all felt that he might be straining himself too hard. He is built on big lines, a very fast mover as I knew already, not at very first sight a stayer. He did, in fact, in the Cwm and higher, often arrive in a state of apparent exhaustion, only to be up, bright as a pin the next morning, discussing the arrangements for the day. Perhaps one might have suspected it, from the strong lines of the face, clean-cut yet not square. My most vivid picture of it is at Camp IV, eyes screwed anxiously behind binoculars, shaven and plastered white with glacier cream even over the moustache.

Combine this thorough-going resolution with an all-pervading charm, and you have some picture of our leader. Only after we got back did I discover that John was a captivating public speaker, with a quiet confidential way of charming an audience. We knew already that he could win over any private listeners. I think the secret lay in his way of treating everybody as a friend, as a potential helper in a worthy cause. He believed immensely in the inspiration of Everest to the world, and officials, manufacturers, diplomats and ourselves had no choice but to agree. Behind this there was a deep religious sense. John once said, round a camp-fire at Thyangboche: "I don't mind admitting that mountains make me pray." And the sense of so earnest a conviction added to the charm of the convinced. On the mountain he could have persuaded the most ambitious that he was doing the one vital job of the expedition peeling potatoes at Base Camp. Such leadership is the art of inducing everybody, even the at first uninterested, to believe that they want to go your way.

One characteristic common to military men is the love of planning. To an expert of the Joint Planning Staff the temptation is irresistible, and Everest needs plans. From the first Party Conference on, we received almost daily sheaves of instructions, programmes, schedules, allocations, emanating from John Hunt and Charles Wylie (a major in the Gurkhas). Before we left England we had a full list of tents for every site on the mountain, together with allocation of personnel at various provisional times. "The Assault," "X-Day" (variation on the theme of D-Day), "X + 1" and so forth. It is a tribute to these plans that so many of them were in the

17

event adhered to,[1] and the few others, like all good plans, were amenable to modification. My last document on the mountain was at Camp IV, a typed list of stores to go up to the South Col. But we had not finished. Even before we reached Kathmandu we were receiving lists of engagements, command performances, miscellaneous invitations and the like. The private army has not, at the time of writing, been disbanded.

John fulfilled Gino Watkins's proposition that a leader should be able and prepared to do all that his team must do. He should never be on his dignity with them, nor above mild ribaldry at his own expense. It is not too much to say that in an expedition of this nature admiration, and even love, of the leader is the largest single factor making for happiness. And this team was a more than happy one.

George Band is a geological student at Cambridge. I had only once met him before, upon the Great Slab of Cwm Silin in North Wales. Balanced on impossibly steep rock, he was "playing about" on what turned out to be a new start to the Outside Edge. I knew also of his feat of doing the North Ridge of the Dent Blanche, and even harder climbs, as an undergraduate. Tall, he had an immensely long reach; and bespectacled, with curved nose and smile that flashed suddenly upon the world, he had an air of benevolent learning which added tone to our expedition, especially when he returned one day to Camp IV earnestly laden with geological specimens. Orange beard and panama hat completed the appearance of a bearded Dr. Livingstone. One was tempted, meeting him with a Sherpa team, to make the classic remark.

Two vignettes of George. The first, as he sorted and arranged stores at Advance Base—a job very different from extreme rock work. He had been perhaps the most conscientious Nepali learner on the boat, but found, as we all did, that when it came to explaining the menu to Thondup, Urdu was better understood. I was amazed, coming over to help interpret sometimes, how much he knew about the

[1] See *The Ascent of Everest*, Appendices II and III.

quantities and species of our diet. He had taken on this thankless task because, as he put it in London: "I'm very interested in food." Nothing on an expedition receives such critical treatment, in such strong terms. It is the one field in which all claim a great degree of expertise. The luckless organisers, George and Griff in this case, are taken to task as if on a personal grievance. Yet George never lost his calm, but sat there working on at the endless figures of foods to be transported, slipping in the occasional comic remark. During the weeks in the Cwm his main job, apart from carrying to Camp VII, was the vital yet dull one of food distribution. Again, no complaint.

The other vignette is of the humorist. Space should be greater and memory longer to recall George in that role. As jester, he had a most happy effect on morale. He would think for a moment after any story, then came the flashing grin, the laugh and the finishing touch. When the newspapers were reaching us on the march home, and one of them announced: "According to reliable sources the assault will almost certainly begin with a bombardment by the 2-inch mortar," George added: "With Spitfires circling over the South Col, I expect." He could tease anybody, so nicely that nobody could mind. Only George could have concocted *The Hunt Manual of Man Management*—a volume which, in conversation, ran to several pages, along with a companion volume entitled *Everest Exposed*.

I enjoyed hearing about the most modern climbing. George, at twenty-four, seemed to know everybody and to be rapidly doing everything, both in Britain and the Alps. He has his finger on a pulse, and the pulse is a fast one.

Tom Bourdillon gave me an immediate impression of size and strength. "He does seem to be that very rare thing," David Cox once said, "a big man who can move really delicately on rocks." That was true. On the boulder problems that lined the route to Base Camp, it was a pleasure to see this bulky figure, poised on a slab, wriggle a toe delicately forth, return, readjust handhold, and reach on again. Strength and control. Incidentally he was one of the very few among us who had never fallen off anything. And he had done rock climbs in the Alps such as have hitherto been the closed province of Continental climbers.

Though not as tall as several others, Tom was more immediately, abruptly powerful than any. I never saw him go in at a tent's sleeve entrance with rucksack and crampons complete, as he did once on Cho Oyu, but it was said to have been a memorable sight. Like many heavily-built men, he lost a lot of weight on the mountain—to his own great advantage. Big shoulders supported a square face with square chin; a wide mouth; hair that tended to ruffle into rebellious verticality. Strong tweeds rather than *recherché* lounge suit, and even these tweeds tended to bulge as if with the muscles behind them.

Tom spoke slowly and quietly, almost hesitantly, with an air of having weighed his words. At conference he could be silent for almost the whole session while others spoke, then finish the subject with some Catonic verdict ground out from the mill of reflection. *Delenda est Carthago.* You could be very sure that on no subject would he say what he did not feel deeply. And on his own subject, oxygen, he was uncompromising. Of his ability in it I have no qualification to write; but that the sahibs and some Sherpas managed to use it adequately, that there were enough cylinders and frames high on the mountain, and that Tom and Charles Evans climbed on the Closed-Circuit apparatus, contrary to the expectation of almost all, to 28,700 feet in one morning from the South Col—this story would seem to indicate a certain skill, to say the least.

Sharing a tent with Tom could be like sharing with a bear or a whirlwind. Having decided at 6:00 A.M. that the oxygen sets had better be adjusted inside, he could benignly convert a placid little bedroom into Vulcan's workshop. At the same time he could turn his mechanical ardour to most helpful ends. When there was a leaky Li-Lo valve to be adjusted, or a Primus to be repaired under difficult conditions at a high camp, it would be done without a word, and no word of thanks expected.

Tom was ambitious to go high, in the name of science as

THYANGBOCHE MONASTERY, SHOWING THE
RANGE OF KWANGDE BEHIND

much as or more than for himself. A natural zeal to prove his apparatus lent wings to a strong determination.

At the first conference a small man with close, sandy hair which tended to stand upright was walking round the table, hands in pockets, taking note of the agenda. He said very little at that meeting. What he did say came out in a curious, low voice, which gave it the impression of being a very considered judgment. I have described some of our activities together with the baggage. Charles Evans, who had given up his job as surgical registrar at Walton Hospital, Liverpool, on December 31st, ordered his life on a plan. The expedition was important; therefore he must devote himself to it.

Now he was quite free, and I had sat in admiring audience at the calculation of weights and measures that filled our days. Charles seemed to have given thorough, careful thought to every detail. "Of course we shall need crampons on the acclimatisation period." It was the same on the march and on the mountain, where he was in command of stores. These had to be checked and marked. As his assistant I would feel happier, settling down to read a book, if I knew that Charles was doing the same. If he was at it again, I felt faintly guilty. He was indefatigable, and I think that this was due to a high mental control of bodily faculties. Such control gave him tremendous stamina. He was, of course, also strongly built: much broader than appeared in town clothes, compact and very agile. But these qualities would have been nothing high up, without a will capable of driving them beyond tiredness.

In a round face Charles's blue childlike eyes were direct, enquiring and discerning. Of all the friends I have, he is the one to whom I would least like to tell a lie. Thus he is one with whom humbug, sham and false sentiment receive shortest shrift. Going directly, with the surgeon's eye, to the kernel of any problem, he would cut away overlying tissues and view them with caustic humour. Hence a number of "dicta" which were oft-repeated. He was at first doubtful of the oxygen, particularly of the Closed-Circuit. After an oxygen meeting (for he was the second oxygen expert) he said to me: "I think really the best chance is to find two chaps who can

get up without it." And before the Lhotse Face reconnaissance, in early May, which used Open- and Closed-Circuits:
"We know that it's possible to get to the South Col without
oxygen. The recce is really to see if you can get up there with
it." Meanwhile he was himself being won over, and, to his
own surprise, to the Closed-Circuit. But that is another story.

Gregory (Greg) was the smallest man of the party. His
leanness, similar to Smythe's, allowed him to lose no weight
on the mountain, because he had none to lose. It is fascinating now to look back at the old discussions of the "ideal"
shape for Everest; when there have been figures as dissimilar
as those of Greg and Tom Bourdillon, General Norton and
Wager, Ed Hillary or Raymond Greene and Charles Evans.
Greg scored by his lightness, because he had less to lift. The
one place where he may have sighed for more weight was at
the fording of the fast-flowing Lobuje Khola. Perhaps because of this lightness he disliked carrying (except for cameras) if it could be avoided. I have a lively picture of him
standing in the rain outside a tent, beside his heavy kitbag.
"Hey, what's happened to the Sherpas? This is getting wet!"
And yet he had, when put to it, carried almost as much above
the South Col.

As director of a travel agency in Blackpool, Greg was in
charge of our diverse journeys to Kathmandu. Before the
departure we would receive efficiently typed documents relating to money, tickets, dates and the rest. With Charles
Evans, in the advance party, he arranged the later stages. Besides this he was in charge of still photography, though all
photographed with equal abandon in all directions. A most
common sight was his small figure bent behind the tripod,
eyes screwed up, knees flexed and teeth showing in an intent
snarl. A woollen skull-cap with bobble and two or three
other cameras slung round the shoulders completed the
picture.

I spent a week with Greg and a party of Sherpas, ferrying
loads between Camps III and IV. His pace was exceptionally
steady, his movements had the precision of a very experienced mountaineer. Apart from John himself, Greg was the

oldest member of the climbing party. Every day he advanced to the climb at the head of the second rope (for photographic purposes), as well dressed as if he had just stepped from some Lakeland hotel: perfectly shaven, moustache trimmed, socks equally turned down, two exactly equal loops of nylon line hanging from his two rucksack pockets. Being untidy myself, I admire neatness on a mountain; admire the better and follow the worse.

I knew from Greg's reputation as a climber that he was absolutely safe. If he said that a place was all right, then it could be trusted. He would go as high as he humanly could, without rashly stretching the limit.

I first met Ed Hillary at Kathmandu, but his reputation, from the Everest Reconnaissance and Cho Oyu expeditions, had preceded him. The long face, hatchet jaw and immense smile have now become famous. But my very first impression was of length of limb. Ed was not the tallest, I believe Tom Stobart claimed that honour, but he was certainly our longest. His angular figure seemed somehow made for going uphill; fashioned into the slope as he took long, easy strides up it. "He's a terrific goer," Eric Shipton had told me before we left. "He might even go too hard." But he did not.

Perhaps more than any of us, Ed was a mountain lover to whom the word "passion" could be applied. In camps, and especially when excited at the Everest prospect, he would ripple on in a medley of past peaks, record marches and future possibilities, tales of climbers and climbs. When he stood on the world's highest summit, his eyes turned towards Makalu, and he started even then tracing a route up it for next year. For the sake of Everest he was prepared even to master oxygen, despite a private desire to "have a shot" without. At Advance Base the figure in Foreign Legion cap and check shirt, bent to tinker with an oxygen set or clean a cooker, was a familiar sight. And he had Tenzing's set to care for too. It was clear, as we lay talking of it on the night of May 29th, that on that final climb his mastery had been sufficient for both.

From previous expeditions Ed had picked up enough Urdu

to make his needs known to the Sherpas, who responded to his cheerful address and warm laugh. Any story, capped with the laugh, would receive an ovation. With Tenzing he always spoke English; and from the first climb together the two seemed to adapt themselves, each to the other. Tenzing's English is fragmentary, but even so he must have found Ed an easier job than Raymond Lambert last year; for Lambert spoke no English at all, and yet the two understood one another. Ed was also accommodating, more so than might be expected from one who described himself as "a glutton for leading." Both on Kang Cho (in the acclimatisation period), in the Cwm and on the first stretch of the Lhotse Face I led, in the latter two cases without asking for it. One member of the party once said: "I try to get into the lead with Ed. It's more restful."

To every problem Ed delivered a frontal attack, to every question the direct answer. So it was with Everest. "Let's have at it," and "I must admit I like this Open-Circuit job." The attack was successful, the answer simple. And after it? A man must be modest to be the world's highest "summiter" and remain quite unchanged. When reporters at Kathmandu persisted in asking: "Who *did* actually get to the top first?" he would confess: "I don't like to tell them I did, it sounds precious like swanking." To combine that modesty with the confidence of an acquired skill and the friendly openness of the New Zealand Alps, is to compose a mountaineer worthy of the highest summit.

The name of George Lowe links itself very much in my mind with that of Ed; for my most memorable night of the expedition was that of May 29th, when we all three crushed into a Meade tent on the South Col and talked and talked of the day.

George had been with Ed on the New Zealand expedition to Garwhal in 1951. He had also been a member of the Cho Oyu party last year, after which the two of them had ascended the very difficult Nup La and done some climbs remarkable for their speed and skill on ice. George was of the same long build as Ed, more slender, and at very first sight less enduring. But his feat of spending nine days at work on the Lhotse Face, and then, after a retreat, joining the Ridge Camp carry, was unsurpassed on the whole expedition. Like other New Zealanders he was before everything an ice-man, more than able to retaliate in kind when hair-raising tales were told of perpendicular British cliffs by our rock gymnasts.

The two Georges were the humorists of the party. George Lowe was aided by a body which could easily be made comic, rather ostrich-like in shape, a pointed nose and slightly receding chin; also teeth which could be removed in an instant with surprising effect. His stories of one or two New Zealand country primary schools in earlier days had a macabre twist which enthralled many hours at Lobuje. The most exciting was the school where the only way of keeping the children quiet the first day was by allowing them to organise a concert; whereupon an eleven-year-old girl performed a most sophisticated, hip-wriggling dance, drawing nearer and nearer to the starting eyes of her teacher. The teacher was George. And he was a remarkable learner, too. George learned the ciné art so astonishingly well, that he was able to take all the high shots, and some in the icefall.

His humour nicely sugared an absolute directness and candour typical of him. Indeed both he and Ed gave the impression of facing every problem squarely, attacking it without subtlety and with a laugh. George could never say what he did not think, and never remain silent for "political" or any other reason. One piece of diplomacy, however, deserves to be recorded. At Camp VII we discussed the Lhotse Face, and I praised what he had been doing in making the route.

"Ah, yes," George said, "but people judge you by how high you go, and it doesn't look now as if I'll make the South Col."

"Surely they don't. Surely it's the work done that matters."

"Well that's what I think. You see."

And I believe that an idea, carefully concealed, was already brewing: he was the person to carry the Ridge Camp to 27,900 feet.

If I devote less space to Griff Pugh and Tom Stobart, it is certainly not because they are less important people; indeed to the scientific and film worlds, two major constellations of our universe, they are probably the most important of all. But we inevitably saw less of them, since they were not members of the climbing party. Very often they hunted together, on their own.

To some of us the idea of taking a physiologist was repugnant. If you answer the question "Why climb?" with "Because I like it," then the idea of scientific aims will be incongruous. But there is a more weighty objection, put by Eric Shipton. An extra, non-climbing member of the party means more food, more transport, a greater liability in case of sickness or of difficulty on the icefall. A physiological expedition to Meade's Col on Kamet, by all means, Eric said, but not to Everest. Everest is a job of its own.

It is Griff's master-stroke that he reconciled us, if that were possible, to his art; partly, in the first place, because he did not practice it so rigorously as we had feared. I myself fully expected a kind of vampire, lurking at Camp III in readiness to absorb our blood and deflate our lungs as we heaved wearily over the icefall. In practice, apart from a thumb-prick at Camp IV, an occasional weighing and a long questionnaire at the end, we suffered nothing. At the beginning Griff suffered himself, I think, from altitude. Later, when he had bravely overcome this difficulty, he made his own body and the surrounding temperatures, tents, oxygen and the like his objects of experiment more rigorously than the climbers.

Griff's results will be both interesting and helpful. It is not generally known to what extent our expedition built on the physiological knowledge he gained on Cho Oyu; much was learned about food, drink and the effects of oxygen, to mention only these. Without this knowledge Everest might never have been climbed at all. But climbers are notoriously lazy people. They accept the tools of their trade from the workshop, grumble at the inconveniences imposed by scientific gadgets, and think they are getting up entirely under their own steam. I know Griff will publish something to expose the real case, and our human weakness.

Physiology aside, he was a great asset in many unexpected ways. He was an expert on equipment, studied with troops during the war, and had devised or modified some of our clothing. He had organised our food. He was an extra doctor, very necessary when Tom Stobart fell ill, or when the Sherpas were descending into the Cwm. Above all he had a vast range of scientific knowledge, an astounding head for figures (how many calories in a packet of Grape-Nuts?), and a wealth of stories, told in the slow academic voice, and usually ending on a note of startling frivolity. On our return to Kathmandu the flaming red-headed figure clad in dirty grey pyjamas (most hygienic for walking in, Griff claimed) and gym shoes, shook hands with the King of Nepal in his own royal palace: a proper rendezvous for princes and physiologists.

Everybody was happy when it was learned that Country-man Films would be able to send Tom Stobart as camera-man. He was known to be a good companion, and a climber himself. Before the war he had made an attempt on Nun Kun, in Ladhak.[1]

Tom was very tall, with fair floppy hair and a round face which most put at twenty-five rather than thirty-nine years. On the boat I thought that he would have great difficulties. He had only recently come out of hospital, and could not even accompany us on our dilettante runs round the deck. But a devotion to his science kept him going on the march. Sometimes, photographing with Greg, he would wait two hours for the right light to strike the scarlet rhododendrons, and only catch us up after everyone else had breakfasted. *Ars longa, vita brevis.* Tom was the most absorbed of devotees, intent that nothing should stop him, and that devotion made him forget his unfitness until he had finally become fit with-out realising it.

During the acclimatisation period he went many miles in search of local colour; then, at Base Camp, acclimatised slowly, and by ill-luck caught mild pneumonia on May 1st. There was some anxiety as to what would happen to the film,

[1] 23,400 feet, climbed by the French, August, 1953.

since the icefall was offering wonderful shots every day, too good to be missed. But Tom was determined. By May 14th he was filming at the lower end of the Cwm; and in the ensuing days one rarely escaped in or out of the Advance Base without the familiar whirr, the familiar tall figure poised at the tripod, with an attendant Sherpa ready to pick up or put down the magic boxes. He did go beyond Camp V, but found that he had not recovered sufficiently for Camp VI. The film in its final form shows to what excellence Tom's art had attained. It brings home to the plain-dweller, as no other medium can do, the outward life and the surrounding beauties of our expedition.

Tom too was a raconteur, a most entertaining tent companion. There seemed to be few parts of the world he had not visited, filming big game or the Antarctic and Mediterranean shores. No story could nonplus him. It was said that, if somebody rushed into the tent saying that they had just seen a pink rhinoceros, Tom would look up, eyes screwed from his cigarette, and ask: "The long- or the short-tailed variety?"

At Cambridge, Michael Ward had been known as an outstanding rock climber. He was of medium build, a closely knit body, obviously flexible and promising tremendous agility. His face too could be startling flexible, almost india-rubber. In 1951 he had been with Eric Shipton on the Reconnaissance of Everest, where he was perpetuated in photograph beside the tracks of the Abominable Snowman. Last year medical examinations and Army service had kept him away from Cho Oyu, and this year he emerged as our doctor on the boat, almost ink-stained from the trials of the examination chamber. But he browned quicker than any of us, being the darkest person I know. London's pallor was soon Indian mahogany.

Mike was as serious, if you could get him to talk of it, about the medical aspects of the expedition as about his surgery. As an instance, his suggestion that he and I should on May 26th go up again to Camp VII as support party, originated in a determination to take alveolar samples (samples of air from the bottom of the lungs) at 24,000 feet. It proved a happy inspiration. At the same time a dislike of outward seriousness and the privilege of switching the conversation with a story (as broad as you like) are among the Englishman's most cherished characteristics. Climbers do not like living permanently on heights. It occurred to me later that one reason for the success of the expedition *as a party* may have been that very failure to linger on the sublime emotional and philosophic planes. Some may criticise this as unworthy. But Everest needs no sentiment. At a high camp, to listen to stories is relaxation; to juggle with emotional or sentimental complexities would be exhaustion.

Mike was the easiest and pleasantest companion, aware that his post as doctor limited his activity, yet not perturbed by this limitation. The under-seriousness made tent-talk about physiology and pathology, as well as the meaning and implications of the expedition, a satisfying pastime. It was equally satisfying to climb together. Our rhythms seemed to suit one another; not too fast, not too slow, and he had an understanding of the stresses caused by height.

I should perhaps add in conclusion that, after the preliminary coughs and throats and diarrhœas which for a time weakened the Sherpas, our health bill was excellent, a fair comment on the medical faculty. A good deal one takes for granted, but it is most cheering to read an account of the physical condition of, say, the 1933 Expedition after the climb,[1] and compare it with our own. Opening a parcel of medicines Mike exclaimed: "Heparin! I hope I don't have to use that!" And he never did.

Michael Westmacott and George Band were the two members of the party who had not climbed in the Himalaya before. Perhaps for this reason, and for their youth (Mike was aged twenty-eight), they were "run" by several newspapers as the first summit pair. A very dramatic but mythical account of a first "failure to reach the summit" appeared. One

[1] F. S. Smythe, *Camp Six*, Hodder & Stoughton, London, 1938, pp. 285, 286.

other feature (presumably unconnected with this story) they had in common: they both wore glasses.

Mike is a statistician at the Rothamsted Experimental Station, and served with the sappers in Burma. Hence two skills invaluable to the expedition. From being financier to the baggage party across India, involved in more complicated dealings than I could ever have contemplated, he found himself paymaster in charge of coolies to the first party marching out. As far as human brain could, he kept an account of the baffling complications of our personnel: Sherpanis appearing from nowhere; coolies who dropped off like plums without warning, perhaps not appearing to claim their loads at dawn; packages whose failure to arrive spelt an anxious afternoon.

On the mountain Mike was to be in charge of tents and structural apparatus. Tents were a constant problem; because we only had a narrow margin, and, had two men been taken seriously ill and sent down, there would have been less than no margin at all. Therefore each individual tent's position must be watched with the eyes of a lynx, whose eyes Mike fortunately possessed. In calculation, as in conversation, an accurate mind spotted and righted the misplacement.

I never had the fortune to climb with him, except for one "sapper" day of putting up bridges on the icefall. But I could see from "Mike's Horror"—a steep step edged on to a crevasse, that he was an ice-man no less than a rock climber. He took his climbing, as his mountains, with all John's seriousness, though outwardly in lighter vein. With John also he shared the interest of butterflies, attacking this subject with some thoroughness on the marches out and back. He caught and murdered over forty varieties; I believe that the British Isles possess only sixty in all.

Determination and unselfishness: two qualities that I suppose Everest demands supremely. Mike acclimatised with a determination wonderful for a first experience. Then, suffering badly from a cough and the wretched diarrhœa, he made daily attempts, after May 10th, to reach Camp VI. He was defeated only after expending everything in him. Going down, he was so far from giving up that he became, possibly, the saviour of others' lives, certainly of their peace of mind. He turned all his skill to the icefall, and the tiring but vital task of adjusting and lengthening bridges, taking down porters, sometimes finding a completely new route where the old had become dangerous. Thanks to him we returned safe in one day, down through the very different June scene, from Camp IV to Base.

It is difficult to describe a good organising secretary without the uneasy feeling that he would do better describing you. *C'est son métier,* among other things. Charles Wylie was the veteran of the expedition, having been appointed organising secretary by the Himalayan Committee in September 1952 and released by the Army for that appointment. When I first met him he was quietly getting on with the job at the Royal Geographical Society during October. I knew of him that he had made an attempt on Nilkanta in Garhwal, that he had been a prisoner of war in Malaya, and that he was a major in the Tenth Gurkha Rifles.

Charles had perhaps the hardest and busiest job of all and he took it as a labour of love. It would have been difficult to find two more gentle, gentlemanly military men to rule over us than Charles and John. During the months of preparation he was necessarily at the hub of every wheel, his help was being sought by telephone or express letter in every problem: equipment, publicity, Sherpa arrangements, Press and B.B.C. contacts. I seldom went into the Everest office at the R.G.S. without hearing at least one telephone ringing, more probably two simultaneously, and perhaps Charles's efficient helper, Ann Debenham, informing somebody that the expedition was *not* out to advertise brands of strengthening foods or underwear. "Hectic but unruffled" is my impression of the office in those days.

Being an officer in a Gurkha regiment, Charles spoke Nepali well. The value of appeals to the Sherpas in one of their own languages was incalculable. Indeed we could never understand how the Swiss managed without a linguistic member of the party, conversing through Tenzing in English. As transport officer, Charles was responsible for an infinity of arrangements not all equally agreeable to the Sherpas, and he remained immensely popular. I think this was because he showed himself exceptionally considerate of the needs and susceptibilities of Sherpas, equally with those of sahibs. He was very gentle with them, and never seemed to lose his temper, despite exasperating situations. As I see it, the art of treating Sherpas, or any hill people, is to let them know that they are companions, fellow-travellers; to do as much as they and conquer by example rather than precept. This practice Charles had acquired already, and he demonstrated it supremely on his ascent to the South Col with thirteen of them. Toward the top of the Geneva Spur his oxygen gave out. One of the Sherpas had failed, his load must somehow be carried the remaining feet over the Spur. Charles carried it.

I have a disquieting sense of repeating myself when I speak of members of the party taking a very serious view of the expedition and their responsibility to its "ideal." But with Charles this must be said again, for he especially, with more direct interest in the peoples than anyone except perhaps Charles Evans, saw the expedition as a social act quite as much as an act of mountaineering adventure. This combined effort of several nations was worthy of having more than a year of life devoted to it, and as much continuous, good-humoured exertion as one man could put into his job. Perhaps that was why, when in difficulties, I would find myself looking round for the tall figure in red Braemar sweater and handsome beard of the style of Charles the First.

Tenzing we always regarded as a member of the climbing party. But since he has become a public, indeed almost a controversial, figure, I hesitate to give his portrait. I might draw down upon me the wrath of those who purport to know his "life story" better than he knows it himself. I might be accused of distorting him for my own guileful and obviously political ends. I must plunge, however, pleading that I am giving no more than a brief personal picture of how I saw him. And I am confident that he would allow it, with that flashing smile which he readily and courteously accords.

Tenzing is tall for a Sherpa (he is really a Bhutia) and

heavy, weighing over ten stone. He appeared before us with the energetic air of an efficient climber; his every garment, and the axe that Raymond Lambert had given him, reminded you that he had served with expeditions. He knew his way about. For at thirty-nine he had for some years ceased to carry his Sherpa load and had set himself up as "sirdar" or chief of Sherpas, the sergeant-major to expeditions as it were. He had for a time instructed ski-ing for the Army. As sirdar he distinguished himself on the French Nanda Devi Expedition of 1951, reaching the top of Nanda Devi East. And, of course, he had taken a leading part in the two Swiss expeditions of last year.

It struck me from the first that the dark eyes under the jet-black hair brushed straight back became thoughtful when summits were mentioned. This characteristic distinguishes Tenzing, as I see it, from any other of his race that I know, Angtharkay included. Angtharkay, it seemed to me after 1945, might have a firmer grip on his troops, stand less nonsense from anyone, and be a first-class organiser. But his own duty and aim as sirdar is to give his sahibs satisfaction. That given, his work is done. When Herzog suggested, on Annapurna, that Angtharkay should accompany the summit party, the French were surprised that he refused. But he had done his job. With Tenzing it was different. When on May 26th Evans and Bourdillon were seen at the South Summit, which from the Col looks like the top, everybody was jubilant except Tenzing, who did not conceal his disappointment as a westerner would have done. All honour to him; he regarded himself most seriously as a climber, a representative of the Sherpas who should go to the top, and only secondly as a sirdar. And a fine climber he was, or he could never have been chosen.

He had then a very clear and laudable ambition, though cloaked under a certain oriental vagueness: to stand upon the summit of Everest, over whose northern as well as southern flanks he had already climbed. Apart from this a simplicity, which I as a westerner admire, was very obvious about him, together with a naïve courtesy as charming as it is real. When I once gave him a pair of boots that I did not need, he pre-

33

sented me the day after with a fine red propelling pencil, and the day after that the leads to go with it. "Tenzing is one of Nature's gentlemen," as very many have said, and it is true. Equally charming is his interest in your family and his anxiety, in exchange, to show photographs of his own. This was a natural politeness very pleasing to meet.

When I was in charge of Sherpa food, I suddenly realised why the calculations were proving so difficult: Tenzing does not read or write. Addition and multiplication are not therefore possible, and you must follow a simpler rule. Allow plenty and you will feed well, morale will not suffer. It was a brave band which deposited eighteen loads on the South Col. Tenzing was their leader and their representative upon the summit. If he had been a man of literary accomplishments I doubt if he could have represented them so well.

I should perhaps introduce myself alongside the company, but this is hardly necessary, for only too much of me will appear in these pages. I will say, however, that upon that afternoon of November 17th I felt something of an intruder. One reason for the cohesion of our party was that a number of members had climbed together, on Cho Oyu, on Everest in 1951, or on British hills. I had climbed with none except the leader, though I had met two others. Moreover I had suffered three accidents, the stroke of wind and weather, among mountains. The first was a fall of 200 feet with a damp ledge that came away on the Mickledore Grooves of Scafell in 1937, when I was nineteen years old. The last, in 1946, found me blown bodily by a gust off an easy rib of Great Gable, on to my leg which crumpled and broke under me. As I sat the weary hours nursing that leg, I vowed that it was all over with me, as far as serious climbing went. I recorded that vow in an epilogue to *Mountains and Men,* whose last chapter deals with this accident. When I returned to the Alps and fells, it was often to introduce boys or to explore new corners. Though I still climbed rock, I preferred to be led at "Very Severe."

And now here I was, an impostor joining in a very serious venture indeed. Perhaps it was unjustifiable to make my family anxious. Perhaps I was doomed to betray John's great and moving trust in me. Moreover, at first I also felt an impostor in the world of science, since everybody else seemed to be closer devotees of that goddess than myself. But I think I have said enough of our company to show that a companion was immediately accepted, on the sole merit of being prepared to get on with the job. No questions were asked, no *post mortems* held, on the immense file of disappointed and more deserving candidates.

Two things specially contributed to this feeling of being accepted. First, John's desire that each should be in charge of his "department," in London and on the mountain, so that in that little field he could be happily and supremely king. Secondly, as I have already indicated, he had chosen men who were mutually compatible, and most of whom had climbed together before. For this, as for many things, honour goes to Eric Shipton, who chose the 1952 party to Cho Oyu.

Finally, these were also men easy to talk to, each of whom it was a pleasure to approach and ask for something—the acid test. I have said that conversation had not the tone of an intellectual salon, though there was plenty of intellect present. But the setting of "foreheads villainous low" was, I found, positively helpful; since it is easy intercourse with companions that makes life in high camps a tolerable routine rather than a pain. There intellect is sour and emotion insipid. It is the

> *Empty heads and tongues a-talking*
> *Make the rough road easy walking,*
> *And the feather-pate of folly*
> *Holds the falling sky.*

A.J.VEILHAM

3

The Road to Kathmandu

February 12th—March 8th

1

The comfortable journey to Bombay on board the *Strathe-den* was enlivened, but not rendered uncomfortable, by the hospitality of the ship's officers and our fellow passengers. We had time to pause and think. I used to wonder, leaning over the rail, what was it all about, this mountain on whose top it must be every climber's ambition to stand?

To come on such an expedition a man must make sacrifices, even if he does not think about most of them. I myself must forfeit salary at Charterhouse over these months; also, far more important, for five months the company of wife and small son. Not only that, but I am condemned to give them anxiety which I could avoid, if I stayed at home. The boldest would not claim that climbing Everest is as safe as walking over green fields. To the average person it is a dangerous occupation; however much he may have confidence in the skill of the climber, objective dangers loom large. All this the family will not like to say, for fear of harassing the already harassed. But the terrors are there, and at the back of the climber's mind, too. He does his best for them by paying insurance premiums, a useless precaution since nothing can replace that loss if it comes; and yet these pledges he must give, as an insurance for his own peace of mind.

I could not claim that I was going to Everest for pleasure. Lesser mountains, yes, lesser ranges, where the hiss of the axe, the swing of the thigh uphill, the balanced body upon rock are the physical music of the mountaineer. But on Everest these pleasures are swirled away with the dust of Tibet,

◄ *We could see our loads being swung over the gorge. . . .*

37

in the pain of rarefied air, numbed limbs and storm-bound nights. I was not expecting to enjoy myself (and that I did enjoy myself after all is quite irrelevant). Therefore I was not going for pleasure.

I was going, it seemed to me, because this adventure was one of the fine things of life, an exciting thing. During the broadcasting on the boat before we left, an Italian commentator asked Michael Westmacott whether he felt a great thrill at going to Everest.

"Oh, it'll be good fun," Mike said, or something equally unenthusiastic.

"*È molto emozionato,*" the commentator translated into his microphone. And of course he was right. We *were* very excited, though being English we disliked intensely admitting as much in public. This adventure was apart from ordinary experience, a great compulsory heaving away out of a rut. Normally, modern men have little chance to take part in anything that can be called "great." Everybody must have an urge to break out, just once, from the comfort as well as the monotony of day-to-day; to do it by the proxy of books if the reality of escape is not possible; to live hard and to live fully these few days of life. Further, the sharing of such an enterprise with others will come to mean as much as the original challenge. The idea of Everest as an unclimbed mountain must first be present to the adventurers, and Everest must be climbed "because it's there," in Mallory's phrase. Then to the individual there presents itself the idea of a great common effort, an adventure in the company of others. Finally, there may be added to this conception the thought of Fame. She is, no denying it, a lady who sometimes takes us by the shoulders and spurs such part of our spirit as we can call "clear," away from our inhibitions and laziness. In this case she sets the seal of Everest on a climber's career; to gain the seal she goads him to unpleasant efforts over which he might hesitate if left to himself.

These were my thoughts, sometimes, as the *Stratheden* steamed across a most placid February sea, down through the hotter waters and always on, towards that curious spot marked on the ship's map in one corner of Nepal: Mount

Everest. We studied Nepali with Charles Wylie, rather desultorily I am afraid; played deck tennis and ate enormous quantities of food. I used to wonder occasionally: is it better to make the most of food while one has it, or start tightening the belt in preparation? Or perhaps never tighten it at all, that may be the answer.

Going down one day to my trunk in the baggage-room, I was startled to find that the boot repair outfit had leaked. In London I had worked for three days with Robert Lawrie's bootmakers, learning chiefly how to stick on micro-cellular rubber soles and heels. I came away with a box of tools and a tin of glutinous rubber solution for the purpose. The latter had now penetrated my one respectable suit, in a manner to remove much of its beauty. I wrote off to Rob Lawrie for more solution, and set about the suit with stain removers.

On the boat I read two books about Buddhism. I read of "tumo," the art of keeping warm even naked in the snow, and "lung-gompa," the art of going into a trance and travelling many miles at incredible speeds. It is strange how East and West differ in their approach even to physical exertion. "Relax," says the East, "meditate and lift yourself into the realm of All-consciousness. Your own petty sufferings will fall from you and you will be able to do the impossible." The West says, "Concentrate, endeavour and think hard. Then you can do anything. 'There's nothing neither good nor bad but thinking makes it so,' " and so on. There has been talk of a Yogi ascent of Everest. When it was diverted to so common an end, the mystic's power would surely fail him.

2

We reached Bombay on the morning of February 28th, and were met on board by Professor George Finch, A. R. Leyden, local secretary of the Himalayan Club, Basil Goodfellow of the Himalayan Committee, and George Lowe of our own party. Leyden shepherded us tactfully through the Customs, the most obliging I have ever met. We came away, however, with one query: what happened when we returned without the great majority of the goods that Charles had

39

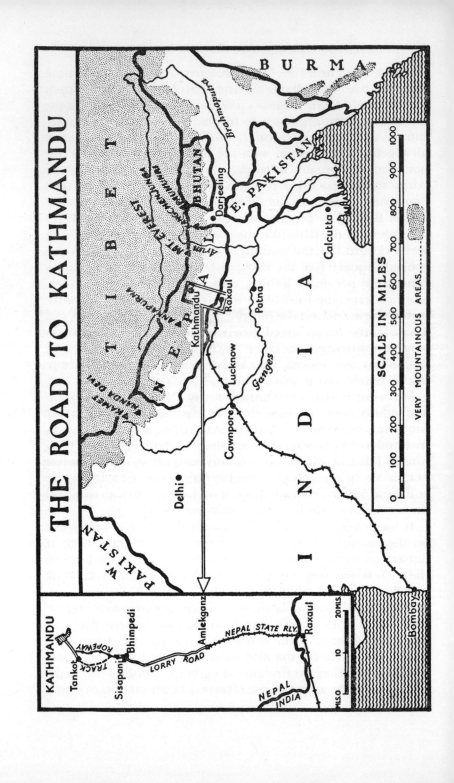

priced and signed for? The Customs officials must assume that we had sold them. At the Taj Mahal Hotel, Finch joined us after lunch for a talk about oxygen. Then I went down to the station to supervise the loading of our baggage into its special goods-wagon. It was the first time I had seen it all together, and I stood with the representatives of Mackinnon and Mackenzie, watching the strangest assortment of oddly shaped packages descend on to the backs of porters, be carried across and dumped in apportioned places on the wagon floor. The procession seemed endless. Some packages were short and small, like the photographic box, some long and awkward like the sections of the duralumin ladder, some robustly square like the cookery boxes. There were kitbags containing personal clothing, and an enormous round sack-cloth package, the bane of all who tried to handle it, containing the New Zealand sleeping-bags. The loading took two and a half hours; we reckoned nearly eight tons of equipment in over five hundred packages (including personal kit). The wagon was then locked. I pocketed the key and went off, hoping fervently that it would meet us safely at Lucknow.

We were royally entertained out at Pali Hill, by Leyden and others. But for Leyden's efficiency over our transport problems, we would certainly have had to stay several days in Bombay. As it was, after a delicious morning bathe with him at Juhu Beach, we were finally seen off at 11:00 P.M. on March 1st in the train bound for Cawnpore. Charles Wylie and Tom Stobart remained, to fly on business to Calcutta and thence direct to Kathmandu, capital of Nepal.

It was a hot journey. The engine broke down at one point on the morning of the 2nd, and the relief engine, when it did arrive, nearly burst itself into pieces trying to push us up the hill. It was very pleasant, at 9:00 A.M. on the 3rd, to be met by E. A. Gaskell, of Burma Shell, in Lucknow, and conveyed to his charming bungalow, where Mrs. Gaskell and he received us with a bath and most hospitable rest after the dusty excitements of the train. Our baggage, we discovered, would not arrive till the afternoon; we could not, therefore, to our great relief, go straight on without spending the night at Lucknow. At 2:15 P.M. we returned to the station to check the transhipping of our stores on to the narrower gauge line running to Raxaul. This time, thanks to Burma Shell employees, we were much quicker; at the same hour next day we ourselves climbed aboard with the pleasantest memories of hospitality, of a visit to the Zoo in the morning and to the historic Residency in the cool of an Indian evening.

We departed with the assurance that our new baggage-wagon had gone on before. As the evening wore on we became rapidly filthier, though rather cooler (Lucknow was suffering a heatwave). During the night I disgraced myself. At about 2:00 A.M. I heard thumpings on the door. I remember thinking through my dreams: "Ah, ticket-collector." I clambered out of my bunk half-awake and opened up. Alas, in an instant and before we could get the door shut, the total population of India seemed to have dumped itself screaming on the floor of our carriage. In vain George Lowe gesticulated and threatened. Families, bearers, merchants, they were all coming on "only for one station more." Occupation, like possession, is nine-tenths of the law, and that was the end of our sleep for the night.

At Samashtipur we changed trains for the last stage to Raxaul, on the Nepalese frontier. We breakfasted in company with Mr. Chatterjee, of Burma Shell, and set off again at 8:30. After the shaking experience of last night we dared not open the doors at all, even for food, and as the train was late, arrived very hungry in Raxaul at 3:30 P.M. But before we could have more than a biscuit and a cup of tea, there was much to do. George Lowe, Mike Westmacott and I were borne off in a jeep, through the flat-roofed village surrounded by hot rice-fields, to the Indian post, where in an upper room a Sikh officer handed me formidable documents relating to the precious mortar bombs. What the Indians thought they were for I cannot guess, but they were very trusting, after we had signed various undertakings on their behalf. Here too we took on more kerosene from Burma Shell.

Then there was the third transhipment, on to the still narrower gauge of the Nepal State Railway. This is a toy-like affair which very nearly met us too soon, when the jeep jauntily topping a rise found it almost on top of us as it ambled along the track. There had met us here a curious little Nepali, distinguished by a stammer and a topee, who styled himself "runner to the British Embassy," but unfortunately had not Mr. Gaskell's control of his men. The loading took a long time; it was 6:30 and almost dark (they had started at 3:30, when we arrived) before we could get off. Even then, nine loads which had not fitted into the two small Nepalese trucks had to be taken off, despite much gesticulation, pushing and general confusion. These we took and locked in a warehouse for the night. With Mike I walked to the dak bungalow, pleasantly sited among trees, and bathed off some of the dirt in a tub. Then we sat down to the first real meal of the day: chicken and vegetable and chapatti. We were now out of the land of bread; the bearer looked at me in astonishment, when I asked for it.

3

Next morning, the 6th, we were at the station soon after 7:00 A.M., receiving the mortar-bombs cautiously from an armed escort. We collected the nine packages, and at 7:30 chugged off, crossing a dirty little stream said to be the frontier between India and Nepal. No passports were demanded: that is not the Eastern way. But at the first station Henry, as I had mentally dubbed our runner, dived out and reappeared after some parley with a grubby piece of paper covered in Nepali characters: our pass. The whole journey of twenty-five miles took two and a half hours, and we might well have ridden, as others have done before, on the front of the engine to observe wild life crossing the rails. By the time we reached Amlekganz, an Indian-type village, but with a background of wooded hills, we were sleepy and yet hungry. Therefore while the train shunted and Henry looked lost among the squabbling coolies, the phlegmatic British pulled out two chickens, potatoes and tomatoes brought from the bungalow, and had lunch.

The last stage to Bhimpedi must be done by lorry; in the end four outwardly respectable lorries did appear. Amid further squabbling the fourth transhipment took place. The porters here were ragged, broad-featured and yellower, skinned than the Indians; high cheek-bones and slanting eyes set in flat faces. We congratulated ourselves on getting away by 12:30, for this very day, according to the schedule worked out for us by Greg, we were due to load our stores on to the rope railway at Bhimpedi and from there walk as far as Sisapani, a dak bungalow on the road to Kathmandu. For the last stage to the capital must be completed on foot by ourselves. There we should arrive on the 7th, for John hoped to begin the march out as early as the 9th.

We distributed ourselves on the tops of the loaded lorries, and set out hopefully on the twenty-four-mile drive. These lorries, it must be admitted, were better to look at than to drive in; the general Indian hill principle of tying things up with tape when smoke actually issues from the bonnet seemed to hold here, too. A special man is appointed for this job. He sits on top of the lorry and descends, tape in hand, to do the tying up when need arises. The road ran through valleys of oak and fir channelled by stony streams cutting their sides. In some places there were curious, upstanding sandy pinnacles.

We arrived in a rain shower at Bhimpedi at 2:50, the Georges (Band and Lowe) later, as their lorry had punctured. The rope railway posts can be seen from the village here, marching up through the woods from an enormous shed, tin-roofed and open at the sides. In this structure coolies were loading packages on to trolleys, which then swung off up the steel rope. Mike Westmacott appeared with the gloomy news that as ours would take at least three hours, they could not possibly load them that day, work ceasing at 5:00 P.M. The lorries had meanwhile dumped everything on an uneven, sack-covered floor, while we ran about rescuing the most precious. What to do? We tried two telephones, rickety contrivances which seemed to have very vague ideas of operating. Then one of the scribes suggested the Indian Engineers' unit engaged in building the road from the plains to Kathmandu. Mike volunteered to walk up to their officers' mess. He had not gone far when he met the Commandant, Colonel Grant, himself, in a jeep. The situation was saved.

44

John Hunt.

THE "EVEREST POSITION" –
George Band, Ed Hillary,
Charles Evans, Michael
Ward, Tom Stobart.

Michael Westmacott.   Tom Bourdillon and Charles Evans.

Griffith Pugh, Wilfrid Noyce, Charles Wylie.

unt, Hillary, nzing, Ang ima, Gregory, we.

THE MARCH—Bouldering. Our leader (perched on pebble), Westmacott and Band. Lowe and Evans watching.

BEFORE EVEREST – The Everest range from Pumori ridge: Lho La (bottom
West Shoulder and Nuptse (

t, South Col, Geneva Spur, Lhotse. The Icefall tumbles down between the
is seen on the extreme right).

John Hunt watches the loads arrive by rope railway.

A budding Sherpani and her brother

THE MARCH – Crossing the Dudh Kosi.

THE MARCH–The view at Manga Deorali. (Westmacott, Gregory, Lowe, Evans, Hillary.) Gauri Sankar appears on the left, and Menlungtse's top between Evans and Hillary.

Right: Coolies cross the Chanawati Khola.

THE MARCH – Namche Bazar. Chorten in front, and yaks. Stone houses behind.
SOLA KHUMBU – The Tenzings and Angtharkays of the future.

Colonel Grant generously offered to put us all up and to set a guard over the baggage; also to check it for us. But we had the further melancholy news that tomorrow, Saturday, was the Nepali holiday, so that the earliest time for loading would be 1:00 A.M. the day after. It seemed we would be lucky in these parts if we escaped a holiday of some sort. There was no point in our all staying, and the two Georges pushed on with Mike Ward, after a most encouraging tea, to Sisapani. Mike Westmacott (treasurer to the baggage because statisticians are to the layman obvious calculators, and therefore financiers) stayed with me to see the loads off and pay any expenses.

The experience of two nights with Indian Army officers was worth having for itself. The mess is a fine white stone building, situated on a bluff near the head of the valley a mile and a half up from the rope railway. It was once the pleasure palace of the Prime Minister, a notably more spacious one than the King's palace nearby. The living-rooms are on three sides of a square, about a central courtyard in which the dining-room stands as a separate upper storey supported on wooden pillars. Here, that evening over dinner, we met the officers in charge of the road, the first road to join India and Kathmandu; and next morning, up at Unit Headquarters, we saw a model of it as it will be when completed, winding many miles over the westward hills. Colonel Grant hoped that this very autumn it would be "jeepable," and finished by the end of next year. The sentimental traveller must regret that Nepal's isolation will be of the past; no longer will this land be the mystery of a few. But that consummation, we must admit with a sigh, was bound to come. The best we can hope is that the invaders will be merciful.

That morning we attended a Durbar, at which the men, sitting in rows in front of the colonel's table, are allowed to put complaints and suggestions to him. One ingenuous suggestion was that the period of service on the road should be shortened, for the altruistic reason "that others may have the wonderful experience of this great work." Then we rested, in preparation for the morrow, and explored the village. It is, at present, an important place, though not large.

45

Some of the houses are of three storeys, plastered with mortar and often half-timbered. The valley bottom which it commands is fertile, and there seems to be little need for the terracing of the hillside common elsewhere. When the road is finished and the rope railway becomes obsolete, Bhimpedi will be "finished," too. As an elderly member of the Rana family, lunching with us, put it: "The good old days are gone." He thereupon bared his backside to show a scar left by the knife of an Indian whom he had defeated at wrestling, in the times when men were men.

All these days of journey across India, Kathmandu shimmered before the mind's eye remote and mysterious as Everest itself. To the traveller by air it is a three-day flight from London. To us, by sea and land, it was a three-weeks' journey with obstacles and discomforts at every turn. We were making for a goal rather than a jumping-off place, for a hidden city guarded by barriers of heat and height in its remote valley. Tomorrow we would see it. We would have done the job. But at the same time one spell would be broken.

4

Colonel Grant had kindly ordered a jeep for us, along with black coffee, at 12:45 A.M. At the bleak hour of 1:00 A.M. on March 8th we found ourselves under the dim electric light of the rope railway terminus. The work started. Load after load we saw piled on to the endless succession of trolleys, to be swung up into blackest night above. Each load must be checked and the trolley number noted. As usual, there were more people present than necessary, the superfluity being there, as is usual in the East, to give advice. The whole process took five hours, 507 packages were despatched in 86 loads. Usually, heavier sacks of rice were put with our loads to give ballast to the trolley. I could not help thinking: This will probably be the last time that this method of transport is used for an expedition. Our grandchildren will marvel at the difficulties of the early pioneers in Nepal, before the road was built.

At 6:00 A.M. we staggered out and had tea, with one large

46

chapatti sandwich, at the tent of the Indian N.C.O.'s who had helped us. Then they took us by jeep back to the village, the start of our eighteen-mile walk to Tankot, the roadhead some five miles out of Kathmandu.

The path across the hills begins with a steep climb up a scrubby, stony hillside to Sisapani. At the top of the ridge, just high enough for crimson rhododendron, there is a fine view of the first big span of railway. We could see our loads being swung on thread-like cable over the gorge, to a scarcely visible pylon on the opposite side. It was a frightening thought that one box of high-altitude boots, dropped a thousand feet and smashed, might wreck the whole expedition. I believe accidents are very rare; but that hardly convinces the purveyor of precious burdens. Fortunately another of our terrors had been laid by Mike's numerical calculations in the small hours: except, possibly, for the odd ration-box, all our stores had arrived safe and virtually undamaged at the trolley terminus.

The walk itself was our first real stretch of the legs. However many times you run round a ship's deck, you cannot feel more than aired. And this walk was taken in country upon which dusty summer had not yet laid a hand. The pink of almond blossom arranged itself charmingly against the yellow mud of which most villages were built. It is very common to have a division: upper half yellow, lower half painted white; and usually a thatched roof. Set in a grove of almond or pear, with the steeply sloping wooded or terraced hills behind, the scene is an idyll. Once, resting on the wayside grass and eating our second chapatti, Mike said: "Whatever happens on the expedition, I really am *happy* today." We both felt that.

As we approached the second of the two 6,000-foot passes, the marks of a bulldozer became increasingly obvious. We learned later that one had passed along this stony, muddy and winding track a few days before: an astonishing feat. The only other mechanical objects we saw signs of were motor-cars—dismembered. It takes thirty coolies about a week to get a motor-car body over the hills to Kathmandu, and we saw three bodies beside the path. I cannot say that we saw one in motion; it seems that the refreshment needed on these journeys is considerable. We ourselves, continuing up a small ravine, were just beginning to feel the hardness of the track on untried feet. It was a relief to top the final pass and look down on the Valley of Nepal—a land which had till this very day seemed remote as the Pacific. The first glimpse of the broad, calm plain, backed by gently rising, wooded hills, would have enchanted any Cortez. But we were not yet there; not even at Tankot, where John had told me over the unit's wireless yesterday that we were to be met. The descent zigzagged interminably through forests of pine, cedar and many tropical trees. The afternoon was now close and cloudy. Many Nepalis came toiling up, the richer carried in a type of sedan chair. They eyed our unusual figures curiously.

The last stretch to Tankot lay along the flat. Here, at our walk's end, we could drink tea in the open-air teashop and hope for our mechanical transport to finish the job. But preferring to walk rather than wait, we set off along the final six-mile road. Two miles along, a beautiful limousine driven by a chauffeur drew up: the British Ambassador, Christopher Summerhayes, in person. It was a most kind gesture. In a very few minutes we had whisked through the suburbs, past statues of the kings, past the high walls that are all you can see of most of the palaces of Kathmandu, and were drawing up in a thunder-shower outside the Embassy. For the first time the whole expedition was together.

A.J.VEILHAN

4

Open Order March

March 8th—March 26th

1

The first reaction of the others, some of whom had been waiting for well over a week, was to leap at the baggage and start sorting almost before it had been unloaded. "Where are the cigarettes?" "Are these *all* the New Zealand sleeping-bags?" "Was it checked with the inventory?" "Where's my rifle?" and so on. The 9th was a busy day for all; there was no time on this outward voyage to visit the temples and ba-zaar of Kathmandu. All were thankful occasionally to retire to the kindly shelter of the Embassy. The Ambassador ac-cepted us as we were, our vagaries and our odd businesses. But for his patience and unfailing help we could never have started at all. The Embassy was a homely place, too. It was pleasant to walk into the drawing-room and find Greg, say, in a large arm-chair reading a book; to be able to sit down for a minute with the daily paper.

At Bhadgaon, some six miles to the east, the luggage was lined up on a parade-ground which we all visited. All except John. He, poor man, had been told to wait for a most urgent telephone call. Having waited, indeed for three hours, for the first call ever to connect London and Kathmandu, he found that it was a certain daily newspaper asking for a story. Disgruntled already by a stupid article which had appeared that morning in an Indian paper, John finished the afternoon hardly in the mood of missionary zeal which should inspire the leader of a quest for the Grail. But the rest of us were happier; each had surveyed his department and opened boxes; the loads were neatly stacked over the open meadow

◄ . . . *along a path that rose
and fell interminably.*

51

of the parade-ground by Charles Evans and Charles Wylie. Above all, we had met Tenzing and the Sherpas; that is to say those of the special, high-carrying Sherpas who had accompanied Tenzing from Darjeeling, or come from their home at Namche Bazar to meet us. These must not be confused with the coolies or load-carriers for the march, who stood or sat in ragged files behind the loads.

My first view of Tenzing was as he ducked from the camera of a questing journalist. There was his now famous shy smile, showing whitest teeth, as he shook hands with the sahibs; he asked me if Angtharkay had not been with me on Pauhunri.[1] Stumbling as it was, he seemed to prefer my Urdu to English. He looked much larger than the other Sherpas; and his dress of military-style shorts and puttees, topped by a green beret, gave him a more commanding appearance. The Sherpas meanwhile bustled about the loads. They were dressed in the most unlikely mixture of garments. Gym shoes would be topped by either plus-fours, shorts, long Tibetan-style trousers, or even pyjamas. Some of the more professional-looking wore boots, and berets or ski-caps. The hat was more usually a trilby; though some of the load-carriers of the march wore high Tibetan hats with fur flaps. There, smiling shyly, was Da Namgyal, in blue shorts and short-sleeved shirt, his long bare legs tapering into gym shoes. There was Ang Temba, a small gorilla both in strength and appearance, and my own orderly, little Ang Dawa I, whom the French christened Benjamin, wearing cloth cap, plus-fours and flaming red stockings above his gym shoes. The cast of the Sherpa face is far more Tibetan than Nepali, having rounded features and narrow eyes, for their home was originally Tibet. Several of them had brought their womenfolk; these carried loads as coolies. In fact, on the march the women carried more than the men, though their position on the pay-roll was never clearly defined. They were dressed in long, heavy black costume; on their heads either an old towel or a Sherpa scarf, for easing the load's headstrap. From their

[1] Angtharkay appears in *Nanda Devi* and other books of Eric Shipton. Also with me in *Mountains and Men,* on peaks of Sikkim. He is often spelt Ang Tharke, but I am keeping Shipton's spelling.

waists hung the characteristic Sherpani apron, spun in the home at Namche and woven of strips of multi-coloured cloth, fastened together and wrapped right round the hips. They wore high, felt Tibetan boots, or went barefoot. The Sherpanis were always cheerful and never seemed to get drunk or quarrelsome. We sometimes wondered whether it would not be possible to staff a whole expedition with them. Besides carrying heavy loads, they gave a dash of colour to the march. Some of them were very pretty; rose red upon the dark bloom of their cheeks, flashing teeth, straight black hair and bright eyes that narrowed to slits when they laughed. There was Daku, *"La plus jolie de nos Sherpanis,"* as the Swiss called her, and "Ang Temba's girl friend," tall and straight, with clean-cut features and the grave gentleness of a Madonna.

In the background of the parade-ground lent to us by the Nepalese Army are cloudy hills, against which soldiers drill. Nearer to the loads our very different, tattered army awaited us. These were the coolies engaged, for the most part locally, to carry as far as Base Camp. In order to be a little less like a battalion, we were to march in two parties, Charles Wylie, Mike Ward and Griff Pugh coming on a day later with two hundred coolies and aided by five Gurkha N.C.O.'s. The remaining one hundred and fifty of them would be leaving with our main party tomorrow, the 10th, under the leadership of one Hakoman Singh, representing the contractor. A few Sherpani aprons peeped out, but most of these carriers were dressed in the Indian costume of the nearer valleys.

That evening we had our second reception; the first had been a party at the British Embassy the night before. The reception of the 9th was at the Indian Embassy, a magnificent palace, floodlit and with a military band playing on the lawn outside. Escorted through a marble hall, we climbed up red carpet to a long upper room. Its high, barrel-vaulted roof was fretted with gilt moulding on white. Even the chairs were of gilt wood, and the chandeliers, enormous structures of myriad glass pieces, were the Nepali version of a Victorian candelabrum. Here we were kindly received by the Indian Ambassador and his wife, and passed on to talk with the dignitaries of the capital in their black, frock-type coats and tight white trousers. Finally the Royal Family made its entrance: the two Queens, the Crown Prince and the Princesses. We soon learned that on the entry of V.I.P.'s special anthems were played, during which one stood to attention. But it was not always possible immediately to tell which they were; after one exhausting bout George Band said: "Well, at any rate, *this* is jazz," and filled his glass, only to find that a specially important personage was being introduced.

2

The last bath. The last of hot running water. How many of the civilities of life are easily dispensed with! Like Christian shedding his sins, we go easily into the new and freer round. The last sorting of personal belongings. Should this and that be left or taken? What about the new toothbrush I had meant to buy? Four months more of this one might be a little unhygienic. And how many books, the eternal problem? I always take laughably too many. We were to carry fifteen to twenty pounds of our own each, and to load some ten pounds more, not counting sleeping-gear, into our personal Sherpa's sack. As I packed, John, whose room I shared, was up already and hard at his *Times* dispatch. He planned to come on next day with the second party, and double-march to catch up the first. For the leader there was much still to be done.

Our bus for Bhadgaon left at 9:45, after the last breakfast to be taken on chairs round a table. A curious, almost physical, sensation seemed to tickle my back. Soon we would be alone together. What pleasures and what pains! Humans appear to delight in flinging their unco-ordinated selves into a crucible of experience, to see what painful but unified creature drags itself up the last few feet of a hill. Certainly it was in part a pleasing vision of tents and a thrill of lonely nights that knocked at my stomach. But there were few moments for thought. The jolting journey did not take long; soon we were again inspecting our private army, now laden and ready for the "quick march." The 60-lb.-load packing

54

system, which the two Charleses had stayed overnight to supervise, seemed to have worked well. Where the packages were underweight, they had been made up to approximately the 60 lb. One of the heaviest items was bullion: coin with which to pay the coolies. This was brought out in metal boxes from Kathmandu by John, and made up twelve full loads. Then there were the awkward six-foot sections of ladder, and an enormous rectangular metal box containing Griff's physiological needs. At last, after a photographic orgy by many visitors, Mike Westmacott and I streamed off with the gaggle. The time was 11:20 and the march to Everest had begun.

Bhadgaon itself is a fine town, with great pagoda-type Buddhist temples. The houses along the stone-paved streets are graceful with the elaborate wood-carving of their wide cornices: work done when the Newars held power in Nepal. They are of reddish stone, and there is often a balconied third storey. In one square, potters were at work, moulding beautiful vases on massive wheels some four feet in diameter. Then we were out on the broad highway toward Banepa, our first stage and some six miles away. The road is still passable by cars, and parties of Nepalis passed us sardine-packed in ancient lorries. It was the season of weddings; several times we saw the bride borne down from some knoll above the road on men's shoulders, to the boom-boom of long, tubular wooden trumpets. Seated on a bank we ate Embassy sandwiches—the last bread. The New Zealanders, Ed and George, joined the lunching party at the roadside; long and lean with a laugh always, and a fine mountaineer's appetite.

We walked on, through fields of rice, onions, potatoes and wheat, into the considerable village of Banepa. Cooled by recent thunderstorms, the day was cloudy, almost English. Many said that these storms meant a late monsoon. We found the first arrivals squatted on a rise beyond the village, and Thondup, our cook, making a fire between three stones. There were some who criticised Thondup's cooking, and it is true that he could not make tea. But then that, with powder milk, would have been something of a feat. I thought his meals good, varied with the little local vegetable we could

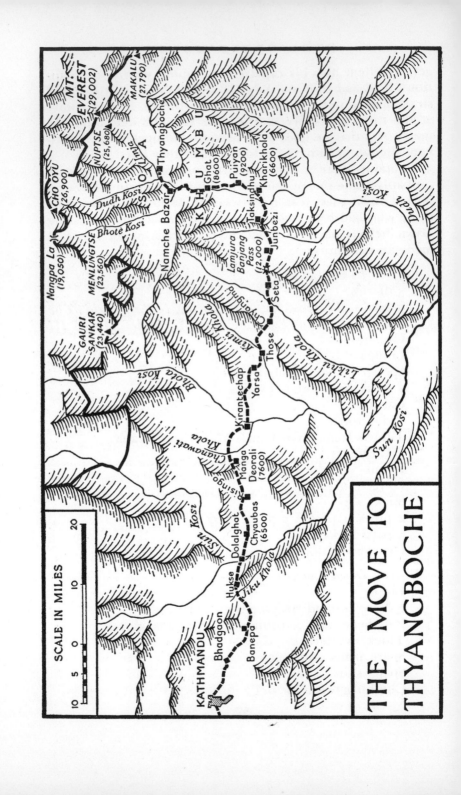

THE MOVE TO THYANGBOCHE

SCALE IN MILES

get; excellent also his capacity for coping with odd conditions. Tall and thin and hawk-like, with black hair brushed straight back and a certain deficiency of teeth, he was always at the camp site early, starting the tea. His defect on the march was that he tried very complicated operations, which kept the sahibs hungry for longer than they liked.

Thondup wore a distinguished costume of bottle-green, probably made out of one of the Cho Oyu sleeping-bags reported missing last year, for it was immediately recognised by those who had been with Shipton. While he made tea, Ang Dawa helped me to arrange my personal kit, of which I made an inventory:

Carried by me (28 lb.)
　　3 diaries
　　9 books, the most important being *Il Purgatorio, The
　　　　Brothers Karamazov,* and *Les Misérables, II* and *III*
　　Camera
　　Compass
　　Sponge bag and 2 small towels
　　2 pairs thin cotton pyjamas
　　Gas cape
　　Vidor torch
　　Tablets from Mike Ward: Multivite & Water
　　　　Cleansers
　　Iodine & Mylol Insect Cream
　　Oxygen mask
　　Sticky tape
　　2 pipes, 1 packet pipe-cleaners
　　5 pairs socks
　　Gym shoes (worn sometimes instead of boots)

In Ang Dawa's sack
　　Li-Lo
　　2 New Zealand sleeping-bags and hood
　　Polythene bags, 1 containing extra silk gloves
　　Thick sweater
　　Spare pants and vest
　　Spare shirt
　　Climbing breeches

I intended to march in an old pair of climbing boots, being suspicious of gym shoes. I was the only one who did not wear this now fashionable footgear for the whole journey.

Everybody seemed busy. Tom Stobart and Greg were photographing before an admiring audience of locals. Tom Bourdillon was looking at oxygen masks. Mike Westmacott, in charge of coolie operations, wrote up the coolie book. There Charles was discussing the route with Tenzing. The really experienced expeditioners, Ed and George Lowe, had their Li-Los inflated and were deep in Peter Cheyney, adopting what came from frequent use to be called "The Everest Position." George Band pulled tins out of the Compo box, and I joined him to interpret our needs to Thondup. Soup, steak and kidney, with local potatoes and spinach, cake and coffee. These Compos were arranged with a different menu for each day; the tinned cake, a great success, held the field as sweet for five days. The remaining two days we indulged in tinned peaches.

We usually turned in early, for the plan agreed by all was to start about 6:00 A.M. on biscuit and tea, then halt for breakfast after some two hours, preferably near a stream in which to bathe. Mugs of tea therefore appeared soon after five, borne to each of us by his own Sherpa. While we sleepily packed up, the coolies arrived in groups from the village, and with inimitable coughs and grunts got down to their loads. Alas, we had no machine to record the lung-splitting "early morning cough." Meanwhile the big tent, in which some slept and all ate, was due to come down. We had two of these, high, metal-strutted affairs, extremely quick to put up—and take down, as Ed, in charge of them, demonstrated that first morning. It paid to be out before the guys were loosened.

The march to Dolalghat, on the main Sun Kosi River, was one of the longest. A pass shortly above Banepa gave a first uncertain view of the high Himalaya; then a long drop through pines followed by Himalayan oak, to the Jiku Khola, a stream flattened out in a broad plain and given up to rice-fields. A few of us ahead seemed to walk interminably over this, growing hotter and thirstier. At last a village, and

Thondup consented to deposit us under a huge pipul. These great trees, the "sacred fig" of India, stand watch and ward of every Himalayan village. Their spreading branches and huge corrugated stems offer shady welcome to the traveller. The question suggests itself, which came first, the village or the pipul?

It was 8:55, and George Band and I wandered off to watch a treadmill: a simple affair, a long beam arranged see-saw fashion, with one end having a downward projection which fitted into a hole. In this hole the grain is manipulated by hand or stick. The other end is "trodden" up and down. At 9:45 appeared a very indignant Greg and Tom Stobart. We had gone far too far, the photographers had been very busy and had had a horrible time catching up, etc., etc. A compromise was made for the morrow, while we waited another forty minutes for an elaborate breakfast of porridge, sausage-meat and eggs, chapattis, butter and marmalade.

We went on over a small col, then down along another valley, also tributary to the Sun Kosi, on a path that rose and fell interminably. Walking with Charles Evans, I agreed that a host of large langur monkeys swinging up and down the steep hillside oaks could not possibly be mistaken for Abominable Snowmen. (Some have suggested this solution of the mystery.) We were very hot when we reached the broad river at Dolalghat, only 2,500 feet above sea level, and slipped gratefully into the most delicious of bathes. After three times in, we washed the odd handkerchief and lay on the beach. One great advantage of starting early is that you arrive comparatively early in the afternoon, hence can spend the rest of the day on your own pursuits: writing, reading or butterfly-catching with John and Mike Westmacott. It was here, as we were supping in the dark, that John caught us up. Here, too, most began to sleep out. Under the brightest of stars and watching the shrunken moon that we had seen rise that morning, I glimpsed again the less mundane feature of the expedition. Poetry, she had had to hide her head, with all the flurry of oxygen masks, equipment sorting, baggage worries and the like. Now she peeped out with the drone of distant voices over innumerable camp-fires, inviting me to measure the starry sky, lulling me asleep to the river's tune.

It was always pleasant to lie and drink tea, even Thondup tea, in the early morning, with the stars dimming and the coolies' cough ringing its familiar bark over the meadow. But then one had to be up and enter the packing scramble before the tent came down. Usually I stayed with Mike to see the last loads off, for if there had been *chang* (native rice beer) at the village, the coolies were likely to be late. Hako-man Singh, looking like a prophet with his long stick and flashing eyes, would speak eloquently of their misdeeds while they slipped shamefaced between the straps. This morning we had a long climb out of the Sun Kosi bed, to Chyaubas at 6,500 feet on the next ridge. The marches, because coolies carrying 60 lb. could not go too far, were not long; today, for instance, we arrived at 12:45, having breakfasted at 9:30. Before leaving England we had been strongly urged to wear oxygen masks during the march, in order to get used to them. I usually sneaked off for a spell with mine in the cool early morning, but some, and particularly John, were heroically conscientious. After breakfast, when the sun was getting really hot, they would don these things for a nice long hill, steam their way up it, and arrive in an aura of sweat, virtue and exhaustion at the top. There all would vow that it had not been quite as bad as last time. On this occasion a pleasant walk from the ridge top, over Cumberland-style fellside, led to the camping site, about half a mile short of the village. In the afternoon I joined the butterfly hunters for a hectic excursion over the next ridge. Far away cloud and haze hid the snow-peaks towards which we were heading. But shreds of an impressive ridge glistened whitely through mist.

The next day too was ominously hazy. Some of us were burned from yesterday, and Charles Evans's back was a healthy lobster red. My elbows were slightly sore, but marching in shorts and shirt with dark glasses and no hat has always suited me well. The coolies started with difficulty, as Chyaubas appears to possess *chang*, and I took the opportunity of learning the composition of our entourage: one hundred and fifty coolies; thirty Sherpas, including Sherpanis come from Namche; three guides; three company commanders, each supposedly responsible for fifty coolies; one Hakoman Singh, armed with a whistle and his long stick.

The way lay over a long ridge, 7,500 feet high. Rhododendrons, a blaze of crimson, lined the path. A descent and a valley of rice-fields led to a short climb up to Risingo, on a bluff overlooking the river. Risingo has a well-known *gompa* or temple, in whose very precincts we camped. I was disposed to treat it with respect; not so Thondup, who proceeded to hammer sticks and nails into its side wall for his kitchen tarpaulin, while the Sherpanis spread their bedding on the two verandas. Just as tea appeared we had the first prelude to storm in a hail-shower of stones as large as the traditional moth-balls. Sobered by it we visited the gompa. In the porch there is a very fair modern painting of the Round of Existence.[1]

Inside, high in gloomy darkness at the end, Buddha sits with his wife and disciples. Erotic paintings of tantric gods and goddesses adorn the walls. Before these Tom Stobart's camera-carrier Sherpa prostrated himself. This curious character, a great drinker, nearly toothless and possessed of the lewdest laugh I have ever heard, proved to be a former lama and conducted us round with much ceremony.

When we came out, the real storm was brewing. First a high wind with squalls of rain. All threw themselves outside and flung ration-boxes on to the tent-flap. The gale lessened as the rain increased. We were now all in the big tent, but discovered that, as we were on the flat ground of the compound (we had not liked to abuse a churchyard by digging trenches), water was penetrating the edges from underneath, while slight drips enlivened proceedings from above. At this point supper appeared, as if by miracle, in the hands of two wet and grinning figures who had run from

[1] See Marco Pallis—*Peaks and Lamas*, page 146, for a good specimen and explanation. Briefly, the artist uses traditional forms to illustrate the Buddhist reincarnations. Shindje, judge of the dead, holds the wheel. He wears the "terrible" aspect and the wheel is divided into sections illustrating the various rebirths: gods, Titans, yidags, purgatories, animals, men. Keeping the wheel moving is "Karman," the force of Action.

the half-blown-down kitchen. The rain went on. If the Sherpas were fine, I have never admired the phlegmatic British more. With Li-Los almost afloat, umbrellas up and torches alight, the party continued its study of Peter Cheyney and Tolstoy, Dorothy Sayers and Jane Austen. If those great ones could but know what a spell they cast!

Fortunately the rain stopped at eight. The next march, to Manga Deorali (7,600 feet), was in brilliant sunshine which dried us out. Its chief memories are a splendid bathe while breakfast cooked, and the long grind up to a col giving our first real view of the Gauri Sankar range, which lies to the west of Everest. The contrast of luxury and sweat is characteristic of all Himalayan travel. John and George Band suffered conscientiously in masks. As we approached the col over grassy flats studded with small oaks, we knew that something was coming; but were hardly prepared for that breath-taking view of the range, looking clear and close as the Bernese Alps from Thun. Gauri Sankar itself stood bastion on the left. Next to it came the fantastic, white granite and ice pyramid of Menlungtse, nearly 24,000 feet. Far on the right was the ridge of Numbur and Karyolung cut as in pasteboard against the blue. I took a photograph, which appears as Plate 7(a). A foreground of almond blossom framed the finest camp site that we enjoyed. I could not help comparing these marches with those of previous expeditions, across Tibet. There, temperatures well below zero and bitter, dusty winds over the barren plateau made each day a burden. In 1953 there were no unpleasant days on that march through the Nepalese valleys. Each night most slept out under the stars. Each day we lazed in a friendly way before a fine view, watching the innumerable ragged, smiling coolies as they arrived in their twos and threes through the afternoon.

We were cutting across the grain of the country, for the rivers of East Nepal flow south, to join the Sun Kosi and Arun, whereas the march to Everest lies almost due east. Hence much up- and down-hill work to cross the intervening ridges. On the 15th we descended nearly 4,000 feet to the Chanawati Khola (*khola,* smaller than *kosi,* also means river).

Here we bathed and breakfasted, and Ang Dawa washed my socks. Over the river swung a hazardous-looking chain bridge, a line of wooden slats leading between iron V's and handrails. Tom Stobart, athirst for filming that day, took many shots of it. The rise from here to Kirantechap (4,400 feet) is not great; we were there by midday. We camped on a terrace out of the village, towards a pine-covered headland overlooking the Bhota Kosi, our next river. Here I lay with John that afternoon and made suggestions for the first despatch from the march. As the last light tinged the peaks, I was trying to type my own reports, which I was sending back to three schools. The pale gold on the snow faded gently as the shadows crawled up, obscuring the deeply-shaded fluting of Menlungtse. The peaks continued as a presence, long after they were invisible in a sky of star-patterned mauve.

We descended steeply to the Bhote Kosi next morning, a big river spanned by a fine iron bridge. Just before this John spotted a pointed boulder some thirty feet high by the wayside. Daring routes were made up it, and henceforward bouldering "by the eyebrows" became a popular pastime. From the river we climbed steeply through woods to a little village, below which we breakfasted. Here those desiring to suffer again donned masks. I noticed that the oxygen experts were not among them, but decided they must already know the routine and were exempt. I put on my mask. Yarsa, our halting-place, lies in a wide bowl of the hills under the next pass. Beyond the village bearing this name a stream cuts the hillside in a wide nullah. Here, in the heat of the day, I rounded a corner to the spectacle of Charles Evans looking happiness itself under a fine natural shower. After tea John and I wandered up the charming river-bed looking at birds: the white-capped redstart, commonest as ever, a dipper and a rock-thrush.[1] Meanwhile, the coolies had constructed shelters from branches. In the darkness twenty fires, surrounded by grinning faces, glittered up to us. With all its hardship, they have a happy life. The next step, the next halting-place, the next meal, these are what they think about. When there is not an-

---

[1] The prettiest bird of all on the march was the scarlet minivet.

other job, they return to the village. There the women await them, the rice-fields and the potato harvest.

Often it was dewy, and some of us lay in the tent with only heads projecting. The 17th was a dewy start, and began with a climb of two hours to the pass at 8,400 feet. At its top is a *mane* or prayer wall and a *chautara* or resting-place. These stone structures, simple shelves of slabs very convenient for resting loads, are the bane of travellers. They are erected by benevolent persons of the district, and no self-respecting coolie would dream of passing them without stopping. When there are many benevolent persons in the district, and hence many *chautaras* close together, the journey becomes slow. This particular one was beautifully placed. Far ahead over the rhododendrons a tangle of peaks sparkled at us, but over one gap a small triangle of snow drew and held the eye: Everest. I think that we all looked at it with emotion. My impression of this voyage so far had been of a happy wandering; not carefree—the coolies and many another problem saw to that—but happy in the immediacy of day-to-day. Everest hung for me like a school test over the school holidays; a trial to be looked forward to apprehensively, but which nothing in the world would make me avoid. A dim mysterious shape evoked in dream and then stored hurriedly away, with other dreams and hopes. And now, here it was. It was so high, its top peeped at us over all these nearer ranges, which seemed blusteringly to be trying to hide it. It was so removed from things of this world, that the idea of climbing it seemed as fatuous as sacrilegious. We descended the sunny slope to breakfast, myself very pensive. Are the Buddhists not right in believing Everest to be the home of the gods?

The remainder of the march to Those on the Kimti Khola (tributary of the Bhota Kosi) was enlivened by massive scarlet rhododendrons. Those itself is a big village, with shops. Iron is mined above it, and it is here that the chain bridges which we had crossed are made. Passing through the village you can stop at half-a-dozen smithies and watch the forging of chains and plates. We camped on a grass flat beyond, near an old man fishing for mahseer in the river. I cannot say that he caught anything.

I spent an hour and a half in a gas mask on the walk up to our next pass, a higher one of 9,500 feet. This pass marks the beginning of Sherpa country, and is suitably decorated with a long prayer wall to be passed on the right side. The experts had noted that the *"Om mane padme hum"* (Sacred jewel of the lotus flower) was now written in Tibetan, not Nepali characters. Tenzing suggested that we might visit the monastery a little way up from the pass. This seemed to be a jumble of stone buildings, full of sheep-shearing and cloth-making, but not, apparently, monastic life. Finally Tenzing managed to produce a caretaker, who led us into a dark upper room. The usual erotic paintings, eighteen years old, adorned the walls. Two conch shells and a teapot stood before the Buddha, but of religious life we saw none. It appeared that we were the first foreign visitors to this unknown monastery.

3

We were now in Sola Khumbu, home of the Sherpas. From a delightful meadow camp near blossoming plum trees at Chyangma, 1,500 feet below the monastery, we descended next morning to the Likhu Khola. We had seen our next objective, the 12,000-foot Lamjura Banjang Pass, from Chyangma, but it took a day and a half to reach it. The Himalayan valleys are like that. Seta, some way up the valley side, was the next camp site; from it our path wound up a broad, wooded rib of mountainside descending from the promontory to the right of the pass. As we rose higher in the early morning air we found frost, and were stamping around to keep warm in our shorts before breakfast, until the sun struck us. To reach the pass itself, the path does a long traverse left through rhododendrons, whose stems are twisted and barkless from the snow. They would be the perfect background to a Walt Disney "Babes in the Wood." The people whom we passed now were Sherpas, round-cheeked and slit-eyed, dressed in the homespun cloth robe and high felt boots. The men wore pigtails, the women their hair in buns. Hitherto the Nepalis had worn Indian clothes, or the tight pyjama-like trouser under full coat.

I reached the Lamjura Banjang pass at 11:15 A.M. One charm of these marches is that you can walk sometimes alone, sometimes with whatever friend happens to be alongside. We were in the Sola district, and I dropped through pine woods to a delightful valley that might have been Cumberland, hemmed in on the left by a huge cliff face. Down this we went, through meadows which on our return were thick with irises, down past a yellow, overhanging crag with the *"Om mane"* inscribed in six-foot letters along its base. The village of Junbezi, my favourite of all, lies in a side valley leading up to the snow-peak of Numbur. From slopes bright with primulas you look down towards the rows of neat white stone houses, their wooden roofs covered with stones to keep them down. It was a Sherpa village, quite different in character from any we had passed. Charles Evans and I rescued Thondup, who always had his own ideas about camp sites and had gone half a mile farther to a particularly waterless spot. We returned to the stream below the village for the ritual bathe.

Junbezi is renowned for its monastery and the manufacture of kukris. The monastery is a handsome, square building backing a balconied courtyard, whose effect, however, is spoilt by the dirt of animals. Mike Westmacott and I found here the largest Buddha I have ever seen. Climbing to the first floor to inspect the impressive library and the Great Pandit's chair, we were just level with his head. Outside, the lady caretaker introduced us to a Chinese family camped amid incredible squalor. But I had espied a yet more exciting temple, perched on a rock 400 feet above the village. To this I toiled by a steep path, and was greeted in a little huddle of buildings, round a terrace looking sheer down to the valley, by beaming broad faces: the lamas, barefoot and clad in single red robe. Tremendous excitement ensued when I took out my camera. The old Abbot, lame and half-blind, was hauled forth and rigged up in a yellow brocade robe and hat of astonishing dirtiness, though originally beautiful. On a towel over his footstool the sacred emblems, the bell and dorje, were laid. Incense was lit, and all the monks changed into ceremonial dress. Meanwhile I was being forced to drink the traditional Tibetan tea, scented with rancid butter, out of a silver cup. What was the disappointment of all when the pictures did not roll straightway out of the camera! I feared I might be expelled ignominiously, but on a promise to send them, the smiles reappeared. I was ushered out, almost with embraces which would have been unhygienic in the extreme.

After Junbezi you have very much the feeling that you are in Everest country. Also, your objective is clear and inevitable before you. Next day we again saw the summit towering over its satellites, now quite subduing the 25,000-foot ridge of Nuptse. The path passes through a more religiously minded country: huge boulders by the streams are given up to carvings of the four sacred words; carefully done as they are, they seem an impressive symbol of faith, but also of a certain monotony of ideas. The next stage, to Taksindhu Monastery, would bring us above the Dudh Khosi, which we would then follow right up to Namche. I lazed and dreamed on a primula slope below it. I found myself asking: What makes a poet? Surely, in his poetic self, a certain inability to *do* things. I had neither inclination nor will-power to capture that butterfly for John, that beetle for George Band, or pick this primula, however rare, for anybody else. I lay and absorbed and wondered. Where the real poet comes in is in turning this luxurious absorption into words.

We crossed the Dudh Kosi by a rickety bridge which worried the Sherpanis, and for the next three days were marching either above or in its deep gorge. It was here that the mountains began to impose their stark presence upon us. The valley-side was bright with rhododendron and tree magnolia, waxy white flowers, perhaps a foot across, that stood out against a hillside like starry clusters. But climbing above these, higher than seemed possible, Karyolung on the left and the Kangtega group on the right dominated us. Snow clung at angles impossible in the Alps to their sharply carved flanks and ice-ridges. At this stage John was beginning to confer, calculate and discuss our plans, both for the acclimatisation period and the mountain. He had even worked out figures for the high carries: a minimum of 110 lb. to the last tent under the South Summit, 300 lb. to the South Col, and 150 lb. for the Lhotse Face camp. All these were discussed around the tea-mugs, as we gazed up at the huge peaks.

The three days to Kharikhola (6,600 feet), Puiyan (9,200 feet), and Ghat (8,600 feet) were filled with growing excitement. One half of me yearned back to the ease of the march, the other spurred forward to the snow-tops. Everest would soon be upon us. We were making the most of the last valley produce, and *alu* (potatoes), with butter and salt were the most popular item for tea; ferns and spinach helped on the supper. At last, on the 25th, we climbed the steep hillside rising from the junction of the Dudh Kosi and the Imja. There was Everest above us in the distance; and as we rounded a corner, in a strange, brown amphitheatre of the hillside, the village of Namche Bazar, capital and centre of "Sherpaland."

Below the village a matronly woman met us with tea of strange taste, and crystal sugar; a charming gesture. The teapot was ornamented with coloured paper, and a friendly throng surrounded us. But we camped above the village, partly to avoid infection, and did not visit it this time. Eric Shipton had warned most strongly of the dangers of flu and other diseases. We were at last among our mountains. Behind us Kwangde, a great wall of rock and snow. On our right, the most beautiful of all, I thought, Thamserku, an outlier of Kangtega. For hundreds of feet the eye followed fluted ridges, stepped one from the other like a giant's razor-edge staircase; the whole topped by the summit's glittering sword-blade. Among these mountains, as George Band said, any desire to climb was lost. It was enough simply to lie back and gaze admiringly, without planning perilous ascents. To the left and behind Kangtega, from the knoll above our camp, there rose certainly the most startling peak of all: Ama Dablam (22,300 feet). It has been compared to a tooth, but to me it is more a wedge, with flat sharp top and ridges rising in one all but vertical sweep. It dominates the scene far more than Everest, which is still peeping over the long ridge of Nuptse, and about twenty miles away.

The mountain on whose sides Namche Bazar nestles is Khumbila, a soaring rock peak which Tom Bourdillon had tried last year. Up its lower flanks I climbed that evening in a mist, and round them we wound the next day, until we started to slant gently towards the river. At a pleasant, stone-walled meadow along this stretch we were met by "Mrs. Da Tensing," wife of one of our trustiest Sherpas, with *chang* in pots. This *chang* was good. It tastes to me somewhere between cider and buttermilk. It is milky and thick, sometimes lumpy, but it adds jovially to the festivities. I noticed that the *chang* brought for our carriers was more watery. At all events, much fortified, and with John riding a minute pony sent from the monastery, we continued our way to the river, to breakfast and the last bathe—a very cold one—for over two months.

Thyangboche lies on the top of a long ridge slanting down to the junction of the Imja and the Bhote Kosi. To my dismay I began to feel very breathless here, on the long 2,000-foot pull up from the river at some 10,500 feet. I certainly ought, surely, to be all right at this modest level? Fortunately there were plenty of excuses for stopping at the photographic scenes. At last I had arrived, along with Tom Stobart and Greg, through a sculptured archway and on to the sudden, flat meadow, the situation for a Garden of Eden rather than for human dwellings. Ahead the mass of Everest, with Ama Dablam standing sentinel on its right. On the left the snow cone of Taweche peeping over an intruding foothill. In front a grass meadow surrounded by woods of pine, tree-juniper and silver birch. And beside us on the left, a cluster of stone buildings leading up the pyramid to the gilt emblem at the summit of the *gompa*. Into one of these buildings we were almost hustled by two hospitable elderly lamas, plumped on cushions and plied with European tea. Then we walked on, to take part in the odd anomaly of oxygen, tins and tools unpacked in the setting of a pastoral idyll.

We were fit and well fed. Above all, and this was part of the plan, the not too strenuous march had allowed us to become friends. A happy party gossiped round the camp-fire under frosty stars.

A. J. VEILHAN

5

Before Everest

March 26th—April 16th

1

Thyangboche, our first Base Camp, was also the scene of the first unpacking. We had three days here, frosty and bright in the early light, later shrouded with hovering mist. The first morning, still sleeping outside, some of the party indulged in leisurely "sleeping-bag climbing" (the Himalayan version of arm-chair mountaineering). Routes were traced up most of the least possible peaks. Then we got down to the day, free of our coolies, who had been paid off by Mike and Charles Wylie on arrival. The many erected tents, red, orange and yellow, were a picturesque background to activity. I noted a day thus in my diary:

> Before breakfast. Walked out and observed musk-deer and ram chikor (like brightly coloured partridge). These are quite tame as the lamas forbid taking of life.
> Gave out crampons to sahibs and Sherpas. Fitted and adjusted. Straps not perfect.
> Sat with John over *Times* report. Drew map of acclimatisation areas.
> Helped Tom to test oxygen cylinders.
> 1:00 P.M. Lunch. Salmon and veg.
> Helped to put up tents for airing.
> 2:45. A break. 50 mins. up hillside above, and felt very different from yesterday. Back 4:00 P.M. packed up spare ice-axes and dud oxygen cylinders.
> Washed teeth in rather dirty water-hole. Wrote letter home.

◄ *We camped that night near Phalong Karpo, on the way to the head of the Chola Khola.*

71

Helped organise boxes in big tent for supper, to sit on. Very crowded supper of sheep (killed by George L. this A.M.) all of us in tent.

Talk by John on acclimatisation plans after supper.

I had sent for the Namche blacksmith to adjust ill-fitting crampons. On the second day a small square man arrived and established himself in one corner of the meadow. I am afraid his banging operations may have been responsible for some of the breakages later, and he was not always very clever. He expended great energy fitting George Band's crampons on my boots. That day too we were invited to pay a formal visit to the monastery. Its most impressive feature was the great library of books, half in Sanskrit and half in Tibetan, adorning the walls. They were written in large raised lettering, and the accumulated dust seemed to indicate a certain lack of study. On the empty thrones of the Abbot, John laid ceremonial scarves. Then we were escorted to an airy little upper room; all squatted round a table and were hospitably entertained with tea, little plates of potatoes, chapattis and a not very good *rakshi* or rice spirit. This, even at its best, always tasted to me like the methylated variety. The Deputy Abbot presided, the Abbot being away on a visit to Rongbuk. One of the expedition flags was offered and accepted.

This Deputy Abbot, solid and round and clad in russet robe, told many stories of the *yeti* or Abominable Snowman. In winter, he said, these creatures come quite low down for food, and have been seen playing in the snow near the monastery. They seem to be about five feet six, with reddish, shaggy hair. At the sound of the monastic horn they make off. They sometimes eat yak, which they skin carefully, leaving the horns stuck in the ground. Once, in Tibet, he said, a village had been very much worried by *yeti*, who used to come and do the same things at night, only in disorderly fashion, as the villagers had done during the day. Thus they would play about in a field of potatoes which had been planted during the day-time. Finally, the exasperated villagers prepared a great bowl of *chang* and made pretence of drinking it. The *yeti,* coming that night, did in fact drink it with the inevitable result, and were easily disposed of. Since that time, the lama concluded solemnly, it has been forbidden to kill *yeti* in Tibet. He looked out dreamily at the superb view from the window, to the slope where *yeti* had played. I thought then how different this scene must be in winter; yet if one had the courage to stay, how rewarding in other ways than *yeti!*

That same afternoon some of us went to tea with the absent Abbot's mother. We climbed upstairs into a long, typically Sherpa room, dark and to European eyes dirty. The mother was a straight, tall Sherpani with fine features, dressed in the ordinary Sherpani dress. The reception was friendly, though less stately perhaps than a bishop's mother might provide. The Abbot of Thyangboche enjoys a prestige in the Buddhist hierarchy almost as great as the Abbot of Rongbuk. Some of our local Sherpas, the stalwart Ang Norbu among them, squatted on the floor, while we sat on carpets raised near the window. An enormous plate of potato, chapatti and delicious rice "twists" was most unexpectedly produced, the women serving us. I had just got a pipe alight, but there was no refusing.

We had now taken to having supper outside; it was more roomy, and in the moonlight infinitely beautiful. By this time everyone had rigged himself, more or less to his satisfaction, in expedition clothing. Greg was stamping about complaining of tight boots. Bright blue wind-proofs and red sweaters were almost a uniform. In our green down clothing we were warm enough, however sharp the frost. George Band had managed to set up the wireless, and seated round a campfire we were treated to the incongruity of Radio Ceylon's commercial programme booming up to the stars, along with the news that Cambridge had won the Boat Race. This would be the last night that we were all together. For the first acclimatisation party, Charles Evans, George Band, Tom Bourdillon and Mike Westmacott, were to set off next morning (the 29th) for the valley and passes this side of Ama Dablam. Tom had partly recovered from the shock of his discovery that many of the oxygen cylinders leaked. The deep, hesitant voice had announced that if the main store of oxygen

73

leaked similarly, "something pretty drastic" would happen to the oxygen programme. For this main supply, despatched by Alf Bridge, was to be brought up to us by Major J. O. M. Roberts, of the Gurkhas, arriving in mid-April. A runner therefore went down with a telegram to the Indian wireless station which we had found to our astonishment at Namche. Tewari, in charge, kindly sent it off. Roberts checked every cylinder before he left Kathmandu, and all was well.

The 30th was preparation day for the rest of us. I must confess that I welcomed this breaking off into smaller groups. We had been too unwieldy a party for real converse, for the real companionship of hills. That morning most of us made an ascent of the 15,500-foot rock knob above the camp, to test out our walkie-talkie sets. It was like a British scramble, but for irritating thorns and dwarf juniper in many places. It was also a strange sensation, to sit in the sun on top and be able to talk to the camp which we could see as a blob, 2,500 feet below. We sun-bathed briefly and descended.

The afternoon was crowded. John had asked me to take on Sherpa food, and there were considerable computations with Tenzing. How much do men eat in three weeks? It was impossible to make out accurate figures for the needs of an indefinite number of carriers. Then there were the needs of the four members of our party and six Sherpas. Ed had retired with a sore throat, but would follow in a day's time. Charles Wylie, Mike Ward and I would start operations in the unexplored valley of the Chola Khola (see map on page 76). We were to have four coolies for the first two days, in addition to our Sherpas. The problem was to make the loads reasonable: four tents, two cookers and fuel, climbing gear, oxygen for testing (two coolie-loads) and food. We held a conference and sent the Sherpas off to sort out their food. Alas, when weighed it made up nearly three full coolie-loads by itself. They were sent off to reduce the weight, on the basis of two pounds per man per day. We could not do the final weighing till morning, when tents and personal gear would be added. Our list for eight days in the mountains read finally something like this:

Cookers	31 lb.
Sherpa food	70 lb.
4 tents	45 lb.
Oxygen apparatus, etc.	58 lb.
3 oxygen cylinders	70 lb.
Food	120 lb.
Total	394 lb.

The food included two days' high-altitude rations as an experiment for all. In addition to these there were kerosene, Li-Los, sleeping-bags, personal gear and the oddments: altimeter, compass, glacier cream, binoculars, goggles and antimist, matches, candles, lantern, torches, cigarettes for Sherpas, camera and film, eight *karabiners* or snap-rings and 300 feet of nylon rope.

2

When we came to load up, the Sherpas, to their great disgruntlement, were still carrying over 70 lb. each; our coolies, including Sherpanis, carried the same, and we ourselves 40 to 50 lb. At 8:15 A.M. on the 30th we set off, first down through forest hung with pendant green lichen, then along the gorge of the Imja dominated by Ama Dablam. At Pangboche, the first village, we found George Lowe and Greg firmly planted and determined on collecting another coolie, for their party's load was as heavy as ours. John, their leader, was far ahead. With some relief we followed suit, thanks to Tenzing's ability to rouse the village. After half an hour, each party set off with two extra coolies and pleasant thoughts of John still carrying his 50 lb. At the junction of the Chola Khola and the Imja we halted for food and to admire Ama Dablam, which now, end on, appeared as a straight-edged pyramid soaring into blue space.

Our ways here parted; John's party followed the Imja, we turned left up the rushing Chola Khola (Coca-Cola as it was generally known). We camped that night in the flat valley-bed against the walls of the little sheep-farming village of Phalong Karpo (14,500 feet). The track for Everest keeps right from here up the Khumbu stream. Our way lay left,

75

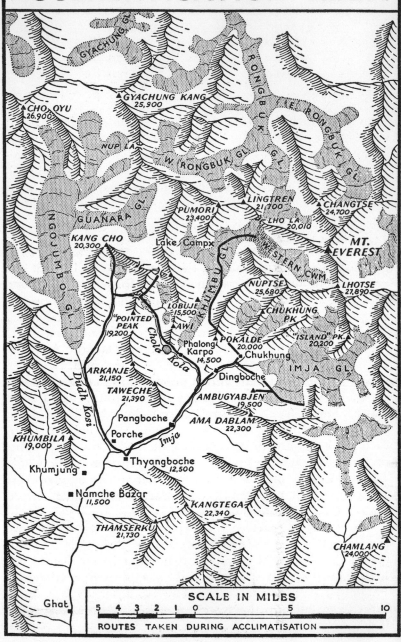

ACCLIMATISATION AREA

SCALE IN MILES

ROUTES TAKEN DURING ACCLIMATISATION ━━━

SOLA KHUMBU – Ice ridges of Thamserku above Namche Bazar and Thyangboche.
The Da Tensings. Mrs. Da Tensing wears Tibetan hat. Top of "Chang" pot in front.

Sóla Khumbu – Four Sherpas: Shepalay, Da Namgyal, Gompu, and Ang Dawa I.

On the march. Sherpanis delouse a Sherpa's hair.

ACCLIMATISATION — Kang Cho from col right of Pointed Peak (4 miles distant). Part of Cho Oyu behind. Route is up right hand ridge. Hillary, Gompu Nimmi, Da Namgyal in foreground.

Final ridge of Kang Cho.

ACCLIMATISATION – Thyangboche camp. A

...otse to the left, Ama Dablam to the right.

ACCLIMATISATION – The author on the Pointed Peak. Practising Oxygen.

ACCLIMATISATION Camp in the Imja. A study in equipment: Ropes, tent, crampons (on rock in front), rucksack, ice-axes.

Dingboche in snow. Part of Kangtega and Thamserku behind.

ACCLIMATISATION – Ambugyabjen. The steep side.

Taweche from the Imja. Tenzing approaching.

to the head of the Chola Khola itself. Mike and I climbed a stony hillside for the view. I wished I was not puffing so much. At this stage one spends much time comparing one's own puffing with that of companions. If my story so far has shown anything, it must have shown how much of the mountaineeer's time is taken with such thoughts of trivial everyday: hopes of tomorrow, worries about cut fingers, breathlessness and above all, food. Perhaps it should not be so, but so we are made.

The scene was impressive. We had come almost completely round Taweche (21,390 feet) which appeared as a huge cone of snow on rock. To the right of it and almost as high, a yet more fantastic peak, called by the natives Arkanje, dropped a sheer right front several thousands of feet to our valley. Stretching to the right again from this ran a line of rocky peaks which we christened, from left to right: Pic Gaspard, the Hump, Pointed Peak, and Twin Tips; to the right again came a bigger mass, with a main summit known locally as Awi. What struck us most was the snowless state of it all. The sun was hot, the peaks stood scorched at the end of the valley like the Tyrol in a dry August rather than the Himalaya in April. We earmarked the Pointed Peak as a possibility and descended.

Next day we intended to leave the beaten track and find the unexplored valley head. The way was obvious, and we had heard of a lake some way up, near which the Sherpa Angtharkay used to graze sheep as a boy. There indeed it was, a frozen surface that groaned and creaked like a bad floor. The way thereafter led obviously over grass and boulder flats towards Pointed Peak; in fact we camped shortly below the glacier snout coming down on its right, at a height of perhaps 16,000 feet. We were behind an enormous boulder (first ascent by the chubby Sherpa Gompu), but it was impossible to avoid the wind, and it became very cold when the sun went down. Despite this our four Sherpanis decided to stay, to the great contentment of the Sherpas, while the other two coolies went down. Nine persons therefore snuggled into two Meade tents, sharing sleeping-bags. How they cooked I cannot tell, but that mystery is common to all Sherpas. We en-

joyed a fine steak and *tsampa* stew. Everybody liked this flour-
like roasted barley as an addition to stew, and particularly
to tea.

Charles had a fair headache here, and took aspirin. Many
people suffer most from mountain sickness in some form or
other between 15,000 and 17,000 feet. The object of our re-
hearsals was in fact to overcome this weakness and "acclimatise" ourselves before we arrived at Base Camp. My chief
suffering from height was a very dry throat; probably my
nose blocked from catarrh, forcing me to breathe dusty air
through my mouth during the night. I sucked lozenges all
next day and preserved the *status quo*. We intended to try to
reach a col which would lead us out of our valley, and also to
find the col reached by Tom Bourdillon and Mike Ward in
1951. They had approached from the Ngojumbo side and
looked down our Chola Khola, but had not been able to
descend. Our other duty was to try out the oxygen. We were
up at six, but not away till 8:35; a delay between breakfasts,
partly due to the Sherpanis's presence. We always had ours
first, and always, just as we were impatient to be off, we
would find the Sherpas tucking into enormous mounds or
blocks of *tsampa*. In parenthesis, the technique here is to add
tea and mould the *tsampa*, as a potter clay, with the fingers.

Charles and Mike wore oxygen, and we made the glacier
snout in forty minutes. I found myself puffing a good deal,
but able to keep up—slightly to their chagrin, I hoped. Here
we roped with the Sherpas and put on crampons. After a
steep beginning to the glacier, we found to our surprise the
slope easing off and an almost flat walk to the col just right
of our Pointed Peak. Rocky on the Chola Khola side, from
this angle it showed a most jolly-looking ice ridge. The time
was only 10:40, and we still had not found Mike's col,
which we guessed must be farther to the right still, beyond
Twin Tips Peak. The glacier here curved round easily under
its face; so at 11:5 off we set, I wearing the oxygen (ordinary
Open-Circuit). "Wearing oxygen" sounds easy. In fact, it is
a clumsy business which we were experiencing for the first
time. A bulky black cylinder must be pushed and wriggled
into its carrying frame; nuts must be adjusted, mask fitted

78

and the weight swung on to the back. But when at last it is set and the switch turned on, all is different. A god has somehow wriggled between you and the outer scene, persuading you, on no evidence, that life is good after all. And one effect that we all found, even at this low altitude, was that we enjoyed the scenery. Instead of breathing hard and keeping eyes on the next step, we looked round and admired the view. The world appeared rosy rather than a dun grey.

We rounded a corner and behold—a stony little col about half a mile away across a long snow-field. The oxygen we dumped and set off, dragging rather heavily, across almost level snow. A nasty two hundred feet over boulders that slipped two down to every one step that you took up, then the level col. Mike identified it as his col without a doubt. At our feet lay an unknown valley, later named the Chugima, and beyond, range upon range of western peaks dominated by the broad mass of Cho Oyu directly across the Guanara.

It was the first glimpse into many unknown valleys and at many unnamed peaks; a wealth which only Eric Shipton's parties have probed. To me it was a world of new shapes, for mountains have always to me been shapes especially, ever since as a child I modelled the Welsh hills in plasticine. The Nepalese mountains were a rich jumble of such mouldings, chiselled and forged and welded strangely as far as the eye could reach, with the vague feeling to the traveller that one shape dominated all, for Everest loomed like an enquiring monster over every ridge not vertically above you. Its presence was weirdly with us throughout these weeks, as if its physical being tried to dominate our sight, as the thought of it mastered our talk.

The time was 12:30 and the height of the col perhaps 18,500 feet. Coming down across the snow slope I was horrified to see one brand-new crampon [1] swing loose—broken. As Gompu had already broken one, I began to be really worried; indeed this was the beginning of the great "Crampon Crisis" which lasted the whole expedition. We regained camp at 3:30. Just as tea arrived, Ed appeared with his Da

[1] Crampons or ice-claws are sets of metal spikes on frames tied to the feet to assist walking up ice.

79

Namgyal. It was splendid to see him striding in, though still slightly suffering from throat. For my own throat, I found that if I slept on my left side, I could keep one nostril fairly clear, and ease the breathing through my mouth. But I often turned in sleep, and that clogged me up. Apart from this, with Li-Lo inflated and sleeping-bag drawn tight under the chin, I slept well. For the next day, three of us intended to try Pointed Peak, while Ed said he would bring our camp up to the first col, perhaps 17,800 feet. He would use one oxygen set and we the other. All went according to plan. The ridge up from our col was of steep ice and snow; in several places steps had to be cut despite our crampons. I tried cutting while wearing oxygen, and to my delight even enjoyed it. As we rose, Everest soon loomed above the intervening Awi; a new view, no longer obscured by Nuptse. To the right Makalu (27,790 feet), a great pyramid curiously similar in structure to its higher brother.

We reached the top (19,200 feet) over a final treacherous rock ridge. The time was 11:30 and we lay three-quarters of an hour enjoying perhaps the best view of the expedition. In this dry April every major peak stood gaunt and grim before us: Numbur, the Gauri Sankar range, Cho Oyu, Gyachung Kang, Changtse or the North Peak, Everest, Nuptse and Lhotse, Makalu, Chamlang. Below us on the col we had the happy sight of Ed putting up our camp. We descended leisurely, very pleased with our Pointed Peak. We later rechristened it Lhakpa Peak, in honour of Charles Wylie's son, Ian, who was born on a Wednesday (*Lhakpa* means Wednesday in Sherpa) soon after. Just above the col Mike stopped suddenly and pointed. Straight across the newly-found Chugima valley stood a splendid ice-peak, the left-hand of two. Its right-hand ridge looked possible. Why not cross over to this, climb it and finish by descending the valley, which must surely join the Dudh Kosi lower down? Ed agreed, and made a prospective descent of the shaly slope below the col. But meanwhile we were having to tighten our belts. I think I have mentioned that we brought two days' Assault Rations for all. The plan was to see whether, as an experiment, we and the Sherpas could live on these and nothing else. Here are the contents for each "man day":

14 oz. sugar
1 pkt. Bovril Pemmican (for soup)
2 oz. cheese
2 pkts. biscuits—1 sweet
2 oz. jam
1 pkt. boiled sweets
1 pkt. Grape-Nuts
Tea, coffee, small pkt. porridge to go with soup
1 pkt. powder milk
1 2-oz. bar Kendal Mint Cake, or chocolate, or Frubix, or banana bar
1 pkt. lemon or orange powder.

These rations were beautifully vacuum-packed, in silver-papered cardboard boxes, the whole costing, I believe, twenty-five shillings. But it will be seen that for a man coming ravenous into camp there is not much to make him feel that he has had a hearty meal, particularly if you are one of those who cannot stomach Grape-Nuts or pemmican. I was fortunate in managing both. We sighed moderately and sat down to the soup and cheese. Four Sherpas we had sent back to our last camp with the oxygen; they would return tomorrow, and having transported us over to a camp as high as possible on Kang Cho (the name of our new peak as we later discovered), two were to return and carry the oxygen right back via the Chola Khola to Thyangboche.

I shared a tent with Ed, and we discussed his great problem of killing time at high altitude, his "battle against boredom." My own very simple method is reading, a long novel for preference. One of the pleasanter tasks of this whole period was that of getting to know each other, and I here got to know Ed: his straight, frontal attack on every problem; his restless energy; his cheerful deep laugh and sense of humour; his staunch feeling for friends. Next morning I was bleary with my cold, my nose had refused to clear in the night and felt like a lump of lead. Mike and Charles were suffering from headaches, Ed from indigestion brought on

81

by the pemmican. Poor Ed! For the next two days he ate almost nothing, despite the hard work of the climb; he seemed to live entirely on lemon powder with great quantities of sugar. This rather groggy party waited impatiently for the four returning Sherpas. It was 10:15 before we all set off, down the horrible shaly slope leading to two small lakes nestled among the moraine boulders below. Here, with great regret, we left our Compo tins under a large rock and turned right, up the stony valley-bed. Our aim was a point at which we could camp in the hollow descending from a glacier which gave access to the snow col between Kang Cho and its right-hand neighbour. We found our camp site shortly below the glacier snout; it is pleasanter to camp on rock, and there was a small stream. Pemmican soup, biscuits and cheese at 5:00 P.M. Then the difficult business of putting on breeches under wind-proof, an agony of thumbs in the small of the back, complicated by the resultant two pairs of braces.

There had been a dribble of snow, but the morning of April 4th was fine. I rejoiced at a good night on my left side, with one nostril free. We said good-bye to Nimmi and Ang Dawa II (off to collect the oxygen) and set off at 7:30. One blessing of Himalayan mountaineering: no 2:00 A.M. starts, as in the Alps. No sooner had we worked our way on to the glacier, than Charles's crampon broke, too. A maddening business. He, like myself and Gompu, went through the day on one and a half crampons. We reached the col at 8:20. Any thought of the right-hand peak faded away, but the ridge of Kang Cho, now seen end-on, still seemed amenable: ice above, steepening at the top to a shoulder. From the shoulder a fairly level ridge rose to the summit, with one mushroom-shaped lump of ice which might give trouble.

Ed, Da Namgyal, Ang Dawa and I were on the first rope. Ed hewed large steps up the steep slope from the col; too large, I thought at the time, as we were wearing crampons. But he was catering for Sherpas. After a stony scramble we changed round the lead; a generous consent by Ed. We were soon kept very closely to the ridge, on a curious honeycomb formation of ice. This helped very much at times; because instead of cutting steps at some of the steepest places, I could place feet in the comb, and for handhold grasp the projections. It was steep work, and the Sherpas looked suspicious. Each side the slopes swept away impressively, but the crest felt to me warm and safe. By noon we were at last on the shoulder; Shepalay (a rather scruffy, unprepossessing Sherpa) and Ang Dawa I decided to stay here. The latter told us later that in 1952 he had been involved in an accident, which had shaken his confidence. Mike, Charles and Gompu started off in the lead, but the mushroom made them pause. It must clearly be turned, on a great honeycomb slab of ice to the left. They struck rather high, and Ed, spying a lower line, forged across at fine speed. But this too provided difficulty, and I suddenly saw a diagonal between the two, a honeycomb shelf upon which, with a few chips from the axe, one could walk. This proved to be the answer; I pulled on to the crest some yards beyond the mushroom, to see nothing except a possible crevasse or two between us and the summit, 300 feet above.

There was indeed a crevasse, finely led over a very delicate-looking bridge by Ed. I remember at this stage that we were all panting hard. We were certainly not fully acclimatised, but apart from thinking that everybody was making me go far too fast, I suffered no very ill effects. There are times when each longs passionately to trip all his companions by the heels. At 1:00 P.M. we were on the snowy top, which we estimated at 20,300 feet, looking down a remarkable drop to the Guanara Glacier. We swallowed Mint Cake, some were brave enough for Frubix. But drink was the chief need; lemon and sugar were more wonderful than wine. Both Da Namgyal and Gompu, seventeen years old, Mike's orderly and the "fat boy" of the party, had climbed splendidly. Lower down, Everest and Makalu had risen to watch us. But already the afternoon mists were floating, and we did not linger long. We picked up the two at the shoulder, and instead of turning left, made straight down a subsidiary ridge leading nearer to our camp, and looking easier. At a misty promontory we turned off it down an ice rib. The month was so dry, there was no snow at all; furthermore the ice lower down had ribbed and wrinkled into bigger honeycomb, more like the ice pinnacles called "penitents"—irritating to tread on, especially when it was the turn of the half-crampon. In the mist they seemed to go on for ever and ever; I remember Charles saying: "I feel as if I was walking in a dream."

At last, at last we were down, and could see the tents below. On stony ground we removed crampons. Then on, on and again on, slithering, very thirsty, the remaining few hundred feet. At camp (3:30 P.M.) we drank endless pints of lemon and tea, then slipped contented into our sleeping-bags and lay talking; the sort of gossip, of climbs and people, which can go on endlessly and with equal enjoyment to all parties. It is one of the most precious sweets of travel. Ed delighted me with stories of last year's trip; then, with the dark, we slowly went to sleep, to dream of the meal we should eat tomorrow.

We picked up our beloved Compo tins, even opening a tin of bully-beef on the spot, then strode happily down the unknown valley,[1] discussing in academic terms the possibilities of Kang Cho's right-hand neighbour. Soon we were off the moraine boulders on to grassy flats which frankly compelled the traveller to idleness. Rising reluctantly, one would see someone else sitting down a hundred yards farther on, and be cordially invited to do the same. The invitation was never refused. We were enjoying the most exquisite pleasure of Himalayan mountaineering: a small party of friends, we were exploring new country among the greatest scenery in the world. We had just climbed a new peak, and were descending an uncharted valley. There was much to talk about, to point out, to ask our loyal companions, the Sherpas. Moreover, we had the easy sense of having done our duty to the expedition; we were acclimatised, and knew more about oxygen and rations.

At last we managed to reach the grassy bluff above the junction of our valley with the Dudh Kosi. We turned left down the side of its steep gorge. The most memorable feature of the day was the dish of potatoes dug up by a tooth-

[1] The Chugima.

84

less man in the field in which we camped. It was the first fresh food for a week; some had not fared too well, and I have never eaten or seen eaten so many potatoes at one sitting. Ed, who had been virtually starving, swelled almost visibly.

In our down clothing we lay very warmly. I had by now given up the pyjama habit, and simply pulled on down clothing as the evening grew colder, taking it off again for bed. Next day, the 6th, we continued in bright weather down to the village of Porche, dropped to the Imja and made the last steep climb back to Thyangboche. By 1:00 P.M. we were hearing how the other parties fared, in their explorations around Ama Dablam and Lhotse. The summit of Everest once again gleamed its challenge over the long barrier of Nuptse.

3

The second stay at Thyangboche was saddened and complicated by the resignation of one Sherpa, a man who had been to the South Col with the Swiss, but whose real *métier* seemed to lie on the horse-racing field. He had given trouble before because of his laziness, and seemed to understand the cause of his dismissal. He asked to be reinstated, but the resignation was insisted upon. Tenzing marched him into the big tent, rather like a sergeant-major before his colonel. John handed him his money. He gave back his clothes and went. Unfortunately he had talked to others, and was followed later on his journey by my little Ang Dawa, of all unlikely people. Ang Dawa had been cheery and helpful both in camp as on the climb; he now appeared, rather drunk, and declared that the Sherpas had been carrying far too much, that they were exhausting themselves before the mountain, etc., etc. Nothing said by Charles and John could shake him; he stayed a short while, then stumped off with his convictions.

I was really happy during these days at Thyangboche, doing jobs and being busily in things. It is natural to feel useless when not active. I repaired boots, whose rubber soles had been knocked from the leather, and blessed screws which are the friend of the unpractised. Besides this, there were many adjustments of packing and arrangements of gear for our departure on the next spell. Some kit would be left at Thyangboche, some sent straight to Base. This time, except for Charles Evans's party, which would return to join up with Jimmy Roberts and the main oxygen load, we were not to come back to Thyangboche. Ed Hillary, the two Georges (Band and Lowe) and Mike Westmacott would start work on the Everest icefall. John, Mike Ward, Tom Bourdillon and myself would explore mountains at the head of the Imja Glacier, trying out Open- and Closed-Circuit. We would then reach the Khumbu over a pass leading from the Imja River. Our party's more detailed list looked as follows:

Pyramid tent	25 lb.
2 Meade Tents	28 lb.
1 Gerry (American) small tent	9 lb.
2 cookers	31 lb.
1½ gallons kerosene	12 lb.
Food, 10 men for 7 days at 3 lb. per day	210 lb.
Oxygen (including Closed-Circuit for practice)	370 lb.
Ropes	10 lb.
Personal (at 30 lb. each)	300 lb.
Total	995 lb.

It was a big load. Prudently, we armed ourselves this time with ten coolies at 60 lb. each (they carried more as it turned out). The six Sherpas took 50 lb. each.

4

I intend to spare the reader a day-to-day account of our second period in Sola Khumbu; to most mortals one mountain is very much like another, and there will by now be some protests: "Why can't we get on to Everest?"

Here is the outline of what happened: One party, Hillary, Band, Lowe and Westmacott, left on April 9th and made their way, accompanied by Pugh and Stobart, Sherpas and over thirty coolies, straight to Everest. Of their doings on the icefall we shall hear more very soon. The second party, Evans, Gregory, Wylie and Tenzing, had as prime task the training of selected Sherpas in the use of oxygen. They explored the glaciers descending from Lhotse into the Imja Basin, and climbed "Island Peak," an ice fang of over 20,000 feet in the middle of it. They returned to Thyangboche to pick up our baggage and come on with Roberts and the main supply of oxygen. Finally John Hunt, Bourdillon, Ward and myself went up to the true head of the Imja Glacier. We tried to reach a snow col just north of Ama Dablam, and on the glacier below two of us wore the Open-Circuit apparatus for five and a half continuous hours. Using Closed-Circuit experimentally, under Tom's tuition, we climbed Ambugyabjen (19,500 feet), a rock peak west of Ama Dablam, on two successive days. We descended to Chukhung, and crossed a high pass leading from the Imja to the Khumbu Valleys. This "yak" pass (18,000 feet) gave access to the ridge of Pokalde (20,000 feet). Thence down to the Khumbu, and up the 16th to the lake wedged between moraine and hillside, where the Swiss last year had their Base Camp. (See map, p. 76, and photograph, Plate 17.)

Having given the mechanics of our movements, I am now free to abandon them; to present you instead with vignettes. Consider that the party is hard-headedly getting on with the training programme planned, and then allow imagination to wander awhile over some of the details of every day, some of the thoughts in whose background you will still find the square-cut black pyramid dominant, even as it dominated every landscape.

Cooking. The four of us are camped at perhaps 16,000 feet on snow-covered sand; the two Meade tents end-on. I undertook the supper last night, having the Primus just outside the tent-door of John and myself, under the nylon inner-lining stretched between the tents. These cookers are a modified Primus, on a pattern designed by C. R. Cooke. Three saucepans can be warmed one on top of the other, heat being conserved by a series of windshields round the whole. As there are circular sleeve entrances to the Meades, cooking meant kneeling for long periods at a time by my method, in a stooping position. Tea appeared successfully but, alas, to my kitchen-proud annoyance, with an upset saucepan as finale. Then supper: soup in one saucepan, pork luncheon meat in chunks and carrots in the next above. Tinned cake for sweet, followed by coffee. How would that do? Not badly, with the usual minor moans about individual and universal dislikes. At the coffee stage the Primus decided just too early to run out of fuel. My fault. John gallantly took on the dreary job of restarting.

When there are Sherpas about, the sahibs tend to shirk the cooking. But there is no denying that it is good discipline, nor that climbers in general could learn much from Boy Scouts. It pays in a small tent to know where everything is; in ours, the Li-Los occupy a large space supporting the sleeping-bags; everything else forms a small chaos up at the ends, of biscuits, tins, novels, diaries, pyjamas, rucksacks, pencils, oxygen oddments, sweaters and the rest. "Where's the methylated?" always starts an exciting treasure-hunt.

Ambugyabjen. April 12th. We were going slowly, up huge hot boulders like the top of Glyder Fach in North Wales. I had been wearing the Closed-Circuit oxygen, for, having only one experimental set, we were taking it in half-hourly turns. Now I had taken it off. We were above 19,000; the breath came in patches and gasps. The rocks were white and dazzling in the sun. Suddenly, there were no rocks in front any more. We were leaning over beside a little cairn, looking down an awesome drop. On this far side Ambugyabjen plunges in tremendous tilts of precipice sheer to the Dingboche pastures 5,000 feet below. It is a sudden and dramatic summit.

And what better summit could an April afternoon ask? Slowly, as became the altitude, we took off rucksacks, spread food between us, settled ourselves in the most comfortable rock arm-chairs to hand. Then, this time with the slowness of enjoyment, we munched the food and pointed out peaks to each other. Mike took me over the ground of the 1951 explorations, to the Nup La and towards massive Cho Oyu and Gyachung Kang. Then we turned south, to the stately snow-spires of Numbur. At our very feet, brown patches were the straggling potato-fields of Dingboche village, and following the valley up below our cliff, the eye suddenly starts to climb rock wall upon rock wall. Up and up it goes, till tough ice begins to cling. Now the ice is there in great streaks and slashes among black vertical rock, now at last it has bulged out into a snow-cap. There, frowning down 3,000 feet, quite on top of us as it seems, the great snowy head of Ama Dablam terrifies us from its advantage point; terrifies and yet fascinates.

I turned away, dazzled by the sun, to that other point that drew the eye as surely as north the compass. Seen from here much more of Everest's bulk is visible over the great Lhotse-Nuptse wall. The square, brown, snow-flecked head is like a giant's as he rises from some magic bath. Indeed the impression of Everest from here is one of hidden but ever-present bulk. It is always there, always asking, and even as we lay sun bathing, enjoying a very ordinary climbing day, it filled me sharply with thoughts of a trial to come.

We soon gave up looking; closed eyes and ate and talked and closed eyes again. Every mountaineer will know the mood of acceptance which is his nearest approach to Nirvana. For these moments, flat upon the rock which becomes part of us, we are at one with the Universal. Eyes closed, we are no longer separated persons. . . . But alas, as Leslie Stephen has said, the Western mind does not lend itself long to such elevation. Thoughts of dinner begin to intrude. Blinking heavily and feebly against the sun, we packed up our sacks and scrambled back over the boulders.

Yeti. At our camp by the Imja I came the nearest I have ever come to an Abominable Snowman. The Sherpas had by now arrived; John, beside me in the tent, was writing letters or reports as industriously as ever. This writing, late into the evening by the light of any torch or candle he could filch, was pursued with characteristic vigour. From down the valley, gently through the tent wall, we heard a whistle. Then another.

"Wonder what that is."

"Must be the Sherpas from Charles Evans. They're under Island Peak. They were coming across for kerosene—but they're very late."

"Perhaps we should go and see."

"Our chaps must have heard. They'll deal with them." We left it at that, having other things to do.

Half an hour later Gyaljen poked his nose into the tent, asking about supper. Had the Sherpas arrived? The ones who whistled? They had heard no whistle, he said. What was it like? On hearing the description he became very excited.

"That was *yeti*, sahib!"

Next day the snow covering the moraine had vanished, there could be no trace. If we had gone out at the first whistle we might perhaps have glimpsed the mysterious denizen of moraine and glacier. But perhaps better not; perhaps better leave him in the mystery he deserves.

Pokalde (20,000 *feet*). *April 15th.* Pokalde is a peak of Alpine proportions set among the Himalaya, a sweep of snow-ridge ending in rock, which might in time become as clean as the south-west ridge of the Mönch in Switzerland. It was an irresistible temptation from the high "yak pass" that connects the Khumbu and Imja Glaciers.

The sahibs led the way from our camp site below the pass; unfortunately we made too far to the left, and had the shame of watching the Sherpas, who had started much later, winding sedately to the pass very soon after our breathless selves. It was a bouldery, rugged saddle, and must be very steep for yaks. Here John decided he must go down; he was suffering breathing difficulty, later diagnosed by Mike as incipient pleurisy. He accompanied the Sherpas over to the Khumbu, while Mike, Tom and I pulled on extra clothes at the sight of long spirals of snow whirling in the wind from the ridge above, against a blue sky. It was a jolly ridge, in the Alpine sense. Snow crest, two rotten rock gendarmes and a steep pull over granite splinters to a narrow summit. Everest and Makalu reared above the clouds like two great canine teeth, "fangs excrescent" upon the jaws of the earth, in Mallory's phrase. Gaunt and yellowy-brown, they seemed to have shaken off the winter snow.

Down at camp by the Khumbu Glacier 5,500 feet below, we felt we were at last on Everest ground. John was much better. Tomorrow across the glacier, to the lake on the other side where the Swiss had set their Base, and the day after, an answer to the question uppermost in all minds. What had been happening on the icefall?

A.J.VEILHAN

6

The Icefall at Last

April 16th—April 23rd

1

For any who have not read books on Everest, I should explain here that we were the fourth party to attack the mountain by this Khumbu Glacier leading to the icefall. The first seven British expeditions, from 1921 onwards, came over the Tibetan plateau and climbed the northern slabs. It was after the Second World War that Tibet became, for political reasons, a closed country to us, and it was a surprise and delight when in 1949 Nepal, hitherto inaccessible, began to give permission for expeditions through its territory. In 1951 Eric Shipton's party reconnoitred the icefall successfully and traced the line up the Lhotse Face which the Swiss expeditions followed in their two tremendous attempts of 1952. This route, of course, covers none of the ground of the earlier expeditions; only at the summit could there be a meeting place.

Here then we were at the lake, the Swiss Base Camp and one stage below our Base, which was the Swiss Camp I.

We had put our tents in the stone-wall enclosures, which sheltered them from a cold wind sometimes blowing off the lake down the funnel between moraine and hillside. If you climbed the moraine which hemmed the lake on the east side, you could gain a good idea of the valley by which we were approaching Everest. Straight over the Khumbu Glacier stood the line of jagged rocky peaks, ending in Pokalde, which are satellites to Nuptse. Behind these the Kangtega spires, and to the right the mass of Awi. But the eye which is wandering along the Pokalde ridge is suddenly brought up, startled, by the most astonishing wall that the Arabian

◄ *Pumori dominates the left bank of the upper Khumbu.*

93

Nights themselves could picture. Hitherto we had been looking at Nuptse in all its length, as the barrier over which Everest peeped. Now we were coming up the valley round to the end-on view; the angle of the wall was apparent. First in little turrets and ridges, finally in one terrifying uprush, too steep even for the toughest Himalayan ice to cling to, the mountain heaved itself to dominate everything around. And the colour! The essential rock is pale, creamy granite. But it is as if some careless giant had taken a brush and daubed his fancy in black limestone. Often there will be a great stain of this, from which the streaks of white still run in tapering veins for many hundreds of feet. And above, against the sky, a narrow strip of snow clings precariously like the icing on a cut cake. (See Plate 17.)

I have lingered over Nuptse, because in a galaxy of impressive peaks it impressed me as the most noble. Beyond its lower, icy perpendiculars the West Shoulder of Everest showed as a rounded snow hump. There was no suggestion of the icefall between. Left again, square-topped Changtse, the North Peak, peered over the Lho La, which we saw as a broad saddle not to be recommended for walking on at night. Its top is a flat white space; but a few steps this way, and you would fall straight over hanging ice-cliffs, down which avalanches thunder, on to the stony Khumbu below. The Lho La's left flank is walled in by one sharp Lingtren peak, while a second and higher (climbed by Eric Shipton and David Bryant in 1935) stands between it and Pumori. Pumori or "Daughter Peak," named after Mallory's daughter, dominates the left (true right) bank of the upper Khumbu, and is, of course, the second most impressive object on the scene. From almost all angles it is a steep cone, its upper part fashioned of pure snow curving like whipped cream into a summit cornice. Below the ridge connecting it with Lingtren it is a sweep of rock with ribs furrowed by ice channels; impossible, as we thought, of ascent.

It was very pleasant at evening to sit on the moraine top and look out into the last light. For some reason the terrifyingly steep ice ridges of Kangtega held the rose flush wonderfully, though Nuptse, of course, towered into the last glow longer than any. Nearer, below and behind us, you might see a Sherpa walking the two hundred yards down the sand, to fill a bucket from the very dirty water of the lake. At the moraine's side the indefatigable Gompu usually built a precarious cairn or two, which all then knocked down with stones. The Sherpas, I am ashamed to say, were better at this than the cricket-educated sahibs. Gompu was one of the most intriguing of the characters. On the march, being rather fat, he had been the only Sherpa ever to have been heard to ask a sahib if he would walk slower. Yet he was one of the two to reach the top of Kang Cho, though only seventeen; and he later carried his load to the South Col. The son of a lama living on the high ridge above the Lamjura Banjang, he took life very seriously. He was also one of the two Sherpas able to write.

Nearer at hand still, you might be lucky enough to glimpse a tailless Tibetan rat scuttling between the stones. These attractive small creatures, built on the lines of a guinea-pig, are said to be the food of *yeti*. Looking back again beyond the boulders you will see Pasang Phutar or Ang Tensing ("Balu") preparing our supper. Both these stalwarts (later South Col men) seemed rather to like that job. Pasang Phutar was a well-built fellow with an enormous grin and an affable expansiveness about his whole person. Balu was big, in a way suggestive of his soubriquet, "the bear," with a sombre, rather frowning face except when his teeth flashed in a smile. There was something Irish about his air of sturdy independence. Tilman had given him very good marks for his work on Rakaposhi, and we regarded him as a dark horse; he might go to the summit itself, he might fade out at Base Camp. He was tremendously strong.

One of these would be busy cooking over a fire of sticks. I still had the job of quartermaster, until we joined up with Ed's party, which had taken up stores, we hoped, for our needs after the 17th. We would be having the usual soup, mushroom or tomato perhaps, then one of the meats and potatoes, followed by cake and coffee. We were not at all tired of the cake, a good fruit one. Then the best moment of the day: coffee and the last pipe or cigarette. We were usually asleep by 8:30.

The day that we arrived, we spent much of the afternoon asleep in the sun on the hot sand, opening an eye occasionally to glimpse the improbably abrupt, whitish-green spires around. John was under doctor's orders to rest the next day, the 17th, and Mike Ward and I therefore volunteered to go up to Base Camp. The exciting question had been agitating us for some days: What had been happening on the icefall? I was also to make a report for John and *The Times* on the doings of the pioneer party.

It was a fine morning. We climbed over the moraine and dropped, to our surprise, on a well-cairned track to the chaotic, boulder-strewn Khumbu below. In places the cairns over the stony ground reminded me of the top of our own Great Gable. But these cairns were tall and thin, built after the tapering Gompu style of architecture. Their line did not continue long. The chief feature of the glacier is the serried formation of row upon row of ice pinnacles, going up to 150 feet high. The first that met us presented a vertical, clean-cut wall of bluey-green, dropping to a little glacier stream, up which we went. Above this two other characteristic features appeared: slivers of ice two or three feet high and often precariously cut at the base, so that a blow sent them tumbling. Scattered over the level shale across which we walked, they resembled *en masse* nothing so much as a large cemetery. Besides these were the "T-Tables" familiar from the Alps: great blocks of stone around which the snow has melted and which remain perched on a stalk of ice several feet from the ground.

All these formations are due to the strong action of the sun on the glacier surface. What is curious is that the "penitents" (so called from their shape, as of kneeling figures) should only occur in some parts of the Himalaya. After an hour's walk we found them pressing thicker and thicker upon us, but a strangely formed, natural trough to the left solves the difficulty. A further half-hour's walk between confining walls leads to a large, stony mound topped by a cairn. We climbed this; there at our feet were three tents perched on lesser mounds: the site of Base Camp, called Camp I by the Swiss, who had their Base at the lake.

Mike Westmacott was at home, also Kirken, our second cook. Kirken looked something of a prizefighter: a broad tough face on big shoulders. Some cast doubts on his cleanliness, but then every Sherpa cook is temperamentally alien to the habits of the hygienically trained British. Moreover it was not his fault if the site was too near that of the Swiss lavatories to be healthy. Mike was suffering badly from stomach trouble and diarrhœa, a complaint common at Base and known, along with a cough and sore throat, as "Basecampitis." Both the Georges were suffering, less badly. When poor Ralph Izzard of the *Daily Mail* had toiled up, some days earlier, he had been greeted by the sombre back of George Lowe, seated in stony depression on a rock. Fortunately, perhaps, credit had been later restored by entertainment to tea from Griff Pugh and Tom Stobart, both of whom had come up with the icefall party. Mike Westmacott told us of their heroic march, on April 10th particularly, when they were caught by the same snow that had found the other two parties at Dingboche. They had a large number of coolies and could not afford to wait; nor could the coolies go on without goggles over the glare of new snow. It was Tom Stobart, I think, who ingeniously started to improvise goggles with big panoramic glasses and his black high-altitude tape. This tape became very popular among the Sherpanis, who used patches as beauty-spots on their round red cheeks. They claimed that these were a charm to ward off headaches, but no males were ever seen to wear them. The tape had not been enough for all the sunshades. Handkerchiefs, scarves and even pigtails had been pressed into the service of keeping out the glare. At Lake Camp there had still been snow, and even with the tents packed full some of the coolies had slept outside, huddled under a blanket. I may say here that "packed full" means something in terms of Sherpas. The highest recorded number in a twelve-man dome tent during the expedition was sixty, and eight in a two-man Meade.

Work had started on the long-anticipated icefall on April 13th. Ed reported it more broken and intricate than in 1951.

Standing in the midday heat outside the tent we could appreciate the problem. Most of the way up from Lake Camp it had seemed quite impossible that there could be this hidden valley between the cut ridge-end of Nuptse, cascading down from twenty-five to seventeen thousand feet, and the round dome of Everest's West Shoulder beyond, supported by glaciers that themselves overhung space. But now, here it was: the frozen torrent, perhaps half a mile wide, of tumbled blocks and mighty fragments. My first impression was that it was not like icefalls in the Alps (nor would one go up it in the Alps), a thing of towers and segments divided neatly by crevasses. It resembled the froth and bubbles scattered over a fast-flowing river, or a myriad sugar-lumps heaped and strewn over a water-shoot. Several days' hard work had been needed to reach a platform over half-way up for Camp II. And today Ed and the two Georges, with Sherpas, had taken stores to spend the night there, tomorrow to explore towards the icefall's top for a possible Camp III. After that it was obvious that a lot more work would be needed before it was safe for laden porters: finding easier alternatives; bridging awkward crevasses, enlarging steps, knocking down dangerous seracs or ice pinnacles,[1] putting up marker flags. Of these last we had a hundred, and I had asked Thondup to go down from Thyangboche and find bamboo sticks for them.

We descended with Mike Westmacott, who hoped to recover at a healthier spot. About a quarter of a mile down, Mike Ward stopped.

"What about this for a Base Camp site?"

We all looked doubtful. But it was clearly better. Instead of many slippery mounds there was one, bounded by a curve in the glacier stream on one side, and a row of shining, 70-foot ice pinnacles on the other. If one did have to climb out in the middle of the night, the risk of breaking a neck was not so great. Moreover, we might be able to use a tributary trickle for water, and here we were farther away from the Swiss site. We decided to move the camp, if John agreed.

[1] Seracs are ice-towers formed by the movement of the glacier. They may be anything from a hundred to a few feet high.

2

John had been spending his "rest" morning disobeying orders by climbing the grass slopes above, from which Tilman in 1950 had the first view of Everest from the southwest. The afternoon was sunny. Mike Ward suggested that what *The Times* would really like would be a photograph of two climbers reposing on Li-Los in the middle of the lake, against a background of the great Nuptse precipice. John looked a little startled.

"No, no, that would give *quite* the wrong impression."

And I have to record regretfully that the photograph was never taken. By now John was feeling so well that he determined tomorrow to go up and see the icefall for himself, though we were not due to be active in it for a day or two. However, he was very much against anybody else going, on the theory that we should all be seeing all too much of it soon. Here a certain mild ribaldry ensued, since the leader would be seeing as much of it as anybody. However, we left it admiringly at that. Mike and I decided to climb the ridge of Pumori from which Eric Shipton took his well-known photograph in 1951. We should see into the mysterious Western Cwm, and be able to tell the conditions on the Lhotse Face.

Here let me pause to differ from those who rename this valley, maintaining, quite rightly, that the word "Cwm" or "hollow" is a Welsh word appropriate to the valleys of Wales. If mountaineers were logical people, their mountain world would be a dull place. As it is, the Western Cwm conjured up for us the figure of Mallory, peering from the col beside Lingtren. It associated our effort with the greatest protagonist of Everest, who gave its name to this "freak of mountain architecture." For us the hidden valley descending beneath the triumvirate of Everest, Lhotse and Nuptse will never be anything but the Western Cwm.

That night my Li-Lo trouble started. We were now using the big, two-layer Li-Los, constructed on the theory that with only one layer the sleeper either bounces like a pea be-

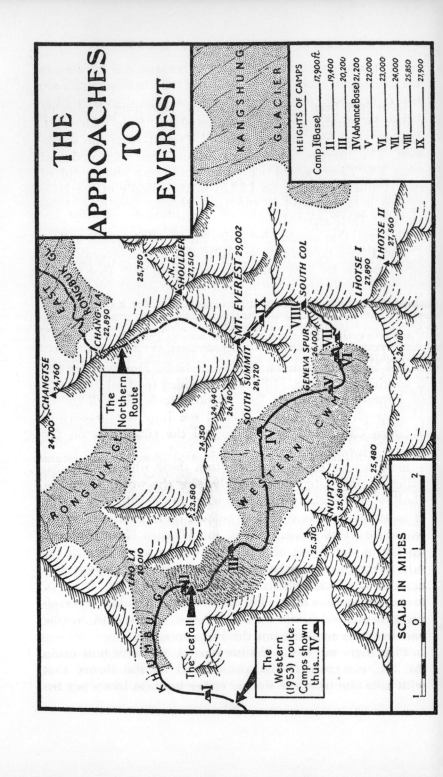

THE
APPROACHES
TO
EVEREST

HEIGHTS OF CAMPS

Camp I(Base) _____ 17,900 ft.
II _____ 19,400
III _____ 20,200
IV(Advance Base) 21,200
V _____ 22,000
VI _____ 23,000
VII _____ 24,000
VIII _____ 25,850
IX _____ 27,900

KANGSHUNG GLACIER

MT. EVEREST 29,002
N.E. SHOULDER 27,510
25,750
SOUTH COL
LHOTSE 27,890
LHOTSE II 27,560
LHOTSE I
SOUTH SUMMIT 28,720
GENEVA SPUR 26,100
26,180

RONGBUK GL. EAST
CHANGTSE 24,760
CHANG LA 22,890
24,700
24,940
24,350
23,580
LHO LA 20,010

The Northern Route

WESTERN CWM

NUPTSE 25,680
25,370
25,480
26,180

KHUMBU GL.
The Icefall

The Western (1953) route. Camps shown thus...IV

SCALE IN MILES

2
1
0
1

cause it is too hard, or hits the rocks because it is too soft. In the case of our models you can have a hard bottom and a soft top layer, theoretically. Some fault in the valves compelled us to pump both layers tight as drums in the hope that at least one would endure till morning. That night I was out pumping at 1:00 A.M. I remember thinking: This won't be much fun on the South Col.

In the morning, the sky looked like snow; we set out (8:10) on the well-tried principle that one could always come back if it did snow. To reach the ridge of Pumori you must first of all make up the valley almost parallel with the Khumbu, across a disused glacier-snout which is now a jumble of enormous blocks. The passage of these was trying, the more so from the folds of mist that hung in places, waiting to obscure the hoped-for view. We seemed perpetually to be poised on one huge, reddish-brown block, or else scrabbling on to the next. It was ground on which no rhythm of movement was possible, but where we blessed rubber soles and our previous practice on the Khumbu and Imja. After a while I occasionally had the curious feeling of having been this way before, and then remembered having done exactly the same type of jump some time back.

At last we could see our ridge, curving round beside a little lake. For perhaps 1,000 feet above us it climbed, stony and rather indefinite. Then a snow-crest took it a further 200 feet, to flatten into the precipitous mountain above. As we rose a long trailer of cloud streamed from Nuptse, at this angle the noblest mountain I know. Its ice-cliffs and buttresses spread downward with the floating beauty of a crinoline. On top of Everest itself a dark sausage of wind-cloud sat like an umbrella. And in and out of moving mist the face of Lhotse gleamed with sinister glints from stray sun-arrows. That meant ice, a lot of work.

We kept rather to the left of the ridge, up a white granite buttress which relieved the legs by giving work to the hands, and in places proved quite difficult enough. Though we had been higher, we were still breathing heavily at this altitude. At last we were over the top, on to a hard snow ridge in which I chipped a few steps. We went on, up and over the ridge, and then down to shelter from a chill little wind. Half shrouded in mist, the brutal black southern precipice of Everest formed a Wagnerian background. The icefall we could see in its whole length, writhing and tumbling its way down that 2,000-foot gorge. Over food we now took binoculars to the view. After some searching we noted figures near the bottom, stopping probably to rope up. Moving up we made out the little yellow patch of Camp II—apparently perched in a wilderness of fragments. Ed's party we could not see at all. But the upper section seemed broken into bigger chunks, any of which might hide them. We reckoned our own height as 19,200 feet, and at 11:45 we packed up and returned talkatively down the ridge, to the desolation of boulders.

Two more happy events took place that day; the first was the arrival of our first real mail, and plenty of it. There is no comparable joy to the traveller; we spent the afternoon reading and re-reading. Secondly, John's reappearance at 6:00 P.M., with the glad news that Ed's party had reached the top of the icefall. John had had a very long day. At Base he had taken on the quiet, willing Ang Namgyal. Griff and Tom Stobart had come up the first bit too. He had met Ed's party returning, some 300 feet below Camp II. He had gone back some way with Ed to look at the route. He was tired but delighted. One obstacle, which might have proved insuperable, had been overcome. Nor had he himself done badly, for a man just recovering from pleurisy.

Next day was the first "off-day" since we left Thyangboche. At 12:30 Ed, the two Georges and their Sherpas appeared, well satisfied and ready for a rest, but still not sure of their route's safety. They complained bitterly of the cold wind blowing at Lake Camp, of the muddy water, and of breakfast not being served in bed, as had been the pleasant habit at Base Camp. It was a lazy afternoon of letter and school-report writing; punctuated by John's appearances to explain the Plan to us. This he had worked out in wonderful detail; my only doubt was whether we could possibly be efficient enough to execute it. The first step at any rate was easy: John, Mike Ward and I would go up to Base and work at the icefall. A higher party would then come through to establish Camp III. John intended to start the "carry" of loads up the icefall into the Cwm on April 24th.

3

The voice of Griff Pugh prophesying woe, or at least a very long and unpleasant job, rang in our ears as the two Mikes (Ward and Westmacott) and I set off on the 19th, firmly resolved to move Base Camp to the new site. We took an early lunch off Kirken and started in. First, tents must be dismantled and goods packed. This and the transport down the trough were the job of our five Sherpas, led by little Gyal-jen. Gyaljen was one of the most vivacious and likable of the Sherpas, a good organiser, but not strong enough, I thought, to be a "top" carrier. Poor Kirken had just completed a monumental stone cook-house with stone walls and tarpaulin roof; but he transferred his labours with a good grace to the new site. Next, and most important, space must be levelled for the big tent. This job took three hard hours, partly owing to Tom Stobart's fine determination to avoid one error of the old site; the ice there had been too near the ground-sheet, which ripped when luckless visitors slid across the floor. Its nearness also made the tent colder. Therefore we must build with stones of the right size and shape, broad and flat. We began to realise the labours of landscape gardeners. Fortunately Gompu's cairn-builder training had given him a good eye for large flat stones and a great enthusiasm for carrying them about. Working all together, we had by 5 o'clock erected a large, fairly flat platform. On this the tent took its stand. It was a little shaming, however, to see the Sherpas knock up platforms for the other tents in ten minutes.

It had been ordained that water should be taken from a small tributary above the site, and that rubbish of every sort should be jettisoned on the down-stream slope. The two Mikes had even hacked out a passage to a toilet-place beyond the river. Unfortunately this sort of hygiene was not easy to drill into the Sherpas. Though they obeyed the principle, they did not go very far. By the time we left in June, the whole area breathed a nauseous odour. But in the first days new Base Camp seemed a palace and a positive model of hygienic beauty after the old. To my mind, it had other beauties, too, and James Morris of *The Times* surprised me when he described it as an ugly spot.

Let us stumble out of the big tent for a moment, at a time when the whole expedition is there. We must go carefully, especially in the wool-lined expedition camp boots, for the starlight is not strong, and the stones around the camp lie loosely on ice, waiting to let the incautious down with a thump. Our tent is right up near the big ice pinnacle. The first day I cut steps, which still remain visible, up the shoulder of this pinnacle. I went over it into a weird and wonderful valley of ice, along which I wandered until it was possible to get back to our trough, somewhere near first Base Camp. Also in this pinnacle you can see the first cave, dug under the command of Tom Stobart. A narrow passage leads to a chamber perhaps six feet square, where Tom's photographic kit is stored. Several people tried sleeping in this, beginning with Tom until he caught pneumonia. The advantage is an equable temperature, six degrees below freezing; and at night, by candlelight, it is a pretty spot. But in the day-time it is a cheerless place to work in, and some are a little frightened by ominous prophecies that we shall all be living in caves, when the tents go up into the Cwm.

Below our tents is a crowd of small platforms supporting the Meades. Down a little towards the river stands the second big tent, occupied by the icefall Sherpas. These fourteen stalwarts, with one or two more as reserves, have come up simply to carry our loads as far as Camp III. They are equipped with normal mountaineering kit, but not high-altitude boots or down clothing. They are mostly locals, and, of course, if especially good, will be taken higher. Two of them already stand out: Dawa Thondup, a small wizened man and the doyen of Himalayan porters; also Ang Norbu, who comes from nearby. Below the tents is the cook-house, a fine stone building roofed with tarpaulin. One wall is made up of ration-boxes. Here Thondup operates, sometimes on a wood fire, sometimes on a double Primus burner if the wood situation is poor. The cost of wood was always another financial worry to John. Each load meant so many coolies from the lower valley: so much pay for each. They usually stayed the night, particularly welcome if there were wives or sweethearts of the Sherpas among them, and consumed food. Thus, a "carry" of wood cost in all about £1.

Descending below the cook-house we reach the stream. This winds round the camp site, and on the right is the little passage carved between the pinnacles, to Mike Ward's idea of a hygienic lavatory. Unfortunately it is a very distant one, and perilously slippery in camp boots in the middle of the night. Now we climb back up the very dirty southern slope of the mound, past the structure which Tom Bourdillon has erected out of oxygen-boxes for his experiments. We won't visit Griff's tent, a little way up the trough; he was anxious to pitch it on ice, to see whether that is really as unpleasant as everyone says. Instead we will turn to admire the peaks. Despite the yellow lights blinking warmly through the tent walls, I am reminded of de Saussure's words, which might well have been written here rather than of Mont Blanc:

> The sky was then perfectly pure and cloudless, and the vapour could be seen no more except at the bottom of the valleys. The stars were bright, but shorn of any vestige of twinkle. They shed over the mountain summits a very weak, pale light, but it was sufficient to distinguish masses and distances. The quiet and the deep silence which reigned over this vast expanse, magnified too by the imagination, inspired in me a real kind of terror. It was as if I were the last survivor of the Universe, and saw its corpse stretched under my feet.

The stars are bright, but the moon is by now tipping the black, straight-cut edge of Pumori. Far down the valley the Taweche peaks dream above the "vapour" of lightly shifting mist. At our valley's head the Lho La, noisy in the day-time, is a white satin cushion, the footstool of giants. Nearer, the ice pinnacles shine silver above the jet black of the uneven ground over which we have been walking. Night softens roughnesses, as it livens the sense of that outward beauty which is knocking all day at our hearts in the Himalaya. For now the worry of doing is gone, leaving us at evening a blank coin ready to receive an imprint.

4

The icefall. We had heard and read so much of it, this dragon that guards the Hesperidean garden of the Cwm. My first venture, on the 20th, was part of an engineering expedition. We left at nine, rather late owing to a delay over Sherpa food. The task of co-ordinating with me had now been given to Nimmi, a competent-looking little Sherpa whose heart prevented him from going high. He could write, after a fashion, which was an advantage, but was vague about the quantities of food required, particularly when it came to six weeks on the mountain for thirty-four Sherpas. *Atta* (for chapattis), *tsampa* (roasted and ground barley), the staple food, rice, butter, dried potatoes—all had to be carried on the backs of coolies up from Namche. He was sent off at intervals to buy these, as well as sheep and fresh potatoes, for both of which sahibs and Sherpas alike had a craving. I finished the figures rather hastily and sent Nimmi off.

I set out slightly ahead of the two Mikes, to attach flags to their sticks at old Base. Mike Westmacott appeared soon, bearing a large spanner with which he attacked the duralumin ladder-bridge. The burden of the five lengths of this was bravely borne that day by Gyaljen and Pasang Phutar. In their company and shod already with crampons we set off finally for the icefall at 9:45. The first stretch lies along glacier trough, roughly at right angles to the icefall proper. The original route had followed this a long way, then turned sharply right. But George Band had made a cunning short cut, hard to discover at its beginning.

"What about this?"

"No, I'm fairly sure we haven't got there yet. Climb that mound if you like."

"Can you see anything?"

"Looks a possible line all right, but I can't find tracks. Let's go on a bit."

"Would this be it?"

"There should be a mark here, but the snow may have wiped it off. I think it was the first place after all. We'd better go back."

And so on. At the most likely-looking spot I planted a flag awkwardly in a tiny crack. All along I found this flag-placing as good an excuse for a halt as photography. One had only to stop and start scraping a hole, for everybody else to stop, too, thinking doubtless: "Ah, what a conscientious chap!"

Gradually our line of frozen tributary stream, winding its confused course, approached steepening icefall. High on the skyline, above where Camp II must be, fantastic fingers of ice seemed to totter already over and down the chaotic descent. To find a way up this, how impossible! We were still unroped, and soon left the level, to begin winding more steeply up little walls and terraces and gullies of powdery snow, sticky to walk on. Wherever possible I pasted the route with flags. Already this April we had begun to suffer a depressingly regular afternoon snowfall, obscuring the morning's tracks and leaving almost a fresh route to find. These falls were heralded by high, wispy cloud banners at night, followed by brilliant early mornings. Up thick snow we ploughed, occasionally losing direction, until Mike Westmacott suddenly uttered the cry of a lost mariner. Two hundred feet above he recognised the steep edge of a crevasse, notched with steps: "Mike's Horror," his lead of some days previously. We roped, climbed a frothy, laborious little slope, and found ourselves on a steep, rounded ice-edge, overlooking on the left a promising young crevasse. We ascended cautiously, digging axe-points into the snow and at the top holding the laden two Sherpas tight on the rope. It had been a fine lead, worthy, we decided, of a fixed rope for following porters.

Above this section we were very soon confronted with a really large crevasse. This had been previously avoided by a detour. Mike intended for it two sections of our ladder, which Gyaljen dumped enthusiastically. These were spannered together, and the resultant twelve-foot length lowered over the chasm. It was amusing to think later in the expedition how cautiously we then crawled across, roping the loads one by one, in the manner of good Scouts. When they were used to it, and especially descending, the Sherpas often walked upright over here even in crampons, and always when the ladder was replaced by two pine-logs. If somebody looked like falling in, he was regarded as a great joke. On we went, expending another length on a smaller crevice, till we arrived at another obstacle, already well-known: this time "Hillary's Horror." It is curious, the mountaineer's liking for connecting the steepnesses of his hills with particular people. This one consisted of a wide crevasse bridged by a broad leaf of ice coated with snow. Nobody liked the leaf greatly; the thought of having to tread it for two months filled some with gloomy unease. It led the way on the other side to a steep wall of fifteen feet, up which steps had been cut and a rope fixed. (See Plate 21(c).)

At the top of this we halted, after fixing our flag. It was past noon, the day was hot but the black snow-clouds were already boiling up in the valley. We decided to go no farther, but to improve the route achieved thus far. Mike Westmacott and Pasang Phutar enlarged the steps of the top wall; Mike Ward and I spotted an ice tower shortly below, which looked as though it might later totter to our destruction; a diamond-shaped block perhaps fifteen feet high poised on a small base. We attacked it as one would a tree. First we manœuvred a rope round it, upon which it was Gyaljen's job to keep a constant pressure. Then, in turns, we hacked cautiously at the base. Suddenly there was a crunch, a split, and the great thing slumped with a disappointingly dull thud on to the level snow.

By the time we were back at 3:40, following our flags easily from above, snow was already falling fast. It was depressing every single day to see the great cloud sacks spreading up and depositing the first loads on the Taweche peaks. Gradually the whole mighty cirque of the Khumbu's head would be filled with brown murk. The sun would wink good-bye, the flakes would fall, faster and faster; and at a certain stage one would sigh and put on a wind-proof. For that is my chief

CAMP FIVE, LOOKING DOWN THE CWM

memory of the icefall; heat, not cold. Already the huge rock walls around seemed to be radiating the sun's rays on to us, tiny creatures trying to climb the burning glass. This close heat induced a not always unpleasant lethargy. It is an agreeable sensation to know that one has every excuse for being in by four, to spend the rest of the evening in the "Everest Position." Certainly we felt well stretched by the time we took off crampons in the trough below old Base Camp.

John arrived this afternoon from Lake Camp; the first as ever. Some time later the two Georges, Ed and their Sherpas appeared, looking like snowmen, to help on the fug in the big tent. Next day, the 21st, this icefall party would go right through and secure the route above II. Hunt, the two Mikes and I would improve the track below it. It was a cold night, for the first time I felt chilled in one sleeping-bag, and of course "on the rocks" again under the sinking Li-Lo. Again we were off by nine. Again I went a little ahead to tie on more flags. Again it was hot and close on the slope leading to Mike's Horror; but familiarity with a route has a strange faculty of decreasing its difficulties. Here we drove in a long steel shaft from the structural apparatus, and attached knotted hemp. Above Hillary's Horror we were on fresh ground. One approaches over flatter snow the left (true right) bank of the icefall. Then, 400 feet above, the largest of ice fingers appears far on the skyline, dominating this lower steep. A mighty tangle of blocks between. How to find the way? Straight below the finger a wide snow gully makes some sort of impression on the tangle. Up this, known as "Hell Fire Alley," we continued, catching sight every now and then of a confirmatory flag left by the pioneers. Occasionally a Swiss flag, far out to the left on some vast, impossible block over a chasm, would show how much the glacier had changed over the winter.

I was leading the first rope, with Mike Westmacott gallantly carrying a length of ladder left yesterday at Hillary's Horror. The awkwardness of this, its pleasure in hitting every knob and catching in every hollow, was a foretaste of things to come. At the top of Hell Fire Alley you must pass out to the right, under overhanging eaves, up through a wilderness of piled chunks. Occasionally, as you step upon them, they subside into their crevasses to a rumble of gargantuan laughter below. One spot, a cleft between vertical walls through which you must pass to climb out and up an easier flank, had been christened "Hillary's Folly," Mike told us. Here Ed had dropped an ice-axe and spent half an hour upside down exploring the depths to recover it.

Always you are expecting the angle to ease. It is a long time, perhaps an hour from the "Horror" before it does. Then, standing on a cake-slice block, you look up a rounded valley, like the long valley hole of Hindhead Golf Course. The concave trough of this is split by a maze of small crevices. John said that the change since last week was startling. We wondered anxiously how much it would have changed in two months. This time we wound slowly up the left-hand side, noting one awkward jump fit for a pole bridge. At the head of the valley a really deep cleft called for a section of duralumin bridge. Here the choice was between making one athletic jump, of which none of us was really capable, or treading upon a sliver of very thin ice wedged most uncomfortably above the depths. For some reason I found myself treading this thing, and a few seconds later digging a platform for the ladder on the farther lip. We then fixed the bridge and tied it down with ice pitons. Two hundred yards to the right, round the right-hand wall of our valley, we came upon the tents. At this time Camp II (19,400 feet) still seemed a high, mysterious place. We had not yet come to scorn it as a disagreeable night halt low down the mountain. There were the four yellow and orange tents on a broad platform, almost overhung, as it seemed to me, by two large and lumpy ice towers about fifteen yards beyond.

Ed and George Band had arrived with their ropes of Sherpas. The unfortunate George Lowe had been overcome by severe "Basecampitis" on the way, and had to descend. John asked Mike Westmacott to stay, with himself; Mike Ward and I, after seeing them settled in, turned to descend before too heavy snow. As we walked along the last stretch of trough I said to Mike: "If anyone asked what we've been doing today, I certainly shouldn't feel like saying, 'Climbing

Everest.' " We agreed that it had never occurred to us that we had been spending the day on Everest. We concluded that perhaps it is because climbers are short-sighted creatures, and can never see beyond the next handhold, ledge, or at most, camp.

Yet when I came to think of it afterwards, the same thought is true of the whole expedition. Contemplate that photograph of Tenzing standing with the flags on the summit; and think back to Thondup peeling potatoes at Base, Roberts checking oxygen cylinders after Alf Bridge had seen them off, ourselves knocking down seracs. What was everybody doing during this time? Climbing Everest; that is to say, making the photograph possible.

Base Camp was transformed in the falling snow of 4:00 P.M. that afternoon. Jimmy Roberts, a Himalayan veteran, had arrived with the main store of oxygen. With him was James Morris of *The Times*, "a very parfit gentle journalist," as I should like to describe him. Nothing could be pleasanter than pouring experiences into a sympathetic, placid ear, and knowing that they would be turned into good English. Besides these, Charles Evans's party had brought up all the main expedition's stores. There was Charles himself, busy already painting camp numbers on the various boxes; and Charles Wylie, the centre of a talkative group of Sherpas. Figures never seen before, like Phu Dorji in his bright orange balaclava, and little Dawa Thondup shyly introducing himself, were now wandering about the site. Tom Bourdillon was already constructing his oxygen department, and a relay of hands worked away at the ice-cave. We were now an officially constituted Base Camp.

The one disadvantage was a squash at meal-times in the big tent. Men wearing down clothing seem twice their normal selves. Also, as spoons and forks were breaking fast, we were reduced to improvisation. James remarked once, in his quiet way, that to a stranger it had seemed very odd to find a national expedition without a mess tent, and the leader eating his porridge from a fork off the floor. I once discovered Charles Wylie, at Camp VII, consuming Grape-Nuts with a spanner. He seemed to get very few in each time.

The nights were cold still, probably some way below zero. But Ed had quite early trodden successfully on a large thermometer and I am unable to give the customary accurate readings. Breakfast at Base was usually a leisurely affair taken at about eight, when the warming sun had peeped over the Lho La. We would sit outside on packing-cases, while Kirken bustled around with porridge, bacon (a peculiarly uneatable sort, likewise the sausage-meat), and eggs if we were lucky. James had pitched his tent on a little mound just up the trough. But he came over to eat with us.

The next day, the 22nd, was an ordered rest day for all who were down here. But Mike Ward and I had spied an irresistible variation to Hillary's Horror. We departed in warm sunshine and reached the spot in fifty minutes from old Base. The variation was simple. We crossed the same crevasse, but lower on the left, where it was narrow enough for a stride. We then climbed up to the same ice-wall, but another, left-hand facet of it. I worked at cutting steps from the top, he from the bottom. We swung the rope round to hang in his direction, and soon had a fair staircase with handrail. Coming down, pleased with ourselves, in time for lunch, we sat sunbathing for half an hour. It was seaside weather. The drowsy eye was astonished, half opening, to behold the immense sweep of Nuptse rather than the blue of a calm Mediterranean.

On the 24th the Low and High Level lifts were to start operating. On the evening of the 22nd John arrived back at 6:00 P.M. with George Band. Good news! They had found a site for Camp III at the head of the icefall, and George Lowe had made wireless contact with it. Ed and Mike Westmacott had stayed up to improve the route, for on the 24th two teams would come up: the Low Level ferry carrying loads as far as III, and seven Sherpas led by Greg and myself, to be based on III and do the higher carries into the Cwm. We were known as the High Level ferry. The 23rd therefore was occupied with preparation for taking up the High Level team with Greg: discussion of rations, repair of boots, letters written home, conferences about stores for III with Charles, sorting out of our Sherpas. The day was memorable for the most delicious scones. Thondup at his best could turn out something delectable, to be remembered for days, and anything like bread was especially welcome. The addition of butter and jam raised the scones to one of the spheres of Paradise. We all made pigs of ourselves whenever such scones, and more rarely fresh cake, made an appearance. It did something to cheer us over the slow, soft snowfall which was again covering and damping every possession that we had. Supper that night was a depressing meal. We had eaten too many scones, but besides that, what of the snow? How would this affect the icefall and the High Level carries?

A.J.VEILHAN

7

High Level Carry

April 24th—April 30th

1

I was disconcerted, climbing out before the dawn of April 24th, to find myself suffering from incipient "Basecampitis." There was nothing for it but to hope that absence from the place would remove the disease. At 7:30, in hot sunshine, life became extremely busy, almost unpleasantly so for the next three hours. I was to take the High Level team to Camp II that night, thence to Camp III next day. Greg would take the Low Level team, which would then be brought down on the 25th by Mike Westmacott, while Greg and I stayed. John and Charles Evans, with Tenzing, would go up to III and there join Ed to reconnoitre the Cwm. All this time Ed and Mike were working from III, improving the route and looking upward.

To prepare for a week's stay at a high camp means a deal of work and calculation. The Sherpas of our two teams must be summoned, and as Greg had the less Urdu, I must tell them of their task and organise them into their loads. Their rations must be given out for the period. Then there was the Great Crampon Worry. It was not only that the crampons broke, but they tended mysteriously to vanish from outside tents; while the thought of bringing them into the tent was uncomfortable. Both the Toms were sadly enquiring for theirs, but short of a tent-to-tent search, all that I could do was to improvise and borrow. Then there was payment for a yak (122 rupees), which had been brought up yesterday, and was pitifully eyeing us in the hope of food. None of the Sherpas liked to kill it. As we set off at 10:30, my last view

◄ *Our constant fear was that this
gap would widen. . . .*

was of the two Georges, one apparently being pulled down the Khumbu by the creature, the other anxiously pursuing in the hope of catching it, rather than his colleague, with the rifle before they disappeared.

Then a Sherpa came along with a sore throat and asked to be medicined, or, better still, replaced. The Sherpas were suffering from a plague of sore throats and coughs at this time, and some of the sahibs too. Tom Stobart had been sleeping in his ice cave and came out with a badly blocked nose. ("Need an ice-axe to blow your nose in there," as George Lowe put it.) Some said that he caught his pneumonia there. The doctor was being kept busy; Mike's prescriptions "Try this, it's no bloody good," and "Go down lower," were by now becoming expedition slogans. Fortunately, the remedies were better than this advertisement.

At last, at 10:30, we were off. I noted the day thus in my diary:

> Progress slow. Hot and sunny at first but clouds banking. Gompu's crampon broke (another gone), but tied up. 11:30, snow started and increased. Arrived at first bridge, now replaced by two poles. Sherpas found great difficulty and were nervous. Tashi Phutar on belly and the loads had all to be slung across. Load of flags very awkward. Greg not pleased with his lot, who certainly weren't efficient. Much shouting. On we went. Two hours to Hillary's Horror, which is better our new way. On, with hood up, visibility nil, Sherpa loads coming off, crampon buckles slipping, and my following Sherpa fell at the icy traverse. However, slowly on, four ropes of us, and reached Camp II at 2:50 P.M. Four and a half hours!

At Camp II we found John and Charles entented. They had intended to go on to III, but it was now snowing hard and they had decided to stay. The Sherpas put up three extra tents. We erected the aerial mast for the wireless. I climbed in to join the others, after hailing the genial Sherpa who had the Primus going. John sometimes hinted gently that perhaps the sahibs should share the cooking, but I cannot remember any enthusiast living up to this ideal. Of course, when there were no fit Sherpas at hand, we "made shift to wag along," like Bunyan's travellers. Otherwise we accepted lazily.

Another visit into the cold outer world convinced me that I had better take a pill for my diarrhœa: a clear judgment on my foolish boast that I was the only member of the expedition so far not to have taken any pill. This, with a sleeping-pill of great moment on Lhotse Face, was, however, the only pill I had to take till the march back. Then we snuggled in for the evening of a day lightened by the glory of finally parting mist, with a revelation of Pumori as a sparkling wonder of fresh snow.

2

The 25th was for me, I confess it, a day of internal grumps. Every climber must have such days; thank Heaven they are rare. On them it would give the greatest pleasure if all his colleagues fell into the largest crevasse available. But it had its beauties, too, for it impressed upon me a more intimate picture of a route traversed many times by sahibs and Sherpas; a route intricate, and yet, to my mind, not dangerous, except in the sense that crossing Trafalgar Square is dangerous. I never felt, in three ascents before the High Carry and three after, that I was treading unsafe ground; only that I was treading difficult ground, and the more so because on every single ascent fresh snow demanded a new track. Moreover, the company of Sherpas, apart from tiring the climber by an added sense of responsibility, throws upon him alone the tasks of route-finding and trail-breaking. The moral tug on the rope is as great as the physical.

Today the High Level Sherpas and myself had been left with two lengths of ladder inexorably linked together, since there was no spanner at II. Taking three and a half hours over a climb which normally took an hour and fifty minutes, I had leisure to memorise each feature of the upper icefall; more particularly since the twelve-foot ladder gave me an exact measurement of the gaps, and later, when we tried carrying it vertically, of how low were the eaves under which we must pass. To begin with, I was overjoyed at Tashi

117

Phutar's offer to carry this problem load. He has appeared before as a nervous little Sherpa. Last year he had accompanied Ed and George over the Nup La, where he succeeded, to his terror, in falling into all available crevasses. Yesterday

THE ROUTE TO THE TOP

he had shown the greatest dismay at the bridges. Even on all-fours he very nearly managed to fall into the largest crevasse, and had to be held tightly on the rope. But he was certainly game. He tried carrying the bridge horizontally across his back, and for the first stretch this went well enough, since the ground is open. Later, when we were once again among fallen blocks and the thing bumped and caught upon every ice projection and every snow crevice, I tried

118

for a short time carrying it between two of us, myself the first. This proved equally impossible, for upon rounding a corner one of the pair would find himself squashed against the wall, while his colleague dangled over an abyss. At last Pemba Norbu seized the bridge. Pemba, going to fetch salt with other Sherpas from Namche, had met us on the corner beyond Junbezi and turned back to accompany the expedition, another instance of the ease of Sherpa arrangements. He was tall and straight, with a mass of black hair and thoughtful features. Later he left us abruptly, after an undivulged disagreement with Tenzing, but reappeared reconciled in time for the march home. He was certainly missed, for he was one of the best carriers. He now tied the ladder elaborately to his head strap and carried it vertical; a method which worked well on flattish ground and in narrow passages, but ill when we climbed over blocks, for there seemed always to be one just ahead, ready to catch the antenna-like top of the ladder.

The first stretch from Camp II, done before "sun-up," was always pleasant. Invariably afternoon snow had all but obliterated the track; a faint line of imprints sometimes carried the eye up over the next gently curving satin bulge. Often it was guess-work to the next flag. I have said that two lumpish chunks, perhaps 100 feet high, seemed to have settled into seracs beyond and to the right of the Camp II platform. We always thought the left-hand of these two menacing, and were not surprised to find, on our final descent, that it had crashed, partly covering the tent site. But it was difficult to recognise these things in the very different conditions of that June day. The route wound up to the back of them, up a little valley and then across a wide slope mildly threatened by seracs. It happened on several later journeys that our tracks here were covered by débris from these; but nobody ever saw one fall, and they were too large for attack, except perhaps by the two-inch mortar. From the back of these Camp II seracs, one must head straight up the icefall, still over débris, but of a larger and more amenable nature than before. At last, when things are getting steep, a traverse to the right gives the answer.

It leads over to a soft, sunny wall, now furnished with good steps and a fixed rope. Thence a period of comparatively level going, delightful if one has not a twelve-foot ladder bumping at one's heels or on one's head. Here Tenzing's party caught us up, and I asked him urgently to tell Camp III that we needed a spanner, indeed we needed it more than anything else on earth. The day was now hot, the work of track-breaking, which Tenzing had taken over, was extremely hot. We had come to a small dog-leg between blocks close together, where I was trying the unsuccessful experiment of a two-man carry. This leads to a long and grinning crevasse, our biggest cause of worry on this upper section. It spans the whole line of the route, its upper lip sometimes as much as twenty feet vertically above the lower. Only in one place, towards the left, is a bridge easy, and across this there lay already twelve feet of our ladder. The constant fear was that this gap, like all the others, would widen. Even after replacing lower bridges with logs, we could not spare another duralumin length.

It was here that Pemba Norbu took over. Unfortunately, the next stage is an ascent over steeply piled blocks, where I must guide the ladder end to stop it bumping the eaves. We followed the route gradually leftward, and in doing so passed through a narrow passage where a 100-foot block has split away from the parent icefall. Thence a descent across steep, snowy ice, torturing to Pemba. If he faced outward, the ladder caught the slope behind; if inward, he must lean out to keep its top from hitting the higher blocks. This game continued, with the afternoon snow now beating time, towards another, broader col, set among the high battlements of chunks peeled off from the Cwm. Just below it, thank Heaven at last, Mike Westmacott with the Low Level Sherpas appeared above our now despondent train, looking, with spanner in hand, a veritable *Deus ex et cum machina*. He was descending with a bad cough. Unfixing our ladder, he remarked: "Just at the minute I don't really want to do anything but sleep." I wished him a good speed down to the world of comfortable tents, and our now very heartened caravan moved forward, the ladder solidly in its two sections.

From the top of the second col, a great grey terrace of ruin, the course turned right. In the falling and fallen snow that mantled everything, it was a weird journey. Obviously one made right; the barricade of ice ahead, veined as in a vendor's barrow, was impregnable. It formed the last bastion supporting the flat and comfortable Cwm. To the right, a slice from the upper glacier had heaved away, leaving a gap of several feet like the space between the pincers of a nutcracker. Towards this we steered, more than ever feeling like pygmies crawling over a giant's sugar-lumps, which the giant has considerately sprinkled with castor sugar. I remember vowing in exasperation that *somebody* must have put these things here on purpose. On each block I fumbled for footing; then prodded forward with the axe to make sure where was the solid part of the next. At last, after one or two errors, but helped by thoughtfully placed flags, we had traversed warily and jumped down on to a platform, from which a length of rope, fixed by *karabiners* or snap-rings to pitons, led across the right-hand glacier side of the Nutcracker, as in fact it had come to be called. A line of big steps was carved underneath; even so poor Tashi Phutar nearly spoiled the "Nutcracker Suite" by slipping from a foot too timidly placed. The line ends with a stride across to a leaf of ice; thence up to the continuation of ice-lumps beyond.

But now the worst was well over. A wide semi-circle is necessary before you can reach the main wall again, at a point above which the splash of yellow tents is almost at long last visible. The wall itself is, as I have explained, the first tottering plunge of the Cwm, down towards the valley; it is the edge of chaos. We approached the projection of it from the side; instead of using a narrow, icy crack climbed by the first party, we found ourselves at the bottom of a twenty-five-foot rope ladder, a fine affair presented to the expedition by the Yorkshire Ramblers' Club. Here Pemba excelled himself by making two journeys, coming up a second time with the load of Tashi Phutar, who seemed nervous that he might be toppled backwards from the ladder. It is quite vertical and the wooden rungs catch at the crampons. At the top of it, suddenly over the snow, there were the grins of Kancha and Tenzing, come out from camp to meet us. Soon the last gentle slopes were crossed, a final crevasse, and we were seated on packing-cases drinking tea at the long-hoped-for Camp III (20,200 feet).

3

The site was very beautiful. At this point the flat floor of the Western Cwm Glacier is just breaking over into the ice-fall. Huge slices, some of them extending a great part of the glacier's width, are leaning valleyward, waiting their turn to topple into confusion below. It is up the last of these that the rope ladder had been fixed, by Ed and Mike Westmacott. Topping it, one suddenly saw, instead of interminable chaos, the strangest valley imaginable. A stretch of snow, that to tired eyes looked gentle flatness itself, led up towards Lhotse. To the right Nuptse, a cascade of falling ridges as it plunged from its topmost level to the Khumbu. Already its rock wall facing into the Cwm was visible: sheets of ice that darted their light between enormous vertical bastions of creamy granite streaked with black, for all the world like the steel laid under the bronze of a Florentine sword-hilt. To the left the most immediate presence was, of course, the West Shoulder, seeming to hang over us, and yet kept safely apart by a trough running down the glacier side.

Camp III (20,200 feet) was a cheery cluster of tents, pitched on flat ground a little way from the edge of the ice-fall. I shared a Meade with Tenzing, a most considerate companion. He had just wedged my boots with his own to keep warm between the Li-Los when we found John, Charles Evans and Ed preparing to set off and fix the bridge brought by us, together with the other length previously arrived. Last year, the Swiss had great difficulty with the huge crevasse above III; to ease that task was exactly the purpose of our bridge. We, the last party, had arrived at 2:25; it was now 3:30.

"Shall we go, too?" I said.

In a minute we were fastening our crampons. From Camp III the route leads leftward, towards a huge ice-mass clinging under the West Shoulder and later destined to crash in jagged blocks into the flat below. About 300 yards from camp an ice-wall ravine wound up towards this, but where it narrowed, it was dangerous from overhead fire. At its wider section therefore the other three were busy joining three sections of our ladder (18 feet). We lowered the far end with a rope and all crawled safely over. It had been a simple operation. A further zigzag among more crevasses. Then a wide gap, similar to the first but not so steep-sided. I was just making up left with Tenzing, when John behind us suddenly appeared to be descending. He had spied a possibility and was cutting steps on the steep drop into the gap, breathing hard over the work but going down steadily, held by the other two from above. He reached the bottom, then more easily the far side. It was nearly 4:45, approaching the magical hour of wireless communication. John called back:

"I'm going to be a pig. Would you mind going back, Wilf, with Tenzing, to take any wireless messages?"

We stood for a moment on the chasm's edge, looking up at the mysterious valley, now at long last revealed between the clearing mists. The others would be going on to look at it; I could see Tenzing's face falling sadly, his brown eyes take on their worried expression. However, wirelesses must be attended to, and we hurried back.

At this stage an added aggravation to our wireless at III was that we had to stand out on a windy knoll in order to get clear reception. For those not radio-minded, such walkie-talkie conversations are the nightmare of all dialogue.

"Camp III calling Base Camp. Report my signals."

"Camp II here, not Base. Can you hear me?"

"Base Camp calling Camps II and III. Please report my signals, Camp II first."

"Camp II calling Base. Can only hear you strength One. Suggest I give my messages to Camp III first, as I am receiving them loud and clear."

"Base Camp calling Camp II. I have a message I particularly want to get to you quickly. Can you hear me better now?"

"Camp II calling Base Camp. No."

"Camp III calling Base Camp and Camp II. Do you both realise that my nose is rapidly freezing off and I'm standing in a sixty-mile-an-hour gale? I suppose you're in sleeping-bags. For God's sake let's get on with it!"

And so on for the next half-hour. The game becomes faster and merrier when there are seven camps, some in communication with all, some with only one other. Our difficulty was not lack of subject matter, as with the Sherpas on the one occasion when I heard them try it. Then: "Oh Tenzing"—"Oh Da Namgyal"—"Oh Tenzing"—"Oh Da Namgyal" rang out for several minutes over the air, but further conversational matter they did not seem to have, and both protagonists retired ruefully. With the sahibs, there was always a mass of confusing detail ready to be poured into your frozen ears at the moment when you were praying at last to be able to switch off. The longest conversation I can remember being forced into lasted forty minutes.

The night on which we arrived at III was one of the coldest nights we had. The tent roof sparkled in the candle-light from the ice crystals of our breath. The cup of coffee. The last cigarette. The final luxury, equalled by few physical pleasures, of snuggling down into the sleeping-bag for the night, exposing no more bare flesh to the cold. This was marred only by the exertion of adjusting down coat, so that it did not rise to encumber me round the shoulders. Or perhaps, more drastic still, the Li-Lo needed pumping; hard work at this height. I was sleeping soundly now, in reasonable control of my nostril arrangements. Usually I awoke with a heavy nose and dryish throat, no more.

4

On the 26th, John, Charles, Ed and Tenzing prepared to go ahead and make the route to IV. The first three had come back at 6:00 P.M. last night, very satisfied that there was nothing insuperable between us and the head of the

Cwm. Meanwhile Greg and I, with a faint air of conscientious Cinderellas, prepared to follow with our High Level team. The names of these men were: Pasang Dawa, seventeen-year-old Gompu, the big Kancha, Tashi Phutar, small and nervous, Angtharkay (far from the great Angtharkay), Pemba Norbu and Phu Dorji, distinguished by his orange balaclava. They were a merry crowd and all most friendly. We got off at 9:30, after some difficulty in making up full loads from the few stores so far arrived. The sun had hit us over the great West Shoulder at 8:15; it was soon very hot. We topped the snow hump, and one by one crawled across the fifteen-foot gap. The Sherpas seemed each day to enjoy this more; indeed it was a fascinating glimpse down through the rungs, down at the blue lumps and chunks strewing the crevasse bottom. Greg and I agreed that this was a more interesting approach to the day's task than that of the suburban worker.

Soon we were at "Hunt's Gully." I descended first, held by Angtharkay. In excess of zeal he had me so tight that I jerked down like a puppet on a string. By dint of hard shouting I got as far as the ice platform at the bottom; thence an easy snow traverse leads out up the other side. The Sherpas came on bravely. One of the results of our wireless contacts last night was a report of worsened Crampon Crisis. It was impossible to equip a number of the icefall Sherpas. John, therefore, had asked me to send down the High Level Sherpas' crampons, since the stretch into the Cwm looked level enough not to need them for a week; whereas to set foot on the icefall without them would be madness. I was without my own crampons, to see what it was like. Today the Sherpas slipped about on the first flats in the new snow. Later, in dry weather, this whole stretch was easier without crampons than with them.

Above the chasm, one is still close under the hanging blue ice cliffs of the West Shoulder. The route swings naturally right, to the level snow of the glacier's centre. I brought out the flags and started fixing. When we came back, the scene looked like a snow-covered golf course, only the hole-flags and bunkers showing. For there were still many detours, to avoid enormous, apparently bottomless caverns, down which we peered in wonder, or sent chunks tinkling into the depths, never to be heard again. On we went, up and down snow humps great and small, often circling back to round some blue-glinting pit, so that the last flag left twenty minutes ago might be only a few yards away, until we halted before the rise into the upper Cwm.

It was by now extremely hot. Greg photographed the panorama that swung into view. Straight ahead, as in a frame, towered the 4,000-foot wall of Lhotse which must be climbed; as right-hand edge of the frame, the vertical black and yellow streaks of Nuptse's rocks, interspersed with straight slivers of ice that glittered greasily in the sun. The serrated ridge of Lhotse looked strangely frail beside the black, straight pyramid now dominating the whole basin: Everest, its western cliff dropping 8,000 feet to our glacier. Between these two the South Col hung like a clothes-line above its gleaming wall of ice. Meanwhile, I took off all the clothes I could; remaining in a short-sleeved cotton tennis shirt, string vest, cotton pyjama-trousers under wind-proof. Even so I could feel the sweat sticky on my chest. I had on the Lawrie boots which we used up to the Cwm's head; Greg changed that evening into the bigger high-altitude boots. And all this time the sun played with us as in a glass house, storing its heat in the rock cliffs of Everest and Nuptse, to roast us in the oven below. I applied more glacier cream and hoped that it would not wash off with the sweat. For my head, a good growth of hair and a beard still seemed sufficient. I never wore a hat.

We had now reached the right (true left) of the glacier. As we climbed the 600-foot rise known as the First Step into the upper Cwm, there stretched away to the left row upon row of enormous crevasses, the tails of which we still had to circumvent or cross by snow bridges that needed careful prodding. It is difficult to instil real glacier sense into Sherpas. If one sahib has been across the bridge, why not the whole party without wasting time? And if the whole party, why not one treading on the heels of the other? Again, the ice-axe. The sahib says: "Drive the shaft in and hitch the rope round the head." Why should he be cross when I do this even if it's ice and the shaft won't go in? There are exceptions to this rule.

At last the crevasses lessened; we were on flatter ground leading, apparently, straight up to the Face of Lhotse. The time was 12:30, the Sherpas were beginning to wilt under the combined effect of loads and heat, there was no sign of Camp IV or of John's party, whose tracks we were following. We halted to eat chocolate and dates. Perhaps John, in the enthusiasm of his moment, had pushed ever forward, forgetting to leave a Camp IV sign? Camp V itself could not be far away, and if we went much farther it would be a disproportionately long carry between III and IV. We decided to push on another half-hour over the plain, then leave our loads.

It was 1:30 P.M. when we finally turned. The Sherpas lay like dogs panting in the snow, breaking off great lumps of it to eat. Greg and I discussed what it would be like in May, if so hot now at midday. Yet the effect of the descent was that of some quickening drink. We trudged almost jovially down the glacier, until we paused to wait for two small dots that had appeared above: Ed and Tenzing. They came up to us, travelling fast, and reported the Swiss Camp IV site to be half an hour beyond our dump. John and Charles would be down soon, but these two were going the whole way to Base. Tenzing unveiled a tin of half-frozen Swiss orange juice, the most delicious of all imaginable drinks. Then we followed them on, our Sherpas going more slowly now over the level plain with its little uphills. Half an hour above III we had noticed, in a broad hollow below our track, all that remained of the Swiss Camp III: two sacks filled with tins. I took Kancha and Angtharkay, cut down the slope and crossed an ice-bridge to them. Countless tins of pemmican, packets of Scott's Porage Oats, some cheese and "Sunbol," one of the many strengthening drinks in which the Swiss delight. We took as much as we could, and I made a note of the remainder. The expedition could, at a considerable pinch, live on pemmican. In falling snow, which obscured and magnified the outlines of every block and brought the

West Shoulder almost heaving down on top of us, we toiled on. Camp III we regained at 3:45, just before John and Charles.

It had been an important day. The route was established to Camp IV, almost to Camp V, which could only be an hour or so beyond. Tired as the Sherpas were, we should be able to take on the loads as extras from our dump to IV tomorrow, on the principle that a climb becomes easier and shorter every time it is done. All this and more we discussed that evening, a cosy one with the two tent-ends together. I remember, over the coffee, the question of climbing and marriage coming up; John giving weighty reasons why marriage was the only way to happiness even for a mountaineer, Charles the reasons why he had not so far married. Greg and myself voted on the marriage side. It was a conversation of higher tone than those which tended pleasantly to chatter the evenings away.

5

Let us take a day of High Level carry, say two days later, as a specimen expedition day. Greg and I are still at III.

Wakened at 6:30 A.M. by cup of tea projected through Meade door by arm, behind which the round, grinning face of Gompu, now our self-appointed orderly. Can't understand how I can have slept so long; on an average, I suppose, this expedition sleeps ten hours a night.

I lie and read for a bit, another luxury, and watch the condensation of snow showers fall from the red tent roof, tiny puffs that sometimes catch in my hair and beard. My sleeping-bag is stiff with ice outside, some of my things are a bit wet, particularly down coat which I use as a pillow. They will dry out. I don't need to wear the down coat in bed yet, these New Zealand bags are warmth itself.

Out at seven. No great dressing problem. Long pants (at night) I do swap for cotton pyjamas. A nuisance changing in the kneeling position. But as for my string vest and shirt, it's well over a fortnight since I changed them, as I ought to be ashamed to say, but one really doesn't seem to get dirty up here. I always pull on the same sweater, knitted by my wife out of special wool that my friend Philip Marsden provided. The warmest sweater I have ever worn. I climb out to a leaden sky; in the Alps one would say snow. But here we seem to be getting our regular routine of fine mornings. The pure triangle of Pumori greets me opposite, at my feet the white strange world of ice blocks and towers. I say blocks, though some of them are as large as a battleship, shaded perfectly from every tone of green and grey to creamy white.

Breakfast 7:15. A large plate of porridge to which I add Grape-Nuts. Greg had too much of these last year, and up here neither of us can take the next course, bacon. I still don't think this is our fault, but the bacon's. In other ways we are eating well. Only the stew of yak meat sent up last night defeated us; toughness itself. Breakfast done, another climb out to visit the Sherpas. One or two of these will be ailing, sore throat or headache, and will demand codeine. Today it is Pemba Norbu, who wants to stay at camp with a sick headache. Just as well, perhaps, as there are only enough loads here (left by Low Level Carry yesterday) for six: Meade tent, oxygen cylinders, boxes of rations.

We rope up and set off, I in front, Greg leading the second rope so that he can photograph us. We are off by nine, which we reckon quite good time when all the putting together of loads has been done. The usual order is that I lay out and arrange loads at about eight. While Greg and I fiddle with the ropes ready to start, the Sherpas suddenly get down to eating their enormous chunks of "*tsampa* paste." This over, they clamber out and rearrange the loads on a quite different plan of their own. Today it is convenient to leave Pemba Norbu behind, to tidy up the mess and let us get away quicker.

At nine then we set off. Pasang Dawa, behind me, is being "professional" and blasé, following very close and holding many coils of rope in left hand. On the narrow snow-edge of the hump, the Sherpas slip about, still without crampons, forward foot sliding several feet into the soft mass. The route from beyond John's chasm looks more than ever like a golf course, the eighteenth hole well out of sight above the rise. When we finally top this rise, after two and a half hours from camp, the sun is well and truly on us. Who would have thought it could be so hot at 21,000 feet! I watch the sweat drop from forehead on to hand, thence down the ice-axe blade. Distances in the Himalaya are deceptive. It now looks an easy few hundred yards stroll to the slight further rise concealing the site of IV. Actually it will take an hour, and we shall be panting like whales at the end.

I curse the snow that fell yesterday afternoon, completely masking the track. We are as if breaking new ground, nearly to the knees in places. I stop to adjust two flags that have tilted, we rest again, but not so long as yesterday. It is amazing how three days up here have acclimatised us to the height and eased our breathing. We feel, though the ciné-camera will deny it, that we are moving as fast as in the Alps.

At last. A glance to the left and there are the boxes marking the site of IV. Two hundred slow yards and we have arrived, specially relieved since we have taken on loads from our dump. The time is 12:20. The boxes, some cylindrical, some square, are Swiss. One contains food: Ovosport, Vita-Weat, Nescafé, cheese, even a tin of orange juice which the wretched Kancha has already pierced with his axe. I have given out John's orders that no food is to be opened, but kept for the monotonous days when the whole party will be up here. However, we are not above taking advantage of the crime, having abused the criminal. Apart from this we don't feel like eating much: some "raspberry jam snow" and chocolate. It is pleasanter just to sit.

Suddenly there is a noise from the left, from the precipices below the west ridge. An avalanche. A crack, then a slow boom as fragments large as cathedrals detach and lean out from the overhanging ice-cliff hundreds of feet above. Falling, they shatter to powder, which rolls down in wave upon wave to float smokily over the valley floor. Greg pulls out his camera quickly and snaps. I stand entranced, following with my eyes each powdery billow as it slowly settles. Fortunately our camp site is sufficiently in the centre to be out of danger.

As we sit, Everest and Lhotse disappear in a haze of glaring mist. The sun beats through a veil that seems to intensify its heat. Clouds from the Khumbu swing up to engulf Nuptse's cliff. When we start down, snow is already falling, almost hot snow; so stuffy is it that even now we cannot bear to put on wind-proofs, and prefer to watch it melt on bare arms and neck. The mood of the Sherpas is very different. Now they are careering down, shouting and singing, really grudging the sahibs the lead; which lead the sahibs are anxious to keep, in order not to be hurried along too fast. The crevasse-bridges still need caution, the Sherpas still seem disposed to jump and run. Lower down, the afternoon snow really has set in, and we stop to put on clothes. Then on, jolting and prodding, joking and sliding. The crossing back over the plain exacts its detours. There are irritating rises, tiring because body and breath are adjusted to a down-hill rhythm. There, away to the left, is all that remains of the Swiss III, a dreary little pile of pemmican tins. Gloom masks Hunt's Gully and the bridge. We are treading the last snow hump. Suddenly the yellow blur of tents below lightens the murk. A large figure, firmly muffled in down clothing, is walking about: Tom Stobart, clearly on cinematography bent.

Pemba, fortunately, has the water boiling, a slow process when it must be melted from snow. Soon there is tea, followed by soup at Greg's special request, followed by tea again. Heat and lassitude seem to have removed all the moisture from us. We chat of how Base Camp is getting on and congratulate ourselves on being up at this pleasant spot. We arrived back at 2:45, by Himalayan standards a very reasonable day. By 4:30, we are in our sleeping-bags. Soon after that the cold creeps up and we cram on down clothing. Only one excursion is needed before supper: to give pills and cigarettes to the Sherpas, chat a bit with them and tell Pasang Dawa to do plenty of potatoes with

the steak and kidney, to make up for last night's yak. At
6:30 Gompu again, bearing supper. Coffee and a pipe,
and a lot of talk with Tom, who is staying the night. Then
a read by candlelight, but this is awkward. Squirm, wriggle, hip joint wrong, wriggle again and lose the place. By
8:30 I have decided I must pump my Li-Lo for the last
time.

It is a curious Li-Lo. As I have said, the valves are tem-
peramental. If I pump really hard last thing at night, it
may just keep me from the ground till 6:00 A.M. So I pump
away, kneeling awkwardly alongside, and as I do so a
strange whiteness seems to be lightening the tent wall. I
must climb out. In front and across the valley, like a
Dominican's cowl awry, the dazzling white Pumori re-
flects the moonlight; the more ghostly from wreaths of
mist that veil and tangle each outline. Nearer, the slanting
slithering downfall of Nuptse's ridge has caught the light.
Its ice-slopes are of pure silver filigreed with black rock.
The square, wedding-cake chunks of icefall are still a
grey half-tone. But behind, looking up the great ravine of
the Cwm, I can see the jagged black edge of Lhotse slashing the moon's disk.

I remain lost in it, unwilling to lose a detail, until my
frozen feet jerk me back into the world of tents, Li-Los,
sleeping-bags, prosaic companions which up here refuse
to be ignored for long. I climb in again. It is but too true
that the Himalayan mountaineer spends the greater part
of his time on his back. It is comforting that this idleness
is imposed upon us willy-nilly. But no more reading. Sleep,
for the next ten hours.

6

On this particular night it was not altogether sleep; at
10:00 P.M. I woke to a miniature snowfall on my face. It
must have come from the join between the tents, but the
torch failed to find any one spot. Book, bedding and rucksack were lightly coated. After a bit I gave it up, curled

in the unsnowy patches and slept again, hood over head. Like other problems, this one would have to wait.

This useful and pleasant existence went on till April 30th. We enjoyed our own company and that of the Sherpas, liked knowing what we were doing and liked working as a small unit away from the hustling Base Camp, with its inevitably endless discussions of plans, personalities, possibilities; also the slightly guilty feeling inevitable in a large *bandobast,* that one is being lazy when not pushing on with the next job. The Sherpas too were becoming quicker and readier each time. Our best speed up the Cwm was three hours twenty minutes; our best down, one hour thirty-five minutes. Sometimes it would be dead still and baking hot as we reached IV. Sometimes a wind would have sneaked in to chill us. This might produce high-altitude grumps on the last slope. I could feel miserable and furious if Greg wanted to go ahead and break the trail, because then I had to adjust to his pace. Usually the Low Level Sherpas had come and gone when we returned; but sometimes we had visitors, like Ed and George Lowe looming one afternoon through falling snow, come up to renew our wireless headphones. And always the choughs. These birds, the most impertinent and delightful, would strut around pecking at any odd crumb, or messing in the tea-leaves. Their black, full bodies and orange legs gave them an air of Elizabethan courtiers.

On the 30th Greg went down, and I took up a last carry. While I sorted and listed stores dumped at Camp IV, Gompu groused because he was not allowed to open a tin of orange juice. So childlike is this people: sulky in a moment but never for long, and smiling the next; ready very often to steal for itself, equally ready to die defending the sahib's property from others. The High Level team was taken down by Ed and George, while John, Tom Bourdillon and Charles Evans came up to III to start in on the first reconnaissance of our next problem, the Lhotse Face. They would establish V and go beyond.

John was anxious to be away by 8:30 on May 1st; for the whole party was using Closed-Circuit experimentally, and my views about the heat of the Cwm filled Tom with apprehension. I smiled, I must confess it, knowing how ambitious was their hope. It was 9:45 before they finally departed. Much work had to be done by Tom fitting the apparatus together; then there was the Sherpas' clockwork routine, the arranging of loads, ropes, crampons and so forth. The Closed-Circuit set looked even more heavy (36 lb.) and claustrophobic than I remembered it: the three green cylinders, the box-like canister, the "windbag" below. I walked round and round adjusting straps, and waved goodbye, not envying them, as they set off up the hot slopes towards the bridge.

For myself, I waited until the Low Level lift came up so that I could take them down, leaving Charles Wylie and Mike Ward free to go on and join John inspecting the Lhotse Face. I did some tidying, then found myself sitting on a box, out of the wind. Beside the box there chanced to lie the Pelican *Book of English Poetry*. Wordsworth's "Ode" and the "Scholar Gypsy" have never read so well as on that sunny morning, in the consciousness of work done and to do. I was interrupted at one point by a crash from the direction of the West Shoulder: another avalanche. Immense blocks slithered with increasing roar down the rock precipices, to be caught neatly by the trough at the glacier's side. Bricks of ice, each weighing thousands of tons, had been tossed down as if by a titanic child. Cloudy masses of powder snow spread upward and slowly, very slowly, over to the camp a quarter of a mile away, creating a miniature snowstorm which drove me into a tent for shelter.

At 11:00 A.M. my luxurious reading was interrupted by the cries of Sherpas ascending the final rope ladder. It was the Low Level team, led by the veteran Dawa Thondup, and all beaming with enthusiasm. I lit the Primus for tea and waited for Griff, who was technically bringing them up, and for whom I had messages about Da Namgyal and Gyaljen, two of John's Sherpas who were unwell. By 12:15 the team was impatient to be off down again, so off we started. We met Griff Pugh just below the rope ladder "having trouble with Mingma." Mingma, Da Tensing's fourteen-year-old son, was serving apprenticeship as Griff's orderly. When Griff found difficulty with the height he went pluckily on, and would only admit, when questioned, that "Mingma isn't going too well today." Mingma meanwhile might be bouncing about behind, looking the picture of a South Col Sherpa. But today he was "a little below par," and went frolicking down with my Sherpas. I passed on my arrangements to Griff and we continued, making excellent time over the beaten track to Camp II. Below this we met Charles Wylie and Mike Ward coming up to join the Lhotse reconnaissance, already using the Open-Circuit apparatus. By 2:45 P.M. we were at Base.

Only Ed Hillary was present, preparing to do a trial run on the Open-Circuit with Tenzing tomorrow, all the way up to IV and back again. James Morris, of *The Times*, we had met making his first ascent of the icefall (and his first climb), escorted by George Band and Mike Westmacott with the Low Level carry. George Lowe, Greg and Tom Stobart had already gone down to Lobuje, the first camp below Lake Camp at which there were good grass and water. It was our Rest Camp. For we had come to a moment of pause on the mountain. Apart from the reconnaissance party (which would go down later) Sherpas and sahibs were to rest in preparation for the next phase. Even Thondup had departed; the delicious scones which I had been picturing for tea all the way down faded with the day-dreams.

Drinking tea and eating biscuits under the big cook-house tarpaulin we heard more from Tenzing about the Sherpa disagreement at Thyangboche: a disagreement which certain newspapers later magnified ludicrously into a mutiny. The question of food seems to have affected some Sherpas. Originally used to a simple diet, chiefly of *tsampa*, they have been weaned by successive expeditions of various nationals to expect more luxurious foods. This taste becomes progressively more costly for each expedition. Similarly, because the Swiss had allowed their Sherpas to keep down clothing and all personal items of equipment, John had been compelled to do the same. Because the Swiss had given five cigarettes per day to each man, we must give the same. The *Daily Worker* of June 2nd lamented that Tenzing and his compatriots

are protected by no trade union. In fact, the Sherpas are a
very competent trade union to themselves. But it was difficult to be quite sure of the story, some of whose intricacies
were beyond both my Urdu and Tenzing's English.

Tenzing and I attempted some calculations on Sherpa food
needed for the remainder of our stay. We seemed to have
spent a great deal already, and had passed the 2,500 rupees
allocated for the whole trip. Then Ed made wireless contact
with Camps II and III. This contact was, as often, very uncertain. It sounded as if III was in touch with IV, established
by John's party that day. But more could not be heard, the
wireless was put away and I joined Ed in his tent for supper,
a wonderful affair of minced yak. The mincing machine had
solved the problem. We lay and discussed, arm-chair fashion,
the way in which this reconnaissance had developed from a
two-man affair to a big party involving six sahibs. Then Ed
switched on the wireless, and we agreed that the oddities
of Ceylon's commercial programme ring strangely over the
Khumbu. "Have you Macleaned your teeth today?" and
"When you're feeling blue—Enos!" are a strange nightcap for
"the sleep that is among the lonely hills." Strange, but not
sacrilegious, for I think the outlook of mountaineers has
changed in this respect. In the 'thirties and before, more
stress was laid on the hills as an escape from complexities
such as wireless. Now, the Himalaya have become an interesting complexity in themselves; climbing them is a job
not incongruous with advertisement. Indeed, it often demands it. The need to justify by scenic description is cor-
respondingly less. Take the best-seller *Annapurna*. If you
think back to it, the tale is of practical things: of climbing
and logistical problems, of suffering and the cruelties of
surgery, rather than of sunrises and the beauty of snow. So
we listened, not outraged, to the various home comforts ad-
vocated by squeaky female voices. I climbed back into my
tent with a medley of songs and sounds, of avalanches and
advertising anthems, to accompany me to my dreams.

A.J.VERHAN

8

Icefall Escapades

May 1st—May 14th

1

I struggled out at 6:00 A.M. of the 2nd in order to help Ed adjust a nut on his apparatus. Then I went back to bed. He and Tenzing set off at 6:30. We learned later that they had sped up the icefall as if on wings, had reached Camp IV (21,200 feet) and returned through the unpleasant snowfall in the late afternoon. It was on this descent that there occurred the incident made much of in some newspapers. Ed was deceived by one of the innumerable blocks wedged in gaps. He slipped in a crevasse. Tenzing, behind, held him on the rope. It was an instance of "climbing in combination."

The sun soon became hot at Base Camp, too hot for my down coat and hot enough for a wash. This down clothing of ours, coat and trousers, was perhaps the most successful item of our equipment. It was of French make, and climbing into it resembled enveloping oneself in three eiderdowns, coming up rather like a green teddy bear. Its bulk did not matter, for it was amazingly light and could be compressed. In warmth it seemed to equal about four sweaters, and had the advantage that it could be taken off in a moment, or put on again when the air turned chill. Now, having divested myself, I pottered in the sun and changed my shirt for the first time since leaving Thyangboche on April 9th. I greeted Griff, who had been forced to retreat from Camp III. This was the occasion when a box of mango chutney had been carelessly substituted for the box containing his test-tubes. I must say that he took it very well, and gave up the struggle to experiment like a man.

◄ *The little mounds reared up, to become huge terrifying giants.*

In the afternoon I set off for Lobuje. A stream of Sherpas was going that way, too, using these two or three days' "leave" to visit their families. They insisted on taking my rucksack, and I started at three in blazing sunshine, wearing open shirt and with wind-proof slung round my neck. Blue lights darted in and out of the ice pinnacles as I strolled slowly enough to enjoy them. By now the track over the snow-covered ice was almost well worn. Below Lake Camp the afternoon snow started. I had never been on this part of the route, for Lobuje lies on the right, or Pumori side of the Khumbu. You must cross another disused glacier bed, on a line of cairns not easy to follow in mist or snow. Once I lost the way and had to return, for I was now well ahead of the Sherpas. At last you are on grass, descending to a flat-bottomed little valley which is really part of the trough between hill and moraine. This seemed to go on for ever. In the falling snow, with each big boulder looking quite certainly a hutment until my nose was against it, I felt sure I had missed the route and would be spending the night out, with no sweater, among the boulders. I was lost. Perhaps I could reach Phalong Karpo, farther down, at any rate shelter and a fire. Quite suddenly, away to the right, an obviously Scottish stone croft stood out. And beside it, un-recognisable in its white coat, our yellow dome tent. I was soon inside, borrowing sweaters from the others.

Tom Stobart was not well; breathing hoarsely with bron-chitis, later diagnosed as a touch of pneumonia. Of the Sher-pas, Thondup had been joined in the croft by Topkie, suffer-ing from a cough, and later by Da Namgyal, down from the reconnaissance, very sorry for himself. It has always been an astonishment to remember this sickly, terribly thin figure with the swollen eyes and sad grin, and then to think of Da Namgyal carrying the ridge dump with John to 27,350 feet. George Lowe and Greg had the wireless on, Greg being very interested in the F.A. Cup victory of Blackpool, his home town. Lobuje seemed even now a real Butlin Camp, still more so the next morning, when a kindly sun had cleared the snow and invited us out to lie on grassy banks already patterned with tiny mauve primulas. If you walked a few

BEFORE EVEREST – Lake Camp and moraine. Nuptse behind in evening light.
(James Morris, Ed Hillary, George Band.)

BEFORE EVEREST – Ice pinnacles of the Khumbu glacier. Changtse (North Peak) visible in background over Lho La.

BEFORE EVEREST – Base Camp and Lingtren I. Tenzing's tent.

THE KHUMBU ICEFALL – On the lower icefall.

THE KHUMBU ICEFALL – (a) Icefall bridge, with poles. (N.B. the Sherpa's crampons.)

(b) The rope ladder.   (c) On "Hillary's Horror."

The Khumbu Icefall – In the Icefall.

yards to the stream, you could sit for hours watching green weeds waving in the clearest water, redstarts hopping on the boulders, and, if you were lucky, the occasional tailless Tibetan rat or stone marten looking cockily out from little rock fortresses.

At Lobuje everything called to idleness, and this distinguished it from every other camp. There simply was nothing to be busy about, except writing, reading and eating. After two days down here everybody felt enormously refreshed, with that refreshment which comes from the sense of relaxation after and before effort. It is the sense of contrast, perhaps the most quickening ingredient in the joy of any adventure, especially on mountains; the relaxation of having done, together with the zest of being about to do. We were joined that afternoon by Ed, and heard the story of their climb. He had been most impressed by the effect of oxygen on their speed. The descent in the afternoon snowfall must have been extremely unpleasant, and the whole an astonishing feat in one day. The Closed-Circuit part of the Lhotse Face reconnaissance, Ed said, had not fared so well; the apparatus was very hot, and, unlike the Open-Circuit, seemed to leave a feeling of lassitude.

And now it is time that you heard, though from a shamefully unscientific person, a little more about the difference between the two types. You will find it properly explained in Appendix V of *The Ascent*. As I see it, the Open-Circuit goes on the principle practised in 1922, 1924 and 1938. You breathe in oxygen by a tube from cylinders on your back, and what you breathe out is lost to the world through an outlet valve. Thus you are really breathing oxygen plus ordinary air. With the Closed-Circuit, where what you breathe out is borne off to the box or canister of soda-lime and there reconverted, you breathe an endless cycle of pure oxygen, and thus, if all goes well, your performance is much nearer sea-level performance. This apparatus has been worked on especially by Tom and his father. It is heavier than the other, 36 lb. against 27 lb., and has more valves which can go wrong, but if it goes well it gives astonishing performance. Sometimes it does seem to have the effect of leaving a sense of tiredness. It was after his bout with it that John made the remark which deserves to be recorded:

"Do you know, for the first time on this expedition I really feel a little tired."

At any rate, there was the reconnaissance going resolutely into action in the Cwm, and here were we, the lotus-eaters, sitting among primulas by a stream. It was all very satisfactory, for a time. That afternoon we were again driven in by snow, but a more dilettante snow than yesterday; salmon for supper was not so welcome as usual, because most had made pigs of themselves on Thondup's pancakes. Into the desultory conversation afterwards there suddenly loomed a dark, snow-covered figure: the mail-runner. We had given him up for that day. By now we had a well-established system organised by Greg, the runners taking our mail to Kathmandu and then returning. As James Morris had his own system, too, we were usually well supplied. In theory they arrived once a week; and if they managed the journey to Base Camp in six days, an astonishing feat, they received a bonus of 100 rupees. Some managed it; in the case of some others, as they ambled in, the word "runners" was a distinct euphemism. Now, after the threats of everyone to "cut his throat" for being so late, it was noticeable that the cries were all of "*Shabash*" (well done) when the dusky figure appeared, and each dived into his own letters. Photographs of my wife and baby son brought home very close to me.

Mist in the morning, the peaks gleaming through as if their angles had been rubbed off. Most of us spent the 4th still in the tent, talking and pretending to write. Conversation ranged from the expedition books to every conceivable possibility on the mountain. I wandered gently down the valley, to get a glimpse of Pumori and the other peaks that guard the Khumbu's head. From this distance they showed in their true perspective, a noble, jagged outline cut against the blue sky. At 6:30 P.M. I wandered again, after the snow had stopped. Instead of mist, a strange pinkness of the sky tinged all the Kangtega group. An immense peace filled the valley. Taweche had girdled itself with cloud, looking twice the height of any earthly mountain. As I looked, the rose slowly faded to copper, against which the mountains continued to stand out like cardboard models.

The two Georges made wireless contact (between Lobuje and Base) that evening, good going over a distance of some six miles. We still had had no doctor down to examine Tom Stobart, and his state was worrying. Each day he gallantly declared that he was better, and on the third day it seemed at last to be the truth. All but Ed and myself were needed up tomorrow, the 5th, to begin the Low Level ferry of loads again. George Lowe, with Mike Westmacott and George Band, would go up to attack the Lhotse Face. The reconnaissance party would come down and rest at Lobuje. At lunch-time Griff appeared and shared some delicious scrambled eggs. Though not the official doctor (Mike Ward was on the Face), he had most helpfully abandoned an experiment, to come and examine Tom and the Sherpas, who loved the stethoscope. After the examinations a great discussion on the merits of Closed- and Open-Circuit oxygen carried us into the afternoon. The disadvantage of the former seemed to all to be its weight, 36 lb., which would be unpleasant even if efficiency were increased to sea-level standard. Griff said that it was not. My own inclinations were all for the Open-Circuit; mainly because it seemed that, in the case of failure of the Closed-Circuit, I would be far less able, having breathed airless oxygen, to cope with oxygenless air, meaning by air the stuff, or lack of stuff, that surrounds you above 24,000 feet.

2

On the morning of May 6th, feeling much restored, Ed and I packed and made our way, heavily laden, to Base Camp. At the Lake we suddenly saw John, apparently descending from Pumori. Granted John's deserved reputation for energy and zeal, even that did not surprise us. But in fact he had missed the route down, having kept too far to the right and left the glacier too early. He was on his way to visit Tom, though he had refused all persuasion to come and rest at Lobuje himself, away from wireless communication with the higher camps. John told us more of the Plan: for the present, a continuation of both Low and High Level carries till May 15th, by which time we should all be up at Camp IV, our Advance Base. The hot trudge continued; something like glacier lassitude enveloped us in that confined, sun-beaten trough: a great weariness of all the limbs, a general fatigue with the load on one's back. The T-tables and three-foot pinnacles had lost their charm, engulfed in the steam of that May morning. We arrived at last, as did also a sheep brought up by little Nimmi, with *tsampa, atta* (for chapattis), rice and dried potatoes. Nimmi had been ordered to bring two sheep. But they are rare, the villagers are too poor to part with them, and the one extra creature he had contrived to get had gone sick on the way up.

At 3:30 the reconnaissance party returned. Charles Evans and Tom, supported by Mike Ward and Charles Wylie, had camped at the site of the old Swiss Camp VI, a quarter-way up the Lhotse Face. Mike's set had sprung a fault, he had had to come down with a feeling of suffocation. Despite this, general opinion provisionally favoured the Open as against the Closed. Tom and Charles, the Closed-Circuit experts, had stayed a night at VI (23,000 feet) and done brave work pushing up the Face in deep snow. But it was becoming clearer that this route to the South Col was going to be a long job, longer than had been expected. That night, in his tent, John told me something of the plan for the later stages, since I would miss the formal announcement he intended to make the next morning by going up with the Low Level lift. There would be a Closed-Circuit attempt direct from the Col by Charles Evans and Tom, followed by Ed and Tenzing using Open-Circuit and camping on the ridge. The Lhotse Face would have been pioneered by George Lowe, George Band and Mike Westmacott. Charles Wylie and myself would lead Sherpa parties carrying the loads for the Col. Supporting parties for the second summit party, who would need the intermediate camp: John and Greg.

That night I desponded mildly to my diary that my present occupation of bear-leading Sherpas would give me little chance of breaking new ground. I had already decided that, being a writer, that is one whose kink is to transfer experience to ink and paper, I must write my personal tale of the adventure. Of what could I write? Perhaps it was the altitude that gave a dreary sense at that moment of the monotony of adventure. I remember a feeling of disappointment; sticking hands in my pockets, kicking at a stone, and saying: "I don't suppose I shall see any *new* ground." Like a small boy suddenly told to play goal. This thought was in my throat when I came down on the 7th and asked John, if there were any exploration to be done, to think of me. His reply was disarming. Charles Wylie and I were the two who could best handle the Sherpas up to the Col. And the unprecedented effort of getting eighteen (it later proved to be nineteen) loads to over 26,000 feet was of such importance that the final assault would be unthinkable without it. *Après ça que dire?*

3

Many incidents enlivened the icefall. The first, if it may be so described, was Camp II. Nobody seemed to like Camp II, mainly because, being a transit camp, nobody thought it worth fitting out properly. It was never occupied for more than one night at a time, and the resultant air of a rather dowdy *pension* added nothing to the pleasure of the stay. The wireless was usually "off," the sleeping-bags supposed to be left there for the Sherpas were usually missing, it was a stroke of luck if both cookers worked, while large hollows formed by the heat made the tents uncomfortable. Added to this were the possible dangers of the serac above, and the appearance of suspicious cracks in the floor below. On one occasion, at an ominous rumble from the depths, half a dozen heads shot anxiously out of tent doors. During the later stages of the Low Level lift, when the cracks were widening apace in the crevasses, the Sherpas insisted on abandoning II and doing the carry to III in one day. This was not as extreme a measure as it sounds; with familiarity any route becomes shorter and easier. Moreover, after May 13th they did not have to contend with the afternoon snowfall. Once there, a track stayed.

Despite all this, I liked Camp II. At this time (from May 6th) Greg, Tenzing and I were leading the lifts; later, Charles Wylie and Mike would come back after their rest. My company on the lift was varied. I might be cramped with ten Sherpas, or I might have a tent to myself, going out only to inspect the cuisine, chat or light the Primus. It was almost impossible to persuade Sherpas to use methylated spirits. The quick way, they found, was to light straight from the kerosene. After a few minutes of merrily blazing Primus, the cook would shake his head, switch off and poke a cheerful face into the tent: *"Istove kharab hai,* sahib" (the stove is no good). Out the sahib would go, and the stove would light with a smoothness which, however, failed to disconcert the Sherpas. Poor Ed, in charge of cookers, spent much time simply cleaning. After these little excursions I would nestle in, perhaps with a cup of tea alongside. It was here, chiefly, that I allowed myself the secret pleasures of poetry. But owing to the hollows under the body (we had to shift the tents once or twice) it was awkward lying and still more awkward writing and reading. The patter of the afternoon snow inspired depressing thoughts of tomorrow's toil. I would lie and listen; read or write a bit, and listen again. At five it might stop, and I would climb out, to see Pumori's darkening outline blurred by the froth of snow-mist from the valley. Far above, through the drift, the sky was dappled with pink cloudlets. The sun was gone, but its reflected rays still lightened with gentle silver the near curves of the icefall—great folds and white sweeps of it that bounded into sudden, romantic chasms; a surface so soft, that you longed to stroke its velvet; a magnificence wild yet orderly, bricks set in pattern by a giant child's hand. The night would be a cloudless wonder of stars above black, friendly shapes.

I also liked Camp II because here I got to know the Sherpas best. At close quarters (three in a tent on one occasion) and with no other sahibs present, they came forward with their happy selves. It was pleasant, after a night at *very* close quarters with a deeply coughing Utsering (odourous into the bargain) to chat about the photographs of my son over the porridge which he seemed to think sahibs ought to have. My son's clean appearance seemed to surprise him greatly.

I noticed an enormous change in the lower icefall, ascending it on May 7th after an absence of five days. The lower section of trough was now almost a river. Snow beds crackled ominously under a foot, just ready to give way. Tramping the line of previous tracks, I suddenly found myself up to the knees in stream, and chipped my fingers on the crust. The Sherpas (like a Welsh farmer once before) recommended dirt to close the wound. Down the first zigzags of icefall, crystal rivulets now ran. Higher, unsuspected seracs had appeared, every gap had widened. Over the first bridge, replaced by pine-logs, the Sherpas this time trotted almost jauntily. Even Tashi Phutar decided on the upright position. Half-way across, however, courage almost failed. He swayed, one foot wavered backwards, his crampon caught. . . . It was a nasty moment, partly because, however often warned, the Sherpas insisted to a man on keeping coils in the hand, which would here have meant an extra fall. But a jump, a tug from all—he was over, and his comrades were exploding with laughter.

The icefall was a living thing. There it was, nosing its way down, and as it nosed, its skin shifted and cracked. Several times new detours were necessary, to avoid new pits. And the final valley! I compared it before to the long hole of Hindhead Golf Course, modestly bunkered. Now, it was as if an H. M. Bateman colonel had blasted the same golf course with his oaths, so that the bunkers gaped into bottomless pits, the little mounds reared to become huge, terrifying giants. One still started up to the left, crossing a six-foot pole bridge brought up by Da Tensing and Gyaljen that morning. They had been told to accompany me, but had anticipated orders and gone ahead. Then back and forth, pausing, prodding, searching for flags, continuing. In a week, it had become a different route up a different glacier.

On the 10th, emerging at 7:00 A.M. from a snug sleeping-bag at Base, I found myself engaged in lengthy conversation with John at III. (He and Ed had gone up the previous day to take over the two higher carries, between III and IV, and

IV and V.) There were, it seemed, two new danger points: a big block poised to form a serac above Hell Fire Alley, and the crevasse between II and III. This had widened alarmingly, so that the two sections of our bridge had now less and less overlap on to the snow at each side. Would I see to these when I went up with my Sherpas? John thought that for the second problem a rope ladder let down from the upper to lower lip might serve.

It was a sunny morning as we packed up the big tent, hitherto used for the sahibs at Base. The site looked very desolate without it, the cave uninvitingly bleak. The morning was as hot as any, we were in shirt-sleeves. Panting towards the top of Hell Fire Alley I soon made out the offending serac. It was indeed a block, perhaps as big as a small bus, mushroom-shaped and perched on a flat "stalk." It was joined by a massive neck to the green, bulging cheek of ice next door. The first step was to separate it from the side wall. The Sherpas disliked the whole job. It was clearly far better to rest when one did halt. Why waste energy on child's games? However, they consented to hold me on the rope. I clambered up awkwardly. It was easy to cut away the neck, but not at all easy to get at the mushroom stalk in such a position that the block could not possibly fall on myself. I pecked and pecked, bent double. At this height it was hard work; I panted, paused, twisted the axe and went on. I shifted position, but that did not help as my blade hit the side wall at each swing. At last the stalk looked dangerously small, the whole structure something like the Bowder Stone in Borrowdale. I brought the battering-ram into action, an eight-foot pole brought up for bridging. One Sherpa consented to ram with me. We stood together, heaved back, then lunged forward. At the second ram the thing tottered forward, heeled over and crashed on to our tracks below. Broad grins from the Sherpas. There it lay, with its fellows of every day. We had assisted Nature and possibly saved ourselves.

The upper part of the icefall is especially associated, for me, with fresh snow. I always tried to get away before eight when the sun struck it, and we usually succeeded. It was a cold business; loads had to be dug out of the new snow, crampons adjusted by chill fingers. On the 11th, we were away by 7:50. Not a track was to be seen, but it was a pleasure, in those first few hundred feet, to be striding up, crunching the foot firmly down through the feathery stuff, reaching forward at every step to plunge the ice-axe securely in. But when the sun appeared, this pleasure melted with the morning mist. We reached the big crevasse whose span was widening, and dumped the extra pole for attachment to the bridge on our return. As I was examining to the right, the whole upper slope seemed suddenly alive. A section of the higher lip, some fifty feet long, was descending with an immense chuckling rumble into the depths. As well not to think of rope ladders here. We went on, the snow deepened, the toil increased. The others would be having a heavy time in the Cwm. We reached III at 10:15 A.M., to find a note from Ed asking many things; for Ed was in charge of the III-IV ferry, John ferrying from IV to V, right under the Lhotse Face, while George Lowe, Mike Westmacott and four Sherpas were getting to work on the Face itself. George Band, who had been with them, I had found at III on the 8th suffering from a bad sore throat. He went down for a rest to Lobuje on the 9th.

We put up the big tent at Ed's request, and set off for home. Reaching the crevasse again, where we had left the pole, we stopped. The problem was easily seen. The two feet of ladder, which had been comfortably resting on snow at each side, had dwindled to six inches. How to elongate the bridge? Obviously the pole must be tied to the ladder, so as to secure one end and allow the other to be pushed farther up in the snow. I scraped away at the bottom to form a resting-place for the pole's butt, also a more level platform for the ladder base. Toward this end it tilted hard to port, giving an uncomfortable feeling that the passenger was being pressed to jump into the abyss. Then I put the pole down and prepared to lash it to the ladder. I sighed for the aid of a better knotsman. With this rope, still stiff since we had removed it from the Nutcracker that morning, I was less sure of my lashings than ever. The Sherpas were grinning down

149

from the other end. I called to one of them, Chotaray, to come down and tie the top end of the pole to the ladder, while I did the same at the bottom. The pole came to a third-way up the ladder, and there he sat, apparently most precariously poised above black space, tying for dear life. I advanced anxiously to inspect the knots, till we were both sitting opposite one another over nothing. Poor Chotaray was as unscoutly as any Sherpa; he had just got to the third of a series of grannies on which our life was to depend.

Finally we had erected a Heath Robinson affair into a position of apparent security. At any rate, nobody could now be let down with a bump, because the upper end was securely in the snow, the lower end supported by the pole, which was itself firmly bedded. Later, the whole was much improved by Mike Westmacott, who more efficiently tied two poles, one each side, to make a regular gangway. We went on, not stopping long at Camp II in falling snow, to reach Base at 2:15, very ready for lunch and tea combined. A pair of eggs on Thondup pancakes restored me greatly.

Reading my diary that evening, I thought how common-place the day had been, and also, how completely I had forgotten the noble purpose of climbing Everest. I might have been out for a day's bridging with the Charterhouse Scout Troop. Even the magnificence of the scenery my eyes spurned from familiarity. No great venture can keep going, I suppose, at its top level for very long; hence the banality of everyday conversation, to avoid straying too far into the depths. The tinge of morning rose on the pale infinite sky before dawn; and the twinge of a tooth cracking on hard biscuit. The burst of spontaneous song before a scene that sings the glory of Creation; and the bursting crampon which sends a man swearing down to fumble with ice-cold fingers. High sentiment alongside straight farce and the comedy of day-to-day. The plays of Shakespeare rather than of Racine.

That afternoon our heaviest snow fell. It fluttered thickly, coating and caking. Soon every box had a three-inch cap, and through the mist Charles Evans and Tom Bourdillon returned damply from rest at Lobuje. It was depressing. John, submerged in heavy snow up at IV, had suspicions of the monsoon, for in 1936 there had been no break at all. No mention of it had been made in the All-India Radio Report which we were receiving. Every day we had: "Westerly disturbance. Snow showers and squalls high up. Wind in free air at 30,000 feet, 40-50 knots." Perhaps they had forgotten the monsoon. John asked for a special message to be sent down enquiring after its whereabouts. Preferring the cookhouse tarpaulin to the ice caves, the whole party had moved in, driving poor Thondup and his fires into the corner. But before settling down I must make some fresh preparations, for John had asked Mike Ward and myself to go up in turn and help George Lowe in the route-making on the Lhotse Face. With this snow it was desperately heavy going up there. I had agreed gladly: new ground at last. Then we watched the snow, and discussed Open- and Closed-Circuit chances as endlessly and inconclusively as ever. Greg thought the Closed-Circuit attempt direct from the South Col a forlorn hope.

"You *can't* get to the top from there. And if it's a reconnaissance of the South Summit, what's the point? You either come back and say the final ridge looks easy, or you say it looks bloody difficult. So what?"

Meanwhile I sat back and thought, with some amusement, how much would have happened before I saw Base again. It might be a month, it might be more, it might even, impossible as it seemed, be never. We were taking up our belongings to the now established Advance Base. All agreed, back again at discussing chances, that a quick decision would be best of all for health and morale. So it went on, and the snow fell, till it was time to have, as we thought, our last Thondup supper and go to bed.

4

May 13th dawned cloudless, apart from an ominous sausage over Changtse, indicating wind high up. There was much to do; loads to be dug out and packed, and a final estimate of Sherpa food. I was uneasily sure we had not enough for our long stay. Nimmi would be back soon from his pres-

ent forage and must go down for more. Tenzing, taking the
Low Level lift, set off first with a rope of seven. We, consist-
ing of Charles Evans, Tom Bourdillon, Greg and myself,
left at 10:55. By Mike's Horror we had caught up the Sherpas, ploughing their furrow very slowly through the new
blanket. At the level halting-place below Hell Fire Alley we
passed them, and it started to snow. But I can still see Tenzing's helpful grin behind, through the flakes. We took the
lead in turns, and it was laborious work. The flags seemed
insufficient, we floundered along, going in several times up
to the armpits. The route was particularly difficult among
the big blocks before Hillary's Folly, where treacherous
snow had evened out gap and hollow. By 1:50, when we
reached II, the fall had stopped, but through dazzling mist
new snow avalanches were booming strangely, like foghorns.
Above II, the going seemed easier, an easier sequence of
prod, flounder, find footing, step up, gasp. By now there were
complaints of tiredness, hitchings at rucksacks, indefinite
mutterings. But after we met Mike Ward's party going down,
the track was stamped by their descending feet and easier
still.

We arrived at 3:40 in a further snowfall at a very crowded
Camp III. James Morris had come up a second time, Griff
Pugh was perched in his own tent experimenting, Tom Stobart, recovered, was gallantly filming snow scenes. We all
cuddled in somehow. Ed reported that the Sherpas were
eating more than had been expected, at least 1½ lb. of
tsampa a day, besides various Assault Rations. Even with one
maund (80 lb.) of *tsampa* up and three more coming, we
would not have enough. A message went back on the evening
wireless for three more maunds. We were now all in the Cwm
except Charles Wylie and Mike. There was just time for
more food to arrive before the last lift, May 18th.

One of the advantages of Griff's presence was that he
could record the night temperature. It was minus 13 degrees
Fahrenheit, which he said was high. He also tried Ed on
sleeping oxygen as an experiment. A babble of critical and
amused talk from Griff's tent kept the camp wakeful to well
after nine. Ed's excitement overflowed into conversation.

Then at last silence, sleep. When we climbed out to prepare for an 8:00 A.M. start, Ed confessed to a most peculiar night. It turned out that the air holes had been set in such a way that he was not getting much air; the peculiarity was explained. At 8:00 A.M. we started, with James in the party. In the cool morning the walk was a pleasure, but alas not for long. At 8:20 I abruptly realised I had left behind John's binoculars, which he specially wanted in order to inspect with a general's eye the advance on the Lhotse Face. Ed volunteered to accompany me back. By the time we had caught the others up again, and with our kit weighing perhaps 40 lb., it was very hot indeed. Thank Heaven for a flask of lemonade!

The last level stretch seemed immensely tiresome and quite endless. But we were there, at last, at the tents which now formed Advance Base, the centre of operations for the next three weeks and goal of our early ambition. There was John escorting us out of the heat under the shelter of a tarpaulin. And there, specks against blinding whiteness far above, were two tiny figures: George and the Sherpa, Ang Nyima, working on the Lhotse Face.

A.J.VEILHAN

9

The Face of Lhotse

May 14th—May 17th

1

At this time (May 14th) the big dome tent was not yet erected. We ate our lunch squeezed between uprights made of two cylindrical Swiss boxes on end; above our heads a stretch of tarpaulin. Lying at awkward angles we enjoyed the Swiss foods: Knäckerbrot (the Swiss Ryvita), Swiss cheese, and, best of all, Vita-Weat. Ovosport we ate solid; I only once had it as a drink. All these were a sharp relief from biscuits and tinned meats, which had become monotonous with the months. They were also an addition to our food supply, about which everyone concerned was worried. Orders were again sent down by wireless for more, but it seemed as if the Compo, due to last till mid-June, would be finished before the end of May. We should certainly be living off the country on the return journey, but what if we had to stay here another month? And how had it all gone?

As for Advance Base, I liked the feel of it at once, except for the heat, a surprising complaint to make of a 21,200-foot camp. It was too hot at midday to sit outside, even in shirtsleeves, with comfort. The tawny sun in its deepest blue setting seemed to blaze down at the great granite walls and be deflected with redoubled power upon ourselves. There was not a breath of wind. Compare this state with Smythe's account of Camp IIIA on the north side, in 1933. The day is May 7th, at approximately the same height: "A high wind did its best to blow the camp away. . . . Meals took a long time to prepare. Once the "Primus" ran short of fuel, and when I went out to get some more paraffin I had difficulty in

◄ *There was only room for one tent at Camp VI . . . we ate, half lying on our sleeping-bags.*

155

finding the tin as it had been buried by snow. When at length I re-entered the tent, plastered with snow from head to foot, the others laughingly called me Captain Oates. . . . The neck of my sleeping-bag creaked with congealed moisture from my breath every time I moved." And at Camp II, the height of our Base Camp (17,800 feet): "I tried to read, but it was too cold, even with gloves on, to hold a book, and my hands soon lost sensation and I was forced to replace them in the sleeping-bag and restore circulation by rubbing them vigorously." [1] We too had, of course, many degrees of frost at night, and unpleasant days' snowfall in early May. But there was more comfort in life; less wind, and greater, at times too great, warmth on the lower stretches.

Coming out and taking the binoculars we could watch the two small figures of Lowe and Ang Nyima advancing slowly, very slowly, up that shining expanse. In half an hour they seemed not to have moved. George had held a wireless conversation every evening to report progress, and John himself had been up in very bad conditions to see how they were getting on. They were established at the site of the former Swiss Camp VI (23,000 feet), and we could see the orange blob of a tent below a grey square of ice wall. On the long ice slope leading up to VI they had renewed, where necessary, 300 feet of rope left by the Swiss last autumn and had hacked a staircase. It was about as hard ice-work, George said, as he had done. The angle of some slopes had changed very considerably. Now they were moving up, zigzagging between what appeared to be half-moon-shaped walls, shown as steeper than the snow terraces by their blue-green colour against the white. They were taking the lead in turns, and "Ang Nyima makes me feel quite a passenger," George had said. That very day they reached the site of Camp VII (24,000 feet), some half-way up the Lhotse Face. In the deep snow that masked everything the journey took five and a half hours.

I was anxious to go up to Camp V that afternoon, and be in a position to start up the Face, acclimatised to a slightly

[1] *Camp Six*, p. 142, etc.

greater altitude, next morning. I must be fit, acclimatised, to help George, and it is a common precept that sleep at a height is a key to acclimatisation. Another precept, handed on to me by Reggie Cooke and acted upon whenever possible, is that if you go up above your camp and then come down to it, you will sleep better and go better the next day than if you simply go up and then spend the night. On the acclimatisation period I had always tried to climb on, even if only a few hundred feet, in the afternoon, after camp was pitched. I certainly slept very well. And now I was feeling a righteous glow in fussing over myself more than usual. I wanted to be very sure of my sleep, being about to go higher than I had ever been before. However, John's Sherpas had been to V that day, and did not want to go up again. As Ed also planned to accompany me tomorrow, we spent the afternoon (to my secret relief, since the grind to V would have been a fiery inferno) dodging the sun until it went down. Then we started dodging the cold.

2

The plan for the next few days was again discussed that evening over the tea-mugs in the pyramid tent, while the light slowly faded. I would go up and spend the 16th and 17th working on the Face with George, if possible establishing Camp VII on the 16th. Already, you can see, the eyes of the expedition were focussed on that Face. Throughout the afternoon, however the conversation started, it always came back to the question: How soon we could get up, and how many Sherpas should carry the loads vital for the assault as far as the Col? Eyes wandered up, fascinated, to the little figures; or, at a meal, somebody would stamp out between the courses and have a look. "They've rounded that big ice cliff at last!" And there would be a sense of relief in the company.

I was to come down on the evening of the 17th in order to rest, while arranging the first Sherpa lift. John was anxious, desperately anxious, that the two lifts should go through to the Col on the 21st and 22nd, the second led by

Charles Wylie. The Swiss had underestimated the effect of altitude on climbers making so great a rise, when they attempted to climb the Face in one. It now looked as if we might underestimate height and difficulty, though forewarned. Four days, it had been reckoned at first, would be sufficient for the establishment of the route. In the event eleven were needed, and we did not realise at the time one of the reasons. Previously the head of the Cwm (Camp V) had been thought to be 23,000 feet. We think it now to be no more than 22,000, making a rise of 4,000 feet or more to the top of the Geneva Spur (*l'Eperon des Genevois*).

While the Lhotse Face work went forward, Camp III would be almost evacuated, the big tent and others brought up to IV, which after the next four days would house virtually the whole expedition. Greg would be in charge of the IV to V lift, John of the III to IV. Charles Evans would do a carry to VI or VII, while Tom disappeared into the mysteries of oxygen between all four.

By this time we were all equipped with the special high-altitude boots, sorted with some difficulty by John and myself at III. These were to be worn only on the upper part of the mountain, and they gave rise to the usual panics. In one case there seemed to be only one boot, in several others there were no special high-altitude crampons to fit. Much has been written of these boots. Here is a personal picture. Specially made for us at Nottingham, their great object was to be light and warm. To look at, they were black, waterproofed cushions. To put on, they were eiderdown in which the foot enveloped and comfortably lost itself. Worn, they gave the climber the appearance of an elephant-footed biped. The sole was thick with layers of insulating material, which did their job so effectively that I never felt cold in them. Moreover, they were always pliable and easy to put on in the morning. The disadvantages were two, and inevitable. These boots were to be used a short time only, and very soon rents and rips appeared, often from a crampon that had penetrated. Also, being very broad, the sole with its micro-cellular rubber covering had difficulty in feeling the holds. The crampons were of necessity broad, too, and the whole structure clumsy in an ice step. One cannot have everything; warmth and lightness are of all the most important.

At 6:45 A.M. on the 15th we finally emerged, Ed and myself, with Dawa Thondup acting porter for us as far as V. The morning was cold, blue shadows slanted across the Cwm, but high on our right Nuptse's creamy granite was already warm with light. The snow was crisp, the walking easy. A very slight detour, to avoid a crevassed rise known as the Second Step, brought us close under Everest's precipice, not far from the grave of Mingma Dorji, the site of which Dawa pointed out to us away on the left-hand moraine. This fine Sherpa was killed by an ice block on the Lhotse Face, during the Swiss autumn expedition of last year. Ed was not going well, probably because of his sleep of the night before last, and halted twice, an uncommon need for him. Even so we reached Camp V at 7:55. It must be less than a mile up, and the rise is perhaps 800 feet. As we arrived, the shadow of Everest which had been creeping down the great Nuptse wall at last edged across to us. The blinding sparkle of sunlight dazzled and rejoiced. We gave a call, and the face of Mike Westmacott appeared in a tent door.

Mike had had exceptionally bad luck. Even when he left Base with George, he was suffering from a cough which barked warningly through the night. Arrived at V he had striven day after day, with the three Sherpas who were carrying the first loads up, to reach Camp VI. But he was still suffering from "Basecampitis," and yesterday he had been forced to rest. Now he had decided that he must go down; but meanwhile the camp had no matches, and the poor man had been spending the morning trying to raise a light by the desperate expedient of puffing blasts of oxygen on to Meta fuel. This had not worked. It was a long time before a fire was lit and enough water boiled to feed our five selves (for Tom and Charles had now arrived) and the three Sherpas. Meanwhile we lay crowded into the Meade tent, feeling more and more limp with the atmosphere, less and less like going on. The sun was well and truly roasting us when Ed and myself, with Da Tensing, Gyaljen and Ang Namgyal left for Camp VI.

Camp V is on the nearest safe spot to the Lhotse Face. It might be possible to pitch tents higher; but from the right, just right of the glaciated ribbon up which we must go, a three-hundred-foot wall was at that time sending down chunks as big as motor-cars to strew the flat. Two hours we came to reckon a fair time to Camp VI. The first hour is a walk up tedious snow slopes to the foot of the ice-walls. I have likened the total Face of Lhotse to the inside of a gigantic white mixing-bowl, one edge of the bowl having been chipped off to give place to the Cwm. From the centre of the resultant basin a convex structure like a series of blisters stands out and runs up to two-thirds height. It is part of the basin, yet not of it, for it is an irregular mass of lumps and crevices in contrast with the smooth straightness of the slopes on either side. Beyond these slopes, to the left and slanting down from the left, from the bump just above the Col itself, runs the rock buttress known as the Geneva Spur.

At the foot of the steep section is a level terrace, where we put on crampons. A little gully, bounded on the left by icy verticals, led up easily. Into every step powder snow had drifted, or rather been driven by a wind that was here beginning to bluster. At V all had been sheltered and hot. Now, I pulled on my sweater and then wind-proof. We went on. Ed was now leading, and the next obstacle consisted of a snowy traverse round a bulge, again with the steps masked. Having cleared a way across we told one of the Sherpas, Da Tensing I think, to leave a length of rope for fixing later. Onward, up a steep, snow-filled gully, and thence to the foot of the real labour of this section. A rope hung here almost vertically down a wall. Looking up it, and then over to the right, I could see that we were now on the true right-hand slope of our line of bulging blister. Looking further right still, I could see the shining sweep of pudding-basin beyond, ending in the cliff whose débris was the chaos of mighty sugar-lumps below.

This was the "400 feet of rope" said to have been fixed by the Swiss. Theirs had been replaced by our Manilla. Steps cleared on the first steep section sent snowballs thumping noisily on to heads below. Better to wait a little, till Ed's

party (Gyaljen and Ang Namgyal) had passed over the skyline. My breath, which I could control fairly well to the
rhythm of my steps down below, here failed for brief
moments after I had pulled myself up, ice-pick bedded in
the snow, trying not to use the fixed rope—a small spark
of mountaineering pride which had followed me from the
Alps. A pause, to let life swing back into its focus; a glance
out at the blazing blank unreality of white peaks down the
Cwm; a hitch at my rope, wound round the axe-head, to tell
Da Tensing below to come on. A heave of the foot forward,
hands scraping away the snow, to fumble at the next steps.
We were, after all, nearly 23,000 feet high, the height of a
very respectable Himalayan peak. To work at this height
banishes the breath. We could appreciate what a splendid
job George and Ang Nyima had made of this, giving safety
and a staircase even to the steepest climb; and how impressive the Swiss effort had been.

After a hundred feet we were out on the cheek proper,
if I may mix metaphors, of our blister. Up this the route ran
diagonally to the left towards an unseen goal. The usual
method of ascent was to hold the rope in right hand, probe
forward with the axe and clear snow with the left. It was
tiring work, a motion always leftward like a crab's, and
seemed to go on for ever. At last, the rope stopped at a piton;
its place was taken by nylon line. A splash of orange suddenly brightened the grey. There was George grinning out
of the tent, filming us in the intervals of his grins over those
last few feet. It was a favourite trick which he had practised
some days before on John, who ascended to visit him. The
snow was very deep, the work exhausting, and John's attitudes appropriate. He looked just what the movies expect of
a Himalayan climber. He was startled, looking up, to be
confronted by the merciless camera.

There was only room for one tent at Camp VI, a ledge
beaten out above our bulge, protected from fire overhead by
the grey curve of serac. There was not much room therefore
for arm-chair conversation; we stood about uneasily in the
snow. But after a few minutes' rest, the time of arrival being

only 12:25, Ed generously determined to carry tent, cooker, and other equipment for us up to the site of VII. Here we discussed a knotty point, still standing about and trying not to become entangled in the innumerable ropes. Would the final carry from V to VII be too long? George had taken five and a half hours on the first ascent from VI to VII, and even on the assumption that every climb becomes simpler the second time, it was a long way. If we thought an intermediate camp necessary, John must be consulted at once. Then Ed went on, with the three stalwarts. I made my way gingerly round the tent, for the slope below was already almost too steep even for crampons. On the minute, crumbling snow platform at the tent door, I took the crampons off. We squashed into the tent and Ang Nyima made tea.

A word about Ang Nyima. At lower levels he seemed very much the "sporty" unhelpful type of Sherpa, like the man dismissed at Thyangboche. He had an ineffective air about him. But he was one of those people (there may be many) who should be kept well above 20,000 feet, for there he was his real self; not only more efficient, but much nicer. Throughout these days he had shared the work of ice pioneering as well as the tent life with George. Later he was to carry the highest camp. Here we all sat huddled inside over our tea, for the wind was by now coming in aggravating gusts, making the tent canvas flap about our heads. The immediate difficulty was to keep the Primus going; despite its wind-shield the poor thing quivered and flickered at the buffets. Our Meade tents, as I have said, were fitted at both ends with a "sleeve," that is to say, a circular opening three feet in diameter, with a funnel of canvas some two feet long, through which one entered, tying it behind on arrival inside. The tapes fastening this at one of our ends had broken. I floundered about (as it was my end, and the windy one), holding on to it with a hand when I heard a gust coming. Only later in the evening did it occur to me to break off a piece of ribbon hanging from the ceiling and use that. Even this arrangement was not satisfactory. The ribbon had to be untied whenever I wanted to go out, and was usually lost by the time I had settled in again, and I must break off another. The supply of ribbons was limited.

However, we managed to keep the tea going till Ed returned at four, having dumped our loads for us. He had reached the site of VII in one hour fifty minutes, a time which I think remained a record. When he set off again for Advance Base, the sun was still on us, but the air was cold, with the coldness of wind fingers probing at the naked flesh if I poked a head out for a few moments. There was plenty to do. At five George became involved in a lengthy wireless talk about the intermediate camp and other matters. I decided to collect snow, but it was perhaps a quarter of an hour before my decision converted itself into action. I had to go twice, each time a greater effort. I tried to gather a pile of chunk-ice, which I had chipped off with the axe, outside the tent door and within easy reach. Somehow there never seemed to be enough. After a few minutes of this I would retire, kneel on my sleeping-bag, hands in pockets, rubbing them hard against the thighs; a primitive method which seemed to restore circulation quickest. And yet, when I paused for a moment outside, the beauty before me was so compelling that it seemed absurd ever to have groused at cold. The eye passed from our eyrie down the strangest valley in the world, the level white river of the Cwm winding between a phantasia of impossible black buttresses. Camp V was a few toy tents far below; Camp IV a dirty smudge. The perfect background to this, Pumori (23,400 feet) now looked on us as equals. Her cone yielded nothing to the two great masses behind and now overtopping it: Cho Oyu (26,900 feet) and Gyachung Kang (25,900 feet). Often she (for Pumori was certainly a she) would devise an elegant cloud background to blot out the lumpish males. Above the mist masses the sky was pure silver with the dying sun.

Back in the tent it was almost dark before we supped. Each large chunk of snow melted down to half an inch of water, and someone must reach for more. We ate half-lying on our bags, balancing things awkwardly between us. The disadvantage of eating inside sleeping-bags, if your heads are at opposite ends for hygienic reasons, is the greater stretch between, also the greater effort needed to climb out for snow or lavatories. Fortunately the latter are not so often necessary at a height. As we ate, we talked. George described graphically the trials of new snow, I congratulated him on their job below. Very soon we were back on the hoary topic of food. Not enough, and too much Assault Ration. This latter expedition scapegoat had now been divided up into silver-paper bags, each containing all those elements of two days' Assault Rations with which nobody quarrelled. As Grape-Nuts and pemmican (which we could both take) were thereby excluded, there was even less than before for a hearty meal. Each night, George said, he bellowed down the wireless for more tins, instead of all this oxygen. Appetite was far from vanished, as had been predicted above 22,000 feet, for we had acclimatised too well. At any rate we had brought some tins today, and we were also that night using the last of a side of Swiss bacon. This I fried, to the accompaniment of a most painful spluttering probably due to the height.

The wind continued to rise. From inside, it seemed clear that the little tent, lit by very flickering candle-flame, was the sole object of its malice. My improvised door-tape flapped and strained and leaked little patches of the snow that was whipping down from the slopes above. Far away, on the South Col, a dull roar dominated the symphony. Then for a minute or two a gust would seem to be pounding across the "Traverse." Then nothing, until a shiver in the air as of a ghost striking off ice sparks; then a thud, as the little tent shook and strained madly about us and the spattering snow hissed against its roof. A cup of coffee, made with difficulty, waited a long time while we listened. At last the mug was roughly rinsed with a dirty hand and the few dirty drops remaining in the pan. Then blessed sleeping-bag for the last time. But it was an important night. Tomorrow we must establish VII, on which the whole speed of the lift depended. Sleep, therefore, at all costs I must, despite the wind. I had never taken a sleeping-pill, but I had with me some strange little green lozenges advertising themselves as such.

"What about you, George?"

"Perhaps I'd better have one too," George said.

3

Now some are unaffected by sleeping-pills. Greg, indeed, never missed a night above 20,000 feet. We had various brands, red, yellow and the vicious-looking greeny-blue object that I now swallowed. This, I remembered, had had so little effect on Greg at III that he woke at eleven and had to take one of his own brand. In our case it was otherwise. I slept soundly, lulled off in a drift of wind and snow that was all the outside world, while I was all warmth within. I woke at six to a morning of cloudless beauty. The wind had dropped; outside, the tent flaps creaked and crackled frostily as I prodded a head through the sleeve. We had heated extra snow last night, and the Primus rested at George's end of the tent. I gave a push at the sleeping-bagged legs.

"George!"

No answer. "George!" again, two or three times, and a very sleepy figure heaved upright, at least into the kneeling position. I looked out. A perfect day. By the time I had pulled my head back, nose and ears numb, George was fast asleep again, still in the kneeling position. I must pass rapidly over the next three hours. I pleaded, pummelled, abused. Only much later did I discover that George, utterly drugged with sleep, had heard everything I said, although his active half was dead. He was very kind about it, later (for I said a good deal). At the time, he could do or answer nothing, only feel an agony of helplessness and a deep longing for the one thing—sleep. Each time I looked out the sun was higher, the sky bluer, the situation more absurd. Down there, they would be getting out the binoculars to watch Camp VII being established. And on the upper slopes the snow would be stickier, softer, more promising of labour every minute. My anxiety reached fever pitch. By nine

I had had my own breakfast: sardine, tea, biscuit and jam. We *must* go. At last, at last George was heaving into consciousness. Perhaps all was well. His eyes, creased with sleep and closing continuously, he rubbed and rubbed. Slowly the rucksacks filled up. He took a little tea, almost nothing else. By the time we roped at 10:30 and had shut the tent, the sun was at last on us over the protecting serac. (Plate 31(a).)

George led at first. He knew the way, and he could set the pace most suited to his own somnambulatory needs. Though Ed's party had taken up tent and stoves, we were heavily laden with personal kit, wireless apparatus and food oddments. The route wound upward to the left, over wind-driven snow crusted at the top. Into it the foot sometimes sank, on the rippled surface it sometimes stayed. It was obvious that George was still grinding by sheer will against the sleep oppressing him. I took over the lead, for there were tracks to break. One steep little slope had a rope fixed and shallow-cut steps, into which the feet fitted clumsily. We were moving very slowly, and twice George said: "Wait a minute. I must stop." The first time he took off his boots, and we both rubbed the cold feet grown sluggish, I suspected, with the dope. At 11:30, the second halt, he relapsed upon his rucksack—and slept. Another huge, half-moon-shaped wall reared over us. We wound under it to the right. By the time we had reached the steep fixed rope, in a snow-slope swinging you back leftward towards its top, we were ready to sit down again. "Perhaps I'll have something to eat," George said. "That'll make me feel better." He was seated in the snow, propped once more against the rucksack. I pulled out a tin of sardines and opened it. But things were looking black indeed when George actually went to sleep with one of these delectable fishes in his mouth! An unforgettable picture. I felt in my heart then a horrible weight of apprehension, no doubt exaggerated by the altitude: we would not see Camp VII today.

A little further, up the fixed rope and on to the levelled snow above the two-hundred-foot wall, and we had plumped down again. George was asleep. I shook him and shouted, or seemed in that stillness to shout:

"Shall we go on a bit and see?"

"I don't know if I can."

"Well, let's go on a little bit."

But this time it was no more than a few yards, and we were sitting down once more. It was madness, and really my fault in the first instance, a comic fault if you like, the offering of a centimetre of green pill; but it might wreck the expedition. Suppose the weather turned, and we a day behind? Why had I ever had the idea of taking one, or offering one, when neither of us knew his reaction to these artificial aids, only that George had disliked the red pill he once tried before? Beyond the glaring Cwm, Pumori, flat and dull and yellow in the noon-day, seemed to be mocking us, defying us to get higher than herself. The snow edge of Nuptse, riven by the wind, heaved its immense length still far above our heads. There was a dead stillness. Round every mountain pedestal the mist crept up. And here was I alone, feeling utterly alone, with a sick man. Suppose that we could not reach VII, and that George had not the strength to get down? Fears crept and played round the back of my dulled brain.

"How far is it to VII?"

"We're about half-way."

It proved in the event that we were rather less than half, perhaps a third, but that was enough. We could not risk arriving late in the afternoon under VII, failing to reach it. There was still the tent to erect and arrange, a job for two whole men. We got up, turned by silent consent and started down the slope, myself acutely conscious that every eye at Advance Base must now be watching us, wondering what those two so-and-so's were doing. I have never admired George more. He summoned all his remaining strength to manœuvre the awkward, now doubly awkward, boots into the holds. Even so I felt that I was playing a sleep-walker down almost unknown ground; for in places, over the wind-blown snow, the tracks were hard to follow. In comparison with our ascent, however, this journey seemed absurdly quick. Before 2:00 P.M. we were in camp, by 2:05 George was fast asleep on his Li-Lo.

The wireless conversation with John at III that evening was prolonged beyond the customary. Our method at VI was to lie on the elbows, with head protruding but body and lower extremities back in the warmth. After John had told of his anxiety at our plight, but relief that it was no worse, I asked for Griff, Mike Ward being at IV. Griff opined that George would "sleep it off." Perhaps I had guessed as much, but official confirmation was after all reassuring. John urged that we establish VII if it were humanly possible. After this conversation there was Ed at IV, unable, owing to one of the many idiosyncrasies of the walkie-talkie, to communicate directly with III. Both could communicate with me, and I, therefore, miles away from either, spent a quarter of an hour passing messages between the two. Then I wriggled back and set to work on the Primus. What for supper? There was sausage-meat, welcome as meat but now unpalatable. I decided to stew it up in the soup. When it was half-cooked, a not unusual event occurred. The Primus ran out of fuel. I gave many groans, pulled myself upright, unfastened the flap (putting the ribbon somewhere I hoped to remember), wriggled out on all fours and started in with the axe, chopping off wind-drift that had buried the kerosene. Suddenly I stopped.

It was a miracle, after the tedious care of stove-lighting. Little Pumori, darkened with sun shadow, had decked her shoulders with cloud fleece, but she could not this time wipe out her larger background. The long, irregular ridges of Cho Oyu and Gyachung Kang sparkled, shifted, beckoned against a paling, silver-blue sky. The sun shone whitely still into my face, still whitened the dazzling linen of the valley at my feet. What matter kerosene, stoves, sleeping-bags, even the ascent on which our every thought had been concentrated? Something here beyond me, outside me, "far more deeply interfused" than my muddled brain could care to know, lent a magic to the air that made human effort meaningless. I was, for a moment, again near to Nirvana.

Heartened, yet not knowing why, I went back to cook sausage-meat in soup.

4

May 17th again dawned kindly. George had managed to swallow some supper the night before; he awoke at six bright as the healthiest new pin. This time we simply must erect Camp VII. We breakfasted meagrely, grumbling again that Tom's miserable oxygen bottles held the field over good solid food as material for loads. We had had one precious packet of Grape-Nuts between us. Mine I had eaten the day before, George therefore had his half-packet scrupulously doled out, with Swiss Knäckerbrot (Ryvita) and cheese to follow. Against all expectation I preferred cheese to jam above 21,000 feet. It had more taste. There followed the wretched routine of "getting away": packing up sleeping-bags, Li-Los and the rest, making pretence to wash up the cups and spoons with cold fingers in still colder water, drying on a continually vanishing piece of rag; leaving a note, scribbled in a kneeling position, for Mike Ward, whose Sherpas we hoped would carry on to VII the bulk of our gear that afternoon; finally, the more than ice-cold job of putting on crampons that had been sitting in the snow all night. Fingers stuck and tore upon the biting metal. We were away at 8:30, George's best time, he said, leaving the little tent still in the grip of frost shadows.

This time it was a very different affair. I carried the sack, George again started leading, at a fine speed as if his sleep had done him all the good in the world. The wind-crust of the first, straightforward section now held; the fixed rope slithered free on the surface. In forty-three minutes we reached the point which yesterday morning had demanded two and a half hours of leaden toil. We rested. Above this our path wound back again towards the right, along a narrow rib of hard snow. Overhanging the rib and separated by a gulf was a great wall of pure ice, perhaps 150 feet high, fashioned like the sun half-risen from the sea; so close that I could see the veins writhing down into its hard, impenetrable greenness. I was now higher than I had ever been before, higher than Pauhunri in Sikkim, and this had the psychological effect of making me feel more breathless than I probably was. George had been up before. Wretched man, he seemed to go on and on, a machine, an automatic hill-climber. The sack weighed heavier at each step. Thirty of them at a time, fitting breath to the rhythm of the feet. One, two, three, four. . . . Let's halt, as I have a little rope in hand. I watch it run out through my fingers, coil by jerky coil, until—with a sigh and a shrug I must step on again to prevent it pulling George up. Pride would be sadly wounded if that happened. But there are legitimate ways. . . .

"Whoa! I want to take a photo."

George stops, obligingly poised. I take out and adjust camera, focussing very carefully, while breath floods back. I am strong again, wondering what was wrong before. Then we go on, and I soon realise.

Some way along the rib, to my inexpressible secret delight, George stopped for good. He was sadly watching his camera filter gavotting down the slopes below. It came to rest near a just visible zigzag of our track. "I'd better get it," George said. I smiled my secret pleasure, and after most careful consideration suggested that there was no point in our both going down those two hundred feet. He could indulge a noble enthusiasm for descending which I did not share, while I went on slowly, carrying the rucksack, ice-pitons and rope. George and Ang Nyima had made the way plain enough for the single traveller, if he advanced with caution.

I waited a little, breathing deeply and luxuriously over my axe, while he started down. What an admirable sacrifice to the cause of photography! Then I went on, slowly. A short steep section led back left and up to the top of the wall. An awkward fumbling to have a hand free for the fixed rope, the ice-pitons giving a metallic clank at each hitch. Then a slow lifting of one foot into the step, balance, breathe, higher hand-grip, manœuvre left hand slung with pitons and rope-end into place, a curse at their clumsiness. Then up again, to repeat the whole motion. The slope eased, gradually, and landed me in a little hollow frowned upon by seracs. Up and to the right a huge mass overhung, rather like

a battleship bow. I did not know at the time that this was
the serac protecting the site of VII. My pace had now slowed
greatly. Earlier in the day we had been going virtually
without pause. Now, at perhaps 23,800 feet, it was twenty
steps and a breath, while I leaned gasping on my axe. Twenty
steps was too much. Ten and a breath, then six. At each pause
the picture, which had been swaying and shifting with my
heart-throbs, my lung-pants, clicked back into focus. I could
appreciate the blazing white wall upon which we were, the
Swiss ropes still in position out to the left, the heat of the
sun that sent little chunks of snow slithering off to tinkle
down crevasses. And away in the distance that mocked all
human effort, the clouds danced and played their sun-play
over Pumori and other reefs high enough to defy them.

George was behind me now. We went on. Climbing up the
join between serac mass and parent mountain, I found soft,
sticky snow and sunk in to my knees. Four steps and a gasp.
At last, at last we were making a long traverse out to the
right, across the serac's very face. A length of line was there
to be used as handrail, but it was not necessary. We seemed
to be leaving earth altogether, traversing on and on into a
blue empyrean. A halt, abruptly; the traverse had turned,
back again towards the shallow gully of the join on the left.
An awkward step round a corner, round a steep buttress of
the serac. Then a straight slog, with the expectation nagging
every minute that at the next step we would see over the
plateau upon which our site must be. It seemed never to
come, our horizon never to sink. Then there it was at last,
a little jumble of very ordinary-looking packages, on that
strangest of all things—level ground.

The time was no more than 10:45, but there remained a
job to do. Here was the Meade tent, but before we could
lie in its welcome shade, a platform must be stamped and
the thing pitched. In the frothy top-snow, nearly a foot of it,
the stamping took a long time. Then the tent, very slowly,
must be hauled across and set up. At 24,000 feet it was a
tedious business, punctuated with many pauses, and nearly
an hour before we lay gasping like fish under a canopy that
seemed fit for princes. Frozen sardines melted over Meta,

biscuits and Kendal Mint Cake. We did not feel that we wanted much, only the lemon, far sweeter than wine, in our flasks. Foolishly we did not light the Primus to brew more, and later in the day I for one regretted it, for we dehydrated ourselves completely. But for the present it seemed far more agreeable to lie simply and doze, to wake and think and doze again.

At 1:15 George opened an eye and said: "Well." I said: "Well," too, and we dozed off for a few more minutes. This went on for some time. Soon after 1:30 two very sleepy figures had pushed out of the tent rubbing their eyes at the fierce blaze around, weighed by that dream heaviness which makes of every movement a Titan battle with natural sloth. We still had a job—to reconnoitre the route ahead for tomorrow, and particularly the first crevasse. For the situation of Camp VII must now be explained. Perched halfway up the great Face, it was surmounted by wall and terrace of the type we had been meeting lower down. Itself it rested on the broad, flat back of the monster serac on which we had climbed. On the mountain side it was protected by a deep crevasse, perhaps eight feet wide, a gaping mouth into which anything falling from above must fall. But although a protection, this crevasse was also an obstacle. We had no duralumin bridges here. A day late already, we must start at once finding a way on to the upper slopes. It was now the 17th; Mike Ward would be coming up this very afternoon in the hope that he and George could finish the work on the Face by the 20th, by which time I would be up again, in charge of the first Sherpa lift to the Col.

As we staggered out there was no sound of Mike from the slopes below. Slowly we went through the tiresome drill of fastening unwilling crampons, then set off with one accord horizontally to the right along the crevasse. After fifty yards we stopped. At this point it is most luckily choked with snow, fallen down a little couloir which slanted up leftward from a point just round the corner to the right. I belayed George's rope over the bridge, upon which, cautiously, he fashioned big steps one upon the other, and finally disappeared round the corner. I followed, driving my axe as soon

172

THE WESTERN CWM – Sherpa safeguarded across the great crevasse. Looking up the Cwm.

Trouble with a Li-Lo. (Noyce.)   Tired. (Tom Stobart.)

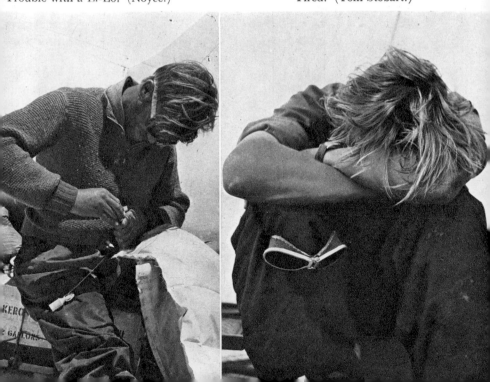

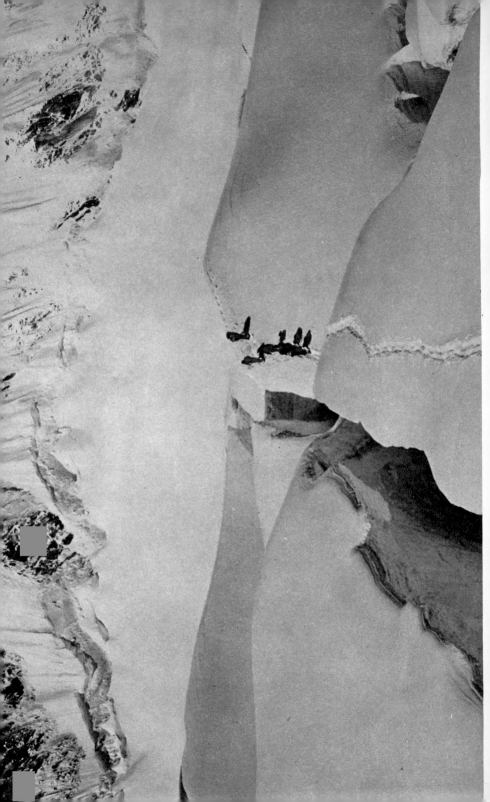

The Western Cwm – Looking down the Cwm, from near Camp IV.

Lobuje respite. Tenzing on right. Pumori behind.

EVEREST   SOUTH COL   GENEVA SPUR   LHOTSE   NUPTSE

CAMP VII

CAMP VI

← CAMP V

To CAMP IV

THE WESTERN CWM – Lhotse Face, showing the route from Camp V to the South Col.
A Sherpa train entering the Cwm. The distance to the Face is 2½ miles, the upper end
of the Cwm being much foreshortened.

THE WESTERN CWM –
Evans and Bourdillon at
Camp V. Notice Closed-
Circuit oxygen set—cy-
linders, square canister,
wind-bag and mask.

THE LHOTSE FACE – May
15th. Ed Hillary clears
steps on lower Lhotse
Face.

THE LHOTSE FACE – May 16th. George Lowe sets out from Camp VI. Notice circular opening of tent. Unwashed pans right foreground.

THE LHOTSE FACE – May 17th. Returning to Camp VII. Camp VII serac on left. The snow bridge is just below George Lowe, who is descending on to it, roped to the author.

The Lhotse Face – Camp VII. Left top, part of Everest. Centre top, South Col. Geneva Spur slants from right top, down to the left.

Camp VII, another view. (Ed Hillary.)

as possible into the firm bank beyond, hoping that each
prod would not reveal a nothingness below. I found George
safely ensconced in the couloir and led on, that being the
easiest thing to do. The snow was steep but firm. The ice-
axe, plunged in up to the head, held me, as I trampled
clumsily at the snow. One step and a halt, to wriggle the foot
in to comfort. Here, in the shadow, I had woken up and was
beginning at last to appreciate Browning's "sheer joy of
living" which had been noticeably absent below. What
fools poets had seemed! Just to the right of our couloir a
giant's nose was dripping noisy dew-drops into our crevasse.
Camp VII had disappeared to the left. Going on, I found
myself on ice. I chipped weakly, but this ice was fortunately
not hard. After fifty feet I brought George up; we stood at
last on the slope to which we had looked up from our tent.
The crevasse was behind us.[1]

The slope itself proved tiresome. It was snow-covered, but
at some steps you could feel the ice beneath. Sometimes the
wind had blown this snow into little ribs and mounds, leaving bare ice to be cut between, and the awkward alternative,
on the mounds themselves, of laying a clumsy boot on their
surface and risking a slip, or stopping to chip a step. I led
on, making ever up and to the left, past our tent which we
could now see below. At last we had crossed out of sight of
it over the slope's top. The way still seemed to lie to the left,
and looking up I found the higher slopes of the famous
"Traverse" deceptively near. Surely we could just go on
diagonally, and we would be somewhere near the top of the
Geneva Spur? A little crevasse stopped us, we trod its crest
to the left again, then on up and across our now gentler
gradient.

I write as if all this were a continuous ascent; but the
pauses were very frequent and long. A few minutes and a
pause; on again, and another pause. At 3:00 P.M. we halted
finally, perhaps 500 feet above VII. For today we had done
quite enough, and we could see no further immediate diffi-

[1] This crevasse became later, for me, Ang Temba's crevasse. See illustration,
Plate 40(b), which shows also the giant's nose. Plate 31(b) shows Lowe about
to descend on to the bridge later in the day.

culties. At the time we thought that we had reached 25,000 feet, but we put our height later at no more than 24,500 feet. Never mind, sufficient to the moment its joy. I think that we both felt far better than below VII. Perhaps it was the zest of new ground, the benefit of sleep, the perfect proportions of the scene westward. We had been stopping no more than every few minutes. Now we sat basking in shirtsleeves, wondering whether anybody had ever so enjoyed a view so high. The black pyramid of Everest foreshortened above us looked for all the world like Snowdon or any other mountain. Directly over our heads the crenellated ridge of Lhotse. Then, far more wonderful than either, the ridge swung from Lhotse to Nuptse, until it became a magic, magnified razor-edge, with all the cuts and whips of the wind perpetuated, and each nick further blazoned by the sweep down from it of a rib of ice, delicately moulded in inverted V's, down to the hump of some monstrous glacier mass that perched all ready to tumble into fragments. Beyond, the bulk of Cho Oyu and Gyachung Kang tilted with the clouds. It was very still. Only little puffs occasionally from Everest, and a faint hum over the South Col, reminded us that there was such a thing as wind.

We descended. As we passed above VII we could already see Mike with four Sherpas. We found him very tired after his quick ascent from Base Camp, and like us dehydrated. In view of the great work still ahead before the South Col could be reached, I wanted to stay on with them. Also influencing me, I must confess, was a dipsomaniac passion to drink several oceans of liquid before I took another step. But the other two and my better self agreed that I ought to go down, since John had seemed most anxious for me to bring up the first rather than the second lift, and there was only just time. But before all else, drink. Every drop had gone from us, we could not even sweat. Da Tensing would stay with the others, using my sleeping-bag, but two Sherpas could go down straight away, Ang Namgyal must wait for me while the water boiled for lemon.

It was 4:30 before he and I stepped out into the entrancing sun-down, every peak clear-cut in greeting. We went down slowly, partly from lack of food, partly because the high-altitude crampons on broad-soled boots seemed more difficult to fit into the holds on a descent. Just before six we were tramping across the last level snow to V, looking forward at the friendly faces of Tom Bourdillon and—none other than Gompu. It had been a day of happy mountaineering.

A.J. VEILHAN

10

South Col: First Ascent

May 17th—May 21st

1

It was a sensation of pure joy, the return in the sunlight that still gilded the flat plain of the Cwm. Wonderful to feel that I had helped to add even a few hundred feet of our route over new ground. However much true virtue may delight in tasks like the bear-leading of Sherpas over the difficulties of a known route, there is a zest of adventure beyond compare in the unknown, however brief. Moreover I had bccn to 25,000 fcct (as I thought) and fclt nonc too bad. Of all this I chattered, probably to his great boredom, that evening with Tom Bourdillon in the orange tent. Tom was to take the Sherpa lift to VII tomorrow; this would become a regular ferry and dump, planned to ease the final carry to the Col. For John was still most anxious not to have two camps on the Face for that carry. Tent problems, food problems, all would be immeasurably increased. If, therefore, the Sherpas were to do the whole Face in two days, their burden would be lightened, could a dump be made at VII, half-way up. Poor Charles Evans, who should have gone up today, was in the other tent suffering from stomach trouble. He was vomiting and most uncomfortable.

Our many problems we discussed over supper of stewed steak and peas; one of the luxuries of descent being freedom from cookery and the idleness of being waited on, with the homely face of Gompu once more appearing behind the soup. I felt very well; if the sleeping-pill had prevented us from reaching as high as our first hope, this had still been a

◄ *I took a quick stride and jump,*
trying not to look down. . . .

wonderful chance to acclimatise. Next morning, the 18th, started with a luxurious lie and late breakfast, while Tom groaningly prepared for the heat of the day. I was using Da Tensing's sleeping-bag, having left mine for him at VII. It was comfortable, but I was wakened by its strong smell of paraffin. Very soon Charles was out, indomitably sorting stores, and we joined up for the descent. The walk from V to IV was one of the pleasantest half-hours of the expedition. Going always slightly down-hill over easy ground, one had leisure and breath to appreciate the splendour of the Cwm, with which we were by now becoming almost too familiar; to take in the details of ice cliffs to which habit was shutting our eyes, of the variegated cream and black buttresses of Nuptse, with their sudden vertical plunges; the rolling waves of hanging glacier sweeping in serried bulges from the West Shoulder and helping to frame Pumori's sharpness.

Camp IV was astir with new life. Charles Wylie and Tenzing were up with the last Sherpa lift from Base. We were now self-contained. Thondup was here, the two big dome tents were in position, Sherpas unseen before bustled about with crampons and cooking gear. It had become increasingly difficult to find things. The day before, Gyaljen II, Tom Stobart's private Sherpa, had been taken down to Base very ill and spitting blood. Poor Griff had once again been diverted from the most important experiments, this time to escort a possibly dying man through the icefall.[1] All this spelt an air of worry, but all this was nothing to the worry of the Lhotse Face. John, come out to greet us, returned anxiously to his glasses. The three little figures on the Face were advancing slowly. They had passed our highest point of yesterday. Then, very soon after, the three of them stopped. There must be an obstacle.

"They're coming down!" somebody cried.

It was hard to believe, but true. Everybody's eyes turned from their jobs to the Face. Poor John! He looked suddenly very tired. Some fate seemed to be holding him from that Col. Another sleeping-pill? They retreated at midday, having

[1] Gyaljen, fully recovered, met us outside Namche Bazar on the return.

set out only at 10:15. Through the glasses we could clearly see the small black shapes standing or sitting on a terrace (in fact rubbing feet) before they returned. Conversation in the big tent, now our mess, drifted back to them uneasily. People would stamp out to have a look. George Band, setting off for V to do the lift next day, was commanded strictly to find out what was happening. Then at 5:30 Tom Bourdillon came trudging into camp with his team, to tell today's story. Mike had indeed taken two sleeping-pills, but these had not caused the delay. The bitter wind which we had experienced two nights before had set about them in earnest. Mike Ward's hands and George's feet, they began to suspect, were stiffening with frostbite; Da Tensing, too, was bothered by the conditions. They went down.

After supper there lasted into the night a fascinating discussion of the chances of survival if the Closed-Circuit apparatus failed at the summit. Could one get back over the South Summit? Would one climber be justified in leaving another if that other were doomed? Could two men possibly work off one apparatus? Griff had very positive views; Tom also, though he listened mainly. It was a lively evening.

Then out, into the starry sky. By now Advance Base was a positive encampment, with six little tents in a row on the West Shoulder side, the big tent on a slight mound, slippery at night towards the icefall. Beyond it a pile of stores. At first this big tent was the cook-house, a convenient miniature crevasse forming the sink-hole, but little by little the sahibs infiltrated, for warmth and space. Thondup, who had come up urgently invited by all the party, saw that it was a hopeless case. The noisy mess in one corner grew larger and larger, more and more disorderly. Sahibs stayed up to all hours. Copies of the air-mail edition of *The Times*, mixed up with old letters, littered a chaos of sleeping-bags. On a shelf a large Cheddar cheese, growing harder with the days but ever popular, disputed standing space with two kerosene lamps. Thondup and his kitchen battery emigrated.

On the Lhotse side of the camp, the first habitation as you came up from below was the big white dome in which the

Sherpas crowded to the most delectable of fugs. Then the tarpaulins, stretched on to staves as only a Sherpa can stretch them, formed Thondup's new cook-house, befloored with the cardboard of food cases. Beside this and forming the last link of the square was a pyramid tent holding three. If you were lucky, you could have one of the small Meade tents to yourself, though some preferred the company of a bigger tent. (See illustration, Plate 42, for tents.) And in the centre of the square thus formed and now dim in the starlight, all camp operations took place. Here Tom Stobart filmed, Tom Bourdillon tinkered with oxygen sets, Charles Wylie harangued the Sherpas, parties were welcomed back or given "God speed!"

That night was unusually windy for IV, but I slept through from 8:30 to 6:45, when tea appeared. The only large inconvenience that I experienced in sleep high up continued to be a heavy clogging of my nostrils; as a result of breathing though my mouth, a slobber of saliva formed which had usually frozen solid over my beard by the morning. Opening the mouth wide took some time, and my beard and teeth were the one part of me that I washed. As each climbed out of his tent that morning, eyes turned as if magnet-drawn to the Lhotse Face. No sign of movement. Soon after nine George Band's party could be seen mounting the slopes below VI. Of the three at VII still no sign. It was not till afternoon, when George Band returned, that we learned they had been nursing their suspected frostbites of the day before, George Lowe's feet and Mike's hands, and had not been able to go out at all. I conferred again with John. There, still, was the barrier, and the first lift must start up this afternoon.

I then had a long talk with Charles Evans, imperturbable as ever amid the anxious scanners of the Face. Here is the last typed document I received, typed for John by James Morris at Base and handed to me at Advance Base. Food details were added by Charles.

Everest 1953—ASSAULT LOAD TABLE
Loads for S. Col.

Item	No.	Wt.	Remarks
Cookers (L)	2 *at VII already*	15	
Fuel	4 qts. *at VII*	9	
Rations	6 Sahibs	24	*at VII*
	3 Sherpa 5 lb. tsampa	10 [15]	*from here*
Oxygen	13 LA (light alloy cylinders)	141	*3 at VII rest at V*
	5 R.A.F. (cylinders)	100	*2 at VII, 3 at V.* See Note (5).
Canisters	4	36	*at V. Wrap up.*
Tentage	1 Pyramid *at VII*	25	
	1 Meade *at VII*	15	OC SP party carries M (eade)
	1 Blister *take up*	5	
Line, 700 ft. nylon			

Total Wt. 380 or 14 loads at 30 lb.

Notes: 1. These stores will be dumped at Camp V by May 15th.

2. They are to be carried to South Col by two parties led by Noyce and Wylie on successive days.

3. Tentage *MUST* be carried by second party, *NOT* first.

4. Both parties stage at Camp VI on way up *and* down.

5. It may be possible to reduce oxygen in ["that" pencilled out and word "initial" substituted] carry by substituting Dræger bottles from Camp VI for RAF.

8.5.53.

Take: 2 cookers, Fuel, Rations, 3 LA cylinders, 2 RAF cylinders, Canisters, Blister.

The words in italics are my pencil notes inserted that morning with Charles. And this document testifies, if nothing else, the thoroughness of John's preparations; even though the bedding, which is not on this list, Li-Lo and all the little weight-adding items, nearly defeated my party. It should be explained that the Dræger bottles were Swiss oxygen cylinders left last year. When it was learned, before we started, that the Swiss had abandoned a number of bottles, some even above the South Col, a brilliant piece of organisation enabled our connecting apparatus to be made to fit the Swiss cylinders.

To have this carried up was my job, and I wandered lifelessly round the hot square, summoning and addressing my Sherpas. How noble if I could keep Everest on the high heroic plane! Alas, the moments of ecstasy are few compared with the hours of drabness; with the dreary effort to drag myself from *Nicholas Nickleby*, which I used to read lying on Li-Lo, head and shoulders inside tent, and be efficient with fiddling details. Yet on the other side, this inertia was just as well. I never remember being excitedly anxious about my capabilities at Advance Base, as I had been before leaving England. How severely would I feel the cold? and so on. These queries had peeled off as unnecessary. Life was a routine existence of meals and arrangements and gossip, with the top layer of the mind comfortably skimmed away, as I now realise. At the time I thought I was as alert as at sea level.

That morning there was a great deal of photography about, of various parties in their various attitudes. Moreover, Union Jacks and the other flags were already being tied round ice-axes in preparation, ready to be unfurled at a jerk; a temptation which Providence, I could not help thinking, would find it hard to resist. Then lunch, two eggs each, Ryvita and the splendid Cheddar cheese. To have four eggs in a day (for we had had two at breakfast) at 21,200 feet in the Western Cwm was an encouraging start. In the afternoon, weighing out 15 lb. of *tsampa* for the South Col with Tenzing, along with the daily ration of 1½ lb. per man, I could feel the physical sense of urgency round. There was Tom tinkering, Ed looking at Tenzing's apparatus, Charles Evans calmly as ever writing notes, John talking to someone, his face plastered almost as white as his hat with glacier cream, one eye cocked every now and then upward. The Sherpas slopped around in the clumsy boots or lay gossiping in their big tent. The assault machinery was geared to start; the next days must provide the starter.

Just after four George Band's party returned, with their story, almost as John and I were setting off to follow my Sherpas. John was accompanying me as far as V, both to see me on my way and to test his apparatus. Mine I was keeping, rather cowardly, for tomorrow. Sufficient unto the day. He suffered difficulty with the two-litre flow rate, and stopped twice, asking me to adjust. Even so we reached V in exactly one hour this time, to find the Sherpas already arrived. John hoped to clear up a wireless problem, but no fiddling could extort an answer from IV. I fussed around hopefully with tomorrow's loads, and in particular fitted the twenty-pound cylinder to my oxygen frame. As usual, something caught annoyingly as the heavy bottle scraped into the container. My eight Sherpas had settled in and were now cooking, for at 5:30 up here it was already cold and windy with the sun still upon us. John and I said good-bye.

"Well, I'll do my best," I think I said.

"Get to the Col if you possibly can, Wilf, that's the most important. We're depending on that."

"I may not be able to get all the loads up."

"Take Anullu and get up alone if you have to. As I think I said, if the others can't make it leave them for Charles Wylie. They'll be strength in numbers with him. You've got an extra oxygen set up there, George Lowe's, and Anullu can use that."

"Yes, I've got George's mask for Anullu."

"Good. Well, good-bye, Wilf, and good luck. We'll be watching you."

"Good-bye, John. Have a good trip down."

That evening I finished my diary:

Very cold as sun went down, and glad to climb with frozen fingers into sleeping-bag. Strange feeling looking up at Lhotse. Is it friendly or sinister? Whichever it is, it's *enormous*. Feel a little lonely and appalled.

2

I arose at 6:30. The great Face, the two swinging slopes of ice enclosing that cut-about line of outcrop, still looked

impassably huge. Away against the blue the Geneva Spur
jutted beside the grey-black cone of Everest, a triangle whose
right side supported a snow banner streaming far out of
sight. As so often happened, I was stamping to be off by
eight; only to find the Sherpas settling down to an endless
enjoyment of their huge *tsampa* cakes. I continued to stamp,
meditating the virtues of patience. It was 8:35 before we
started up the trail, powdered, but not excessively, by a small
fall yesterday.

We were on three ropes, I leading the first and wearing
my oxygen. A word or two about this vital feature of "The
Plan." No oxygen could be spared for the work of preparing
the Face; but Charles Wylie and myself leading parties up it
would use oxygen, for it was vital that the loads arrive, and
leading Sherpas can be an exhausting job. Thus I would
now benefit in my double role of pioneer and carry-leader.
For all except the two assault or summit pairs, the Open-
Circuit apparatus consisted of the portly black cylinder supplied by the R.A.F. and weighing 21 lb., which needed to
be pushed and fiddled into its holder in the very light
aluminium carrying frame. The assault sets consisted of two
or even three light-alloy cylinders weighing 11 lb. each,
having the advantage that they could be discarded one by
one after use. We had all practised oxygen on the acclimatisation period. The awkwardness of the set, on a morning like
this, lay in the bitingly cold business of screwing up connecting valves; then the swing on to the back, mask on, and
the connection of face-tube with the tube from the set. When
you were with another sahib, each fixed the other's, switched
on the oxygen and watched the dial for the pressure. But
with Sherpas this was impossible, because I did not trust
them to read the figures and could not read them myself
with the apparatus on. Finally there was the problem of
resting. The set could remain on your back while you rested
on some fairly level space; but if you had nobody who could
switch off for you, it was impossible either to switch off
yourself or, however elastic you might be, to read the dial
just over your right shoulder without removing the whole
thing. And that meant unhitching, swinging the weight,

made even more heavy by a rucksack on top, off the shoulders, at the risk of following it down whichever steep bit of mountainside you happened to be climbing. Having, at great cost to breath and temper, at last got it off, you must rest it somewhere. If you set it upright, its top-heaviness made a catastrophic crash probable. If you laid it horizontally, it was with the uneasy feeling that the delicate machinery must be catching on every rock splinter.

Experts may tell me that I am making absurdly heavy weather. But to one who is unscientific enough for the whole thing to be clearly magic, every scrape or slither spells possible disaster to the magic box. However, when all is said, and when it is agreed that our apparatus will look prehistorically clumsy in twenty years' time, the result was a plain miracle. When, after all the struggles, the switch was at last turned on, a taste or breath of metallic new life seemed to slip through mouth to lungs, mocking every disadvantage and making life seem good once again.

On the long upward traverse below VI the weight above the shoulders seemed to be trying to swing me at every step down in to the Cwm. New snow had blown over all the tracks. Sometimes I stopped to chip again, more often the angle was just easy enough to take a cramponed foot, if only there were a well-balanced body above it. That proposition the oxygen cylinder and rucksack disputed; the look down at the Cwm beyond the green bulge was alarming. A heave, with right hand on fixed rope, a few steps, then a halt. Below me the Sherpas doubled up and gasped, making me feel uncomfortably luxurious in my oxygen. In an hour and three-quarters we had reached Camp VI.

We spent over an hour at the bare site. In the first place the Sherpas were appalled at the extra load of six Dræger cylinders and other oddments that they were expected to take on. In the carefully calculated list of loads we had not, I suspect, allowed for the full extra weight of Li-Los, sleeping-bags and personal gear, which must have made up 20 lb. Moreover, I had said to Anullu, my sirdar, that we would be travelling light to VI and there picking up further stores. But the Sherpas, living in a child-like present, saw only that they were lightly laden. Therefore there was room for the odd extra comfort. I had been anxious on the Face, seeing how bulky their loads appeared to be already. Now I could positively feel the uneasiness with which they were regarding new burdens. They sat down, shifted, felt the cylinders, and sat again, entangling the rope more hopelessly with each movement.

The second reason for our long halt was the oxygen supply. I was astounded to find that in this brief ascent my oxygen pressure had sunk from 2,700 to 1,000 p.s.i. A leak. I seemed to hear a faint sizzle from the big nuts at the oxygen bottle's neck. But alas, I had no spanner large enough to tighten these. There were, however, two bottles up here in the snow, both, as I hoped, full. Unfortunately with these black R.A.F. cylinders there was no way of telling the oxygen pressure but by fitting and connecting them, at least none simple enough for me. Both cylinders I fitted slowly, cumbrously, spannered one by one into position. Neither was very much better than my own. There was nothing for it but to try what I might find at VII, which on two litres a minute with my present cylinder I ought to reach. But it was a melancholy little party which finally disentangled itself from the ropes.

I always found climbing with Sherpas three times more tiring than with sahibs. As I dragged along I was heartily envying those lucky ones like Tom Bourdillon, who from the nature of their jobs had less to do with bear-leading. At the time I had no pity for what others might miss. And now the moral tug on the rope was so strong that it almost pulled me from my steps; a dead weight of doubt, dismay and reluctance which the Sherpas themselves could never have explained, had they been blessed suddenly with the gift of tongues. We climbed very slowly; the halts were very frequent. "*Aram* (rest), sahib," and the whole caravan would plump panting down in the snow. I found the whole business so much more tiring than the ascent with George without oxygen, that I risked all and increased my flow rate to four litres a minute.

Just below the final serac we met George's party of three

descending. Terrible conditions these last two days on the upper part had prevented further advance, and George, after nine full days on the Face, was overdue for a rest. The only solution was Mike's "Go down lower," and down they were going. They warned me that frostbite had affected Mike's hands and George's feet; also, a far more grave problem at the moment, of the shortage of kerosene at VII. Now kerosene was one of the loads I had not thought to take on from VI, believing it to be sufficient above. "You'll have to take some out of the South Col cookers," George said, but in an unconvincing voice. I knew that these South Col tins were sacred. I looked at the dragging ropes of Sherpas, among whom there was only one as untired as ever. Ang Norbu had done fine work for the Swiss last year, but in the autumn had been operated on, in the neck, by Dr. Chevalley, and might not go high. He was a local man, and his sister, the elder "Auntie," was our best carrier. Both equally square and solid, undemonstrative and utterly dependable. I had noted him already.

"Ang Norbu and Ang Dawa II, you will go down to Camp VI. Bring up the kerosene." (This was a second Ang Dawa.)

Ang Norbu was ready in a moment, Ang Dawa had no choice but to follow his example. I changed the ropes round, to give them a length to themselves. They started bravely down, with George's party.

"See you soon at Lobuje," Mike called back.

We toiled on, slower than ever. The traverse across the pinnacle face upset the balance of heavy loads. A few steps and a halt, bodies doubled up. Fortunately the steps were now bigger, but the fixed rope they found no help at all. For myself, I was at last fully enjoying the oxygen, taking proper belays, looking at my watch, even exhorting the troops, forgetful that I must sound to them like a muffled elephant. It was 1:45 before we reached camp. There remained still the extra Meade and the pyramid tent to pitch, a shuffled, jumbling job, thankfully disposed of by all, so that all could flop exhausted inside. To make tea I poured kerosene out of one of the sacred South Col cookers, and got one Primus going. In my own tent I found the remains of a blessed thermos of lemonade. But alas, as the tent was now end-on with another Meade occupied by Sherpas, and therefore very public, I had to share it. The higher one goes, the lower drops the moral tone of thought and inclination. It was drink that revived us. Kancha told me that they were all exhausted from lack of food, since they had not eaten between 8:00 A.M. and 3:00 P.M. But considering their performance of the day after tomorrow, I believe food shortage was not to blame. The cause was partly thirst and heat, partly the unexpectedly heavy loads; 50 lb. for the first time to 24,000 feet.

Myself I ate, very slowly and with immense pleasure, a whole tin of sardines which somebody had carelessly left in a side-pocket of the tent. To dry lips and empty stomach it seemed the best thing of the expedition, and I was delighted that there were not enough to share with the Sherpas. I was doing everything very slowly. That tin must have taken twenty minutes. How right George had been about the dilemma up here! The more work you do, the more food you need. The more you eat, the more you want. A last lick of the lips. Then I climbed out into the sunshine. The indomitables were labouring up the last slope, our kerosene tied to their backs. Otherwise there were no signs of life, all were prostrate inside tents. I went plodding round, stooping to pull back flaps. *"Thik hai?"* (All right?), *"Bahut bimar sahib!"* (Very ill). I distributed all the helpful-looking pills that I had. Then I asked Anullu to come out.

Anullu was the younger brother of Da Tensing. Returning last year from the Cho Oyu expedition to Darjeeling, he had cut off his Sherpa pigtail and become the sophisticated man about town. He must have shared the cigarette record with Ang Nyima, and yet these were probably our best two Sherpas. There was about the amount that he smoked and drank, as well as the general reserve of the puckered eyes, a veneer of Westernism contrasting strongly with his rugged brother. At the same time there was also in the smooth round face, when it smiled, something that gave confidence; he knew his job and he was fit, though he too had carried his load today. I explained what that job would be, for tomorrow. We must sort the stores, what was to go up, and I must fit Anullu's oxygen set together. He tried George's mask, it was well enough. He, wearing oxygen, must lead one party, I the other. We had six Sherpas intended for the Col, specially selected by Charles Wylie. But because of our weight of loads all must go up who could. I had no illusions about the difficulties of combining the two operations of store-lifting and route-making. If none could go, Anullu and I must concentrate on that second job, if only the cylinders would work.

I turned to the cylinders. Twenty-pounder upon twenty-pounder I wriggled in, connected, tried. Not one but seemed to leak, from the big nut at the neck of the bottle. What to do? I had the whole tent outside in a search for a large spanner. In despair, at the appointed hour, I advanced upon the wireless. A few mundane messages. Then: "I've turned all the cylinders on and they all seem to leak." Alas, it was a capricious creature, our wireless. At this critical point a "break in transmission" caused a sleepless night for Tom Bourdillon, down at IV. The mechanic in him had spotted that I omitted to say that I turned them *off*. Knowing me to be far from mechanically inclined, he suspected at once that I had failed to do that operation. I was told later that John spent the rest of the evening hopping around with the wireless set. "Come out from behind that serac, Wilf!"—and doubtless stronger expressions such as my informant was too kind to repeat. Fortunately they were not justified.

Oblivious of the panic I was causing, I meanwhile was tucking into a supper of soup, lemonade in quantity, biscuits, cheese, chocolate and condensed milk, which we either sucked from the tube or spread like jam on Ryvita. An immaculate Anullu did the cooking, squatted over the Primus next door and seeming to know exactly where everything was. At sundown it became very cold. I had been writing my diary, poetry even, but despite mittens this became impossible. I spent too much time rubbing hands inside the bag to allow any for thought. By eight I was climbing out for the last time, into the moonlight and merciless stars. Everest was still and huge, peaceful and yet mocking "our miserable tents." Only over the South Col a faint boom announced wind. I felt very much alone, oppressed by the impossibility of that star-crowned black pyramid.

3

Compelled to rise at 5:00 A.M. for a journey to the distant lavatory, which meant tottering leftward beyond the curve of our sentinel serac, I was astonished at the wild golden light already splashing upon Pumori and the peaks down the valley; so astonished that even in my dazed state of sleep I felt a longing to perpetuate this, and tottered back to pull out my camera. The painful stoop, the fumble and search, and the heave back to the upright position, show how strong the urge must have been. I took a photograph which appears on Plate 38(a). I had told Anullu that we would not start too early, for fear of frostbite; therefore I now snuggled back with a good conscience.

Tea appeared from the cook's clockwork hands at 6:30. Then another lie, in that suspense which precedes the tearing of a man from peaceful horizontal ease to the painful gasps of the vertical. I must kneel, must pull off the sleeping-bag, must wriggle lumpishly on all fours into the cold air. The eye wandered round the tent roof, seized every excuse, a scrap of paper to be read, a film to be looked at or even the stitching of the tent; anything to delay the moment! It was long before I was out, feet clumsy in the big boots whose laces seemed to catch at every step. The time was 7:45. One or two Primuses were going, but there were no other signs of life, except a number of groans and Pasang quietly being sick. Everything was *not* well, and I pushed in more medicine.

At eight Anullu called across. He had produced miraculous porridge, putting the oats of several Assault Rations together. That breakfast made a great difference later, for the most lively deed is prosaically founded on food. Then more uncertainty. Anullu shrugged his shoulders. Groans resounded from the tents. Some had dragged themselves out; one or two were looking at the loads with an eye which could only be called "wan." I asked who was well enough to come on up, and a stocky figure came forward. *"Jaega* sahib" (I'll go). It was Ang Norbu. But who would go with him? For it was impossible that Ang Norbu, without oxygen, should attach himself to our rope. "Ang Dawa *hai* sahib," he said. I was delighted. Two loads at least would go up. But as I was preparing them, Ang Dawa came up, coughing badly. He could not come after all. It was a sad moment. The alternative plan must take the field. The two sickest Sherpas must go down with a note for John, the rest would wait and acclimatise that day, adding their strength in numbers to Charles's party the next. I felt sorry for Ang Norbu after his gallant offer, and he looked disappointed. It was after 9:30 before all these discussions had finished; before Anullu and I, cramponed and using oxygen at the low flow-rate of two litres a minute, stepped out towards the first snow bridge.

The couloir passed, I led at a not too high speed over the first short traverse, which had packed down a lot since the 17th. In three-quarters of an hour, breathing that invigorating flow, we had reached our highest point of that day. Just beyond it we rested, swinging the heavy cylinders gently off our backs, careful not to capsize after them. Mask off, set balanced against a slope. Then rest, that absurd peacefulness of another world. In movement, in camp, the triviality of day to day is heightened by the extra exertion of each thought and twist. It is the succession of life's burdens magnified through a distorting mirror. But rest is different. All that lurked in our hinterland now comes forward. The mind is at ease, that is to say willing to receive and register. At the time it may not even appear to register, but remains like a painting that waits for the overlying daub of tiredness, some day, to be removed. And then, perhaps, in an evening of future years, the picture will show more clear than it ever showed through the mists of reality.

After rest we went on. Yes, the route did still keep to the left, as an obvious fixed rope showed, but the start looked steep. Not knowing we made for this rope's bottom, and were soon floundering in fathomless snow. We should have joined the rope (left by George's party) some way up, from the right. A little farther on a great half-moon of wall confronted us. Right or left? Right, Anullu suggested knowingly, and we started over to where a wide slant of snow seemed to lead back and to above us, over the wall's top, between this and the next wall. The slant was of nastily hard snow. I chipped and chipped. But no, the snow was going to peter out on ice. There was nothing for it but to come down and not waste time. I was glad that there were no Sherpas being held up behind us. The less promising-looking line to the left did lead, after a minor steep wall, on to easier, leftward-slanting slopes. I noted an aluminium piton with a great coil of thick rope. It appeared later that this was the highest point reached by George's party, and that Da Tensing had left the rope.

We were keeping towards the left-hand side of our Lhotse glacier, but with no prospect of getting off it, though sometimes temptation beckoned on the shining, straight slopes that separated us from the great Spur. A zigzag course in heavy snow now took us to the bottom of another rope, left by the Swiss. None of these ropes did we dare to use, not knowing how the attachment had weathered. I cramponed up beside it to a small platform, really the beginning of a long ledge running to the right across the face. Along the line of flat we edged, painfully aware of the dangling temptation of rope above us, and of the view down the overhang that seemed to push us out and away; and below, almost between the legs, the toy tents of V dotting the plain. It looked as if the structure of the wall was altering rapidly; now a jump would land us among our friends 3,000 feet below. (Plate 38(c).)

It was well that we had not trusted the rope. This particular one hung down, I have said, temptingly. We found on arrival that it dangled from a piton stuck in a little plateau; and the piton, more than half out, waited precariously on another pull, before it joined the ice-fragments capering down towards V. At the time I was too occupied with other things, with mask and movement forward, to be thankful. First, the way. The plateau top was really the top of a narrowing slice, bounded by space on the side overlooking the

Cwm, by a crevasse on the mountain side. Let's try again, in the hope of a bridge. Some way along the crevasse deepened, widened; now I must return. There was no choice but to the right, to regain the parent mountain wall beyond our slice by a step on to narrow uprights of ice-sliver. A few more steps led us finally beyond the line of crescent walls, typical feature of this Lhotse Face of ours. Looking up I could see ever-subsiding hummocks; and then, a few hundred feet beyond again, the ugly black towers of Lhotse rising from polished snow. It looked as if we were up.

I was stepping along, feeling how alert, how full of life I was with the oxygen, now the depressing intricacies of putting on and taking off were over. How different I should have felt without it! Quite suddenly I was looking down one of the most impressive crevasses I have seen, a gash in the soft snow cheek up which we were striding. But it was still a crevasse, and we were accustomed to crevasses. One walked some yards right or left, and there would be a snow bridge. This time therefore we walked left. No bridge. Right then; but there was no bridge here either. The thing clearly crossed the whole snow face. I looked at Anullu, and Anullu, behind his mask, looked back at me. He was pointing. Where he pointed, the crevasse, some eight feet wide, had narrowed to perhaps three. The cause of narrowing was the two lips, which had pushed forward as if to kiss over the bottle-green depths below. The lips were composed, apparently, of unsupported snow, and seemed to suspend themselves above this "pleasure-dome of ice," into whose cool chasms, widening to utter blackness, it would at other times have been a delight to peer. I walked right once more, then left. Nothing. I signed to Anullu that he should drive his axe well in and be ready for me. Then I advanced to the first unsupported ledge. I stood upon this first ledge and prodded. Anullu would have held me, had one ledge given way, but he could not have pulled me up. As the walls of the crevasse were undercut to widen the gap, I would have been held dangling and could not have helped myself out. It would be silly to face such a problem in the Alps without a party of three. But I cannot remember more than a passing qualm. Altitude, even through oxygen, dulled fears as well as hopes. One thing at a time. Everest must be climbed. Therefore this step must be passed. I prodded my ice-axe across at the other ledge, but I could not quite reach deep enough to tell. I took the quick stride and jump, trying not to look down, plunged the axe hard in and gasped. The lip was firm. This time the Lhotse Face really was climbed.

Only lying in my sleeping-bag that night did I realise the implications of one step.

4

Perhaps a hundred yards up, one last small cleft barred our path, but this time a bridge offered itself at once. On the almost level ground beyond we had our first proper halt. I switched off Anullu's apparatus, swung my own clumsily off and switched that, too. I dangled my mask from the ice-axe head to dry, and rejoiced in fresh air on the face. We sat and ate a little, but we needed drink most of all. Anullu had a specially large and welcome water-bottle filled with lemonade. He himself seemed to prefer smoking to eating, and had reeled off two cigarettes by the time I had finished three biscuits and some cheese. We were now at the apex, as it were, of the Lhotse Glacier; nothing barred us from the smooth sweep of slope that bounded the Spur, now seen as a fine jutting eminence, bald-topped and dropping steeply towards the Cwm in an edge of mixed rock and snow. This half-obscured the great rocky cone of Everest, distinguished by the snowdrift racing from it. We had halted at 12:15. At 12:50 we set off again, after the delays of putting on and adjusting sets.

I put Anullu in the lead. A little below our level, at a rock ribbon crossing the face toward the Spur, one Swiss rope could be seen dangling disconsolately. Too low, I thought. Anullu set off at what seemed the pace of a fast Swiss guide (though it can have been no more than half that); a performance more remarkable, since there was still an ankle-deep surface layer. Sometimes drifts had crusted over with wind, and here steps must be cut, to my secret inward relief. Just time to bend and gasp. The word "traverse" is a misnomer; this traverse must rise diagonally across the slope. At last, after an hour's movement upward, we had reached the wide gully almost in the shadow of the Spur, where some slight rock intrusions gave a relief; downward-sloping, half-buried little shelves. It was the first step on rock since Base Camp; a welcome change, though a scrapy business in crampons.

How were we to get on to the Spur? I had been told, keep to the right and cross it at its top, whence a 600-foot drop to the Col. But look, there was a snow gangway slanting gently up under a rock band on to the very crest. If one could reach that, it might be possible to skirt round to the Col without having to descend on to it. We made for the gangway. It was of steeper snow than it looked, and hard. Pecks with the axe, then a pause. Strange how breathless I could feel, even on four litres a minute. Anticipation was breathless too as the crest drew near, backed by the shadow of Everest's last pyramid, now a floating right-handed curve from which snow mist blew. I was leading again, and hacked the last steps on to the crest. Still no view, and no easy traverse; we must go on up to the widening top. First boulders, up which we stumbled easily, then more snow, the broad forehead of the Geneva Spur, and then suddenly nothing was immediately above us any more. We were on a summit, overlooked in this whole scene only by Lhotse and Everest. And this was the scene long dreamed, long hoped.

To the right and above, the crenellations of Lhotse cut a blue sky fringed with snow cloudlets. To the left, snow mist still held Everest mysteriously. But the eye wandered hungry and fascinated over the plateau between; a space of boulders and bare ice perhaps four hundred yards square, absurdly solid and comfortable at first glance in contrast with the sweeping ridges around, or the blank mist that masked the Tibetan hills beyond. But across it a noisy little wind moaned its warning that the South Col, goal of so many days' ambition, was not comfortable at all. And in among the glinting ice and dirty grey boulders there lay some yellow tatters— all that remained of the Swiss expeditions of last year.

We were soon descending the drop to the plateau, only some 200 feet down after all. But first I took out the 500-foot length of nylon line from my sack and started laying it down, from a piton driven in. This was to be a moral lifeline for weary Sherpas returning from the long carry. As we approached, I remember very clearly my wonderment at being here, at walking so easily and comfortably down to this place which held the Swiss prisoners for three days in the spring, which in the autumn they had described as "having the smell of death about it." To me, with one Sherpa and an oxygen mask in a stiff breeze, it bore a strong resemblance to parts of Scafell Pike in winter. A week later the tale was different. But I had no forebodings.

We crunched down to the last of the wind-crust, myself still unwinding the rope. Then the flat. The yellow rags lay in dead little heaps, or flapped forlornly from metal uprights that still stood. Round about was spread a chaos of food, kit-bags, sleeping-bags, felt boots. Whenever people talk of the "conquest" of Everest, I close my eyes and see that ghost-ridden scene. Our tents must now look like that. Meanwhile Anullu, who had enjoyed no such romantic reflections, was suddenly to be seen fastening a fine Swiss rucksack containing felt boots on to his back. "Hey, the other people will need that." But to my every suggestion he returned the laconic reply that Tenzing had told him that if he reached the Col first, he was to have the first spoil. Arguing from behind an oxygen mask is not easy. "What about your oxygen?" No, he would rather leave his oxygen. Foolishly, perhaps affected by the altitude, I failed even to realise that George might need his mask after all, and we left that too. All this, with my photographs, took some time, and the South Col is no place upon which to linger idle. I was wearing only one sweater, and no down clothing, for it had been comparatively warm on the Face. I picked up some matches, a tin of sardines and a box of Vita-Weat, a candle and cheese. I took a photograph (Plate 39(b)). Then we turned to go.

Oxygen helped me, I know, up those 200 feet to the Spur. To make sure that it worked, we tried out our handrail. On the top the wind blew less cold than on the Col, and I must tell what I was wearing: string vest, flannel shirt and thick sweater, thick pyjama trousers and wind-proof suit over all. Two pairs of gloves. Not very warm clothing for over 26,000 feet, I can hear you say, but the truth is that up to the Spur, in the noonday, it was often warm. But not always.

On the crest I stopped, amazed at the swing of the ridge of Nuptse, now below us, with its myriad ups and downs. On each side the cloud billows foamed gently, but the ridge itself, its furrowed sides and dazzling ice edge, sparkled up into a pure sky. So elating was the effect of oxygen, I even pointed out its beauties to Anullu, who doubtless thought me quite mad.

Half-way back across the traverse we halted. I swung my cylinder heavily into the snow, Anullu produced his large flask. It was drink that above all we needed, not food, and neither of us ate. I thought, "Going down I ought not to need my oxygen." I would switch off. It would now be easier, and it was an awkward job reading the pressure without a companion able to help. The perilous crevasse we jumped merrily from its upper lip. Then on, down to the intricacies. But I had been spoilt. I was not going so well. I thought, "Well, I'll put it on again, I won't be so tired and I'll drain the last drop." The heavy swing off, the switch on, the fatigue of the swing of the cylinder back. The fastening of the tubes. Then, at last, the metallic breath. But, oh dear, with oxygen on I can never keep my goggles clear. There they were, misted up again. I peered and rubbed, they were still misted. We were coming down unearthly terraces dimly seen, the circles of Dante's Purgatorio, into the declining sun. Strange shapes seemed to rise towards me. At the shaft left by George we halted to cut a length of the rope, which I took on to fix in the bottom couloir. At last we were crossing the last slope above camp, and there were confused cries from below. It was the reality of Charles's party, and they seemed even to be cheering. However I had an *idée fixe* about this bottom couloir. We were not going to hurry it. I hammered in the spike with axe-head, and knotted two lengths of rope together. Then we dangled them down the couloir and on to the bridge. We crossed the crevasse as the sun tipped Nuptse, then dragged along the flat in an ecstasy of anticipation. Before six we were drinking tea beside the very crowded tents.

11

Medical Support

May 21st—May 28th

1

The party at VII was cramped. Two of my Sherpas had gone down, but that still left six, and there were Charles's seven. Besides these, to my surprise, were the cheerful faces of Ed and Tenzing. It must have been a nasty decision for John. He did not want to exhaust the second summit pair, yet he had seen only two figures start up that morning. Something must have hitched. If the loads did not go up to time, there would be no summit pairs at all. Therefore he had risked much, in the hope that Tenzing's prestige and the support of the two wearing oxygen would make assurance doubly sure tomorrow.

Camp VII therefore was crowded. It was cold now with sundown, and after the tea I nestled in alongside Charles, careless of where or how my belongings lay, in a mood of divine elation bred prosaically of oxygen. The Open-Circuit, as against the Closed, left this feeling of *bien-être* for several hours after it had been taken off. My job was done; there was nothing left but to talk and talk, in the happy knowledge that others would be working tomorrow. To this Charles must listen, for we shared the tent and he is a patient person. Retrospective qualms at the rickety piton and the step over the crevasse vied with fairer pictures of the day, but all, at this stage, very subjective. The mountain was nothing to me just now, my own sensations and satisfactions were a great deal. The misty personality with which Everest had been invested before I ever saw it, which had dominated the acclimatisation periods, now faded into the rock and snow, cliffs and chasms, which make up any mountain and are any mountaineer's meat. Just at the moment Everest was

◄ *Ang Temba was incapable of movement.*

199

a job of work which we were successfully doing. I recalled the immensity of the Col's prospect, the desolation lapping the tatters of yellow tents, and the mystery that was still the final pyramid beyond. But chiefly I recalled our movements. Returning to earth, I promised to draw a diagram of our route in the morning, and meanwhile explained some of its details. Then we supped from Tenzing's cooking, rather meagrely. The most substantial items were the tin of sardines and the Vita-Weat that I had brought down. I lit a cigarette from a box of matches picked up on the Col.

Soon after we had settled down, lights out in the two end-on tents, the wind rose. Again it was hurrying with a low roar across the slopes, again the fabric strained and the poles creaked. But the tents took it magnificently, and for the rest, who cared? In the intoxication of oxygen I lay happily think-ing, thinking, thinking round the day. The South Col—and hazard had brought me the first to it. It should have been George Lowe, of course; he deserved specially to see his work on the Face completed. But altitude abets selfishness, and I experienced only happiness that I had been allowed to tread this new ground, to look down first on that pitiful wreck of man's leavings. At last I had dozed off, and dreamed no more.

I woke luxuriously to the sound of bustle around. This time Tenzing was determined that all should go up; with the light cooking had started, and very soon tea appeared. Into this some mixed Grape-Nuts, and that was all that the Sher-pas had, with occasional biscuits, the whole day. It was here that Charles Wylie ate his Grape-Nuts off an oxygen spanner.

However often the act had been repeated, it was an effort once more to sit up, wriggle hips out of the bag, twist round and at the risk of knocking everything over, climb on hands and knees into the frost-laden wind, take a pencil and try with numb fingers to take note of the stores going up. By the time I arrived this morning, most were already packed; I must go to the back of each Sherpa, pull at the covering cloth to see how many cylinders he had, or what was in the boxes. At 8:40, in very good time, they were off, and I retired. An-ullu produced a plate of porridge, which he must have been hiding from the others up some conjuror's sleeve. Then we did some tidying, very slowly, and I tried to wash out sauce-pans caked with yesterday's *tsampa* as with glutinous mud. Of all jobs at a high camp washing-up is the bleakest, and for the first time I noticed that boiling water up here is not really hot. At 10:20 we ourselves set off; pausing as we rounded the serac before the beauty of it. That maiden courted by princes, Pumori, had once again changed her adornment and was a pure, straight pyramid flaunting a black shawl of cloud against her suitors. Suddenly a beam of golden light from above pierced the black to tip her cone.

We reached V in an hour, IV in a further half-hour. The reception was embarrassing: cameras clicked, hands were shaken, an infinity of interested questions asked. Heaven knew if the answers were right. Then lunch, and all returned to the binoculars. The seventeen small figures were at last, with hour-hand slowness, drawing near the top of the Spur, but one had stopped. At last, at last the others reached its skyline, led by two whom we took to be Ed and Tenzing. Then a considerable pause. But look! Six figures only reap-peared, coming down. Another ten minutes, and still only six figures. Had some of the Sherpas failed to make the slope above the Col on the return? Had Ed and Tenzing decided to stay with a support party? It was a long time before all appeared, before John sighed in audible relief, and we settled down to watch the parties divide. One group of four spent a long time resting on the rocks, while the first party was far ahead. By 5:30 it was seen well below VII, the others strung out well above. The sky darkened to purple, the golden glow upon the slopes dimmed to silver. A long time ago we had seen off the supporting party for the first assault, John and the two Sherpas, Balu and Da Namgyal. We had waved good-bye to Charles Evans and Tom Bourdillon, the first assault pair itself, enabled because of this great carry to set off into action. We had joked in awestruck terms at the 36 lb. Closed-Circuit set which they were using, at the items of personal gear they had piled on top to "make up the weight." Now, at supper, speculation ran on whether the returning parties had met John at V.

"Hello, you folks."

It was Ed, slipping and stumbling on the big tent floor. Off with the gear, and greetings to a tired, brightly cheerful party: Ed and Tenzing, Dawa Thondup the veteran, Pasang Phutar, Gompu and Ang Norbu. With the others, more tired, Charles had stayed at VII: with Topkie, Ang Namgyal, Gyaljen, Pasang Dawa, Ang Dorji, the sixteen-year-old Ang Tsering, Phu Dorji, Ang Dawa II and Kancha, who had just failed to make the Spur. At the time when Kancha failed, Charles's own oxygen was failing. Over the last stretch he had to carry a 20-lb. cylinder without it. But because of this feat, because Charles had tended these men and driven them on by his own example, we had thirteen good loads planted on the Col. Already the first assault was going forward.

2

It was pleasant to climb out at eight on the 23rd and know that for today there was nothing urgent to do. Yet when I looked up and saw John's trio setting out for the Face, a demon of suppressed envy pricked me, now that my own job was done. It only remained for me to carry the tidings, good, bad or indifferent, down to James Morris at Base. It would be nice to go up again . . . but perhaps after all not yet. First breakfast, and I slopped over to the big tent in the high-altitude boots that we used for slippers as well, pulling on down coat (used as pillow) over my day-and-night costume. This latter was always the same theme with variations: string vest, thick flannel shirt, thick pyjama trousers under wind-proof trousers, with sweaters and down suit added or subtracted according to the time of day.

At 11:30 Charles Wylie and the other Sherpas arrived down, tired yet in good heart. George Lowe was busy with the problem of a second carry, for on my answers of yesterday it had appeared that at least five more loads must go up, especially if the climbers were not to carry the heavy burdens of Charles and Tom. Already Da Tensing and Changjiu, a local man, had gone up at five this morning. By 2:00 P.M., to our amazement, they were back from VII, putting the sahibs with their oxygen to shame. It was an astonishing feat, if not newspaper news. They had eased the second carry, but when should that go, and the second assault? John's original plan had been for a gap of only twenty-four hours between the two. But Ed, spending the day in the "Everest Position," admitted that he could do with more rest. Also, twenty-four hours' interval would have given very little time for the South Col Sherpas to recover wind. But after two days, Tenzing said, they would certainly come.

At 4:30, after tea, I went up alone to V, to collect belongings and to check an oxygen point for George Lowe. It was my first experience quite alone on the mountain, and I looked forward to it. To be sometimes alone is to me almost a physical necessity, for then the imagined shapes of the hills seem to speak, as they cannot do when another person, however sympathetic, is present to blur the contact. Solitude enlarges the nervous personality, heightens perceptiveness. Terrors are then more acute, so also is the sensation of being a part with hills, and through them with all natural forms.

This time there were no physical terrors. The route was plain, the crevasses obvious. Twice I felt breathless and stopped, partly to admire once more the silver blades of ice riveted in the bronze-work of Nuptse's rock. When I reached the camp site I looked at my watch; only forty-seven and a half minutes, more than ten minutes less than last time. Perhaps that meant it was good to stop and admire the view when you felt like it.

I settled the oxygen point and turned downward. One object of the excursion was to visit the grave of Mingma Dorji, the fine Sherpa killed with the Swiss last autumn and buried on the moraine to the right as I descended. I turned off and found it easily, a monument of stones a man's length and raised to four feet from the ground. One stone splinter stood upright. I have no hopes or anxieties about the fate of my body after death, but I confessed to myself at Mingma's monument that the thought pleased me of resting here, where the eye passes in an instant from the little stone erection, up the 8,000-foot precipice of Everest to its summit.

Returning to the track I experienced that inexplicable happiness which mountain sunset can give. "Homely" is the wrong adjective to use in such awesome surroundings, yet the human animal does feel himself for a moment at home in that awesomeness. A cloud down the valley pinioned the sun and masked the level snow in blank and appalling shadow. Yet somehow the little cliff of a comical side glacier had caught the straying light and refused to give it up. For a time I was part of the scene, like Leslie Stephen an "animated top of the mountain." But like him, I must return. "One is still of the earth, earthy; for freezing toes and snow-parched noses are lively reminders that one has not become an immortal."

After supper, companionable discussion usually filled the evening until bed-time. That night we reflected how high Camp II had seemed in April, tucked "right up" in a fold in the icefall. And Camp III had been a positive mountain top, at which it was dangerous to stop too long for fear of loss of appetite and sleep. Now, Camp IV itself seemed homely as Base; we ate like giants and slept like logs. The Sherpas had insisted on abandoning II altogether, preferring to do the carry to III in one.

Much of the morning of the 24th, in bright sun, I spent writing a report to send down to James at Base. It was strange how long such things took, although I felt very efficient at the time. Charles Wylie went off to write air-letter cards. By lunchtime he had done just three. From time to time I looked up at the wall. John's party, John and the two Sherpas, set out from VII at 9:45. Tom and Charles were on a separate rope. They were going very slowly, it must be the loads. The second party, with George Lowe taking up five Sherpas, would be strong enough to carry sahibs' personal kit and save the summit pair. In the afternoon all was bustle and packing for this second party. Luxury foods, up to two pounds, were being chosen by Ed. Crampon straps were being adjusted for the Sherpas, Charles Wylie was giving final instructions. Into the midst a sturdy new figure suddenly made irruption, carrying a large load: Mike Westmacott with Griff Pugh's sack, then shortly after, Griff himself. Mike was much better; he had already devoted himself to a

THE LHOTSE FACE – The Sherpas who came up on the 20th. Standing: Ang Tsering, Ang Norbu, Kancha, Angtharkay, Ang Dawa II. Squatting: Anullu, Phu Dorji, Pasang. (With Noyce.) At Camp IV.

Anullu puts on high-altitude boots at IV. General purpose boots beside.

THE LHOTSE FACE – The South Summit and Snow plume, showing the South East Ridge running down to the South Col (right). Geneva Spur on the extreme right.

E

CHO OYU   WEST RONGBUK
PUMORI   GLACIER
(below)

THE LHOTSE FACE – Looking down Cwm from the Lhotse Face; Cho Oyu in distance
(about 20 miles away), above Pumori (in cloud).

The task before us, from Camp VI to the Summit.

Everest from the air, from the West.

THE LHOTSE FACE – May 21st. Sunrise from Camp VII. Taken by the author at 5 a.m. before the climb to the South Col. Cho Oyu (centre) and Gyachung Kang.

"Have you tightened those cylinders?" Tom Bourdillon at the wireless.

May 21st. Anullu near the top of Lho Glacier.

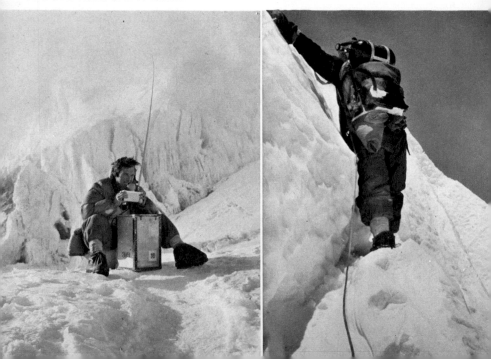

May 21st. Anullu near crest of Geneva Spur. South Summit of Everest behind.

THE SOUTH COL – First view of the South Col—afternoon of May 21st. Remains of Swiss tents. Anullu on right.

The author with Anullu, back at Camp IV.

THE LHOTSE FACE – May 22nd. Wylie's party setting out from VII. Fixed rope on snow bridge visible bottom right— scene of Ang Temba's fall. "Giant's Nose" directly above. Couloir out of sight.

vital and strenuous work, keeping the icefall clear. Together we said good-bye to Ed and Tenzing with their supporters. Greg took Pemba, Ang Nyima and Ang Temba, George Lowe the five Sherpas for the South Col.

The reader will here ask: "What of Everest all this time? What of the hugeness dominating everything which you promised to picture in your introduction?" I have said that for me, and I think for most of us, Everest as a personality had given place to Everest as a thing, upon which we as persons operated. We were too close. Even so the Lilliputians must have recognised Gulliver much better from afar than when they stood upon his chest. Incapable, moreover, at that height, of interest in much more than one thing at a time, we were too concerned with our own movements and sufferings, our camps and co-ordination, to think, except at rare moments, of the mountain creature beyond.

Thus my diary: "May 25th. Nose a little less blocked and unpleasant last night. A very clear day, wind seems to have dropped. Is this the summit day? They could scarce have a better. Climbing out, just caught a big avalanche from West Shoulder cliffs. It sliced off like a great piece of cake, disappeared round rock edge, reappeared as smoke which spread across the whole Cwm." In fact, of course, it was not a summit day. The party had, the afternoon before, pitched the South Col camp with terrible difficulty. They were very tired. Two tents which should have taken five minutes needed, in the wind reigning, an hour and a half. Balu had given up, his main use being to act as ballast, so that the pyramid was not blown away while the others tried to pitch it. It was an exhausting job after the exhausting climb, perhaps the nastiest experience of the whole expedition. No wonder they lay low on the 25th.

On the 24th Mike Ward had first murmured to me the magic scientific words "alveolar test." This medical rite appeared to involve taking samples of the air at the bottom of human lungs by getting the patient to breathe out suddenly into glass tubes, which would then be sealed off. Mike did not know if these had been successfully taken as high as

24,000 feet. Would somebody come up and try with him? It was a tempting offer, but what of the third attempt, supposing it were needed? I was concerned with the organisation of this, though at present nobody seemed to have the energy to think much about it. There was Griff, being allowed to experiment away with a precious oxygen cylinder which we might need for that third attempt. It was absurd, but equally difficult to see immediately why he should not, for it all seemed very remote. I would probably keep my strength better, in case the attempt were needed, down here, since Griff congratulated us on being just below the height at which high-altitude deterioration sets in. And yet—what could I do here? I had with great labour written an article which I had not the mental energy to copy out.[1] I liked climbing with Mike. Why not go up?

3

We planned to be off early, and rose at 5:15 on the 26th. But we did not step out till 7:15, with a very sluggish Pasang Dawa, commissioned to carry our gear. At V, reached in an hour, Mike was of opinion that I was leading too fast for the Sherpa. There was no alternative but to invite him to take over. It was a wily manœuvre, for, as Mike said later, he liked leading because it has the advantage that one sets one's own pace. But I was glad to find, this third time up, that I was on top of myself and better acclimatised. I must say he set a very good pace. Twenty steps and a pause; but this time with greater zeal to go on afterwards. At VII, to our surprise, we saw a movement outside a tent. We were greeted by Changjiu, the local Sherpa who had graded from *dak walla* (postman) because of his extraordinary speed, but who had not acclimatised to this height. George Lowe had left him behind. He accompanied Pasang Dawa down, back to Advance Base, while we settled in to have a little sleep. The air of VII always had this effect on most of us, I think.

We had arrived at 12:30. In the early afternoon we

---

[1] It later appeared in the *Climbers' Club Journal*, 1954.

wakened to the sound of voices coming along from the bridge; cheery voices, soon followed by a rope of three striding jauntily along the level: Dawa Thondup again, Ang Norbu and Topkie. All had that day done their second carry to the Col. Though in his late forties, Dawa Thondup, for some time past quite speechless from a throat infection, was as cheerful as if he were walking along the Namche highway. Ang Norbu remained his placid, comforting self; Topkie, a tubby little person, smiled shyly but with obvious excitement. Their account was confused, but it seemed that Tom and Charles might have reached the top, and that there were others coming down today. We sent them on back to IV.

Towards five we saw the next party descending, very slowly and with halts, across the slopes above the big crevasse. From a good stack of snow blocks outside the tent we made tea, and went out to greet them. Da Namgyal, thin and terribly tired, was being shepherded by the brothers Anullu and Da Tensing, together with Balu, who had failed at the Col. It was only now that I thought, how fortunate that medicine has brought us here! We ought not to have needed that excuse to come up in support. Mike examined them. Da Namgyal was suffering utter weariness, together with a blister of frostbite the size of a penny on the little finger, and swollen face and hands. Balu suffered a general crumpling of the man. He was no longer a big, confident creature, but tired like a little child. And he could not face his tiredness.

Meanwhile I read a note handed to me by Da Tensing.

IMMEDIATE
Wilfrid Noyce

Wilf

1. Just to tell you that Tom and Charles were seen at about 1:00 P.M. passing the South Summit en route for the *top*. Great excitement here.
2. I accompanied them with Da Namgyal to 27,500 ft and left the top camp stores, they may well be carried higher tomorrow by the second support party.
   26th May.   JOHN HUNT.

Of course our speculation was endless. The Sherpas believed that they had reached the top itself, not realising that the South Summit, seen from the Col, conceals the summit ridge. It was certain they had climbed 2,700 feet in one morning. All this while we slowly, tediously made soup, then passed the one working Primus to Anullu, who was catering for the party in the pyramid. Soon the wind cut short conversation, rising at evening to fling snow pellets at us across the silvery stretches. We lay, simply contemplating the dirty mugs, watching the light fade from the tent roof as the canvas swelled and sagged before the gusts. Of what does one think? I wondered in which of the tent pockets were the cigarettes, in which the matches; and decided that it was too much effort to explore for either. I wondered whether they were having as much or more wind on the South Col: the far boom of the "South Col Special" we could hear distinctly. I wondered too what it had been like on the Col, and tried to picture them in wind like this: dazed, muffled figures stumbling about as they struggled with the tents the day before yesterday. "The windiest spot on earth," as the Swiss thought it. How they must have tripped over the rocks, fumbled and fallen at the guys. Then there was their exploit. Tenuous threads of excitement seemed to have been spreading down all day, at the thought of what might be happening overhead. They had reached the South Summit, 28,700 feet. I could only guess the details. I did not know that John and Da Namgyal carried, in fact, 45 lb. to a point 100 feet above the tent used last year by Lambert and Tenzing (a height of 27,350 feet). They turned, very tired, and not helped by the ice which blocked their valves. Meanwhile Tom and Charles on Closed-Circuit went on to the South Summit . . . perhaps had even reached the summit.

Then I mustered mentally the jobs that could be grouped into one climb out, to save two efforts: a stumble round to the Sherpas, a last lavatory, a hacking of snow blocks for tomorrow, body unsteady in the wind, the arrangement of my sack as pillow. There remained the last breathless tussle of the sleeping-bag and the hitching of down clothing, which would try to stop the bag coming above the waist. For we wore our down clothes in bed, to save weight by having only one sleeping-bag. At last I was in. I lay, chin up, with only an occasional wriggle and puff to get more comfortable.

The night continued gusty. Only at 8:20 in the morning I climbed out, thinking that the Sherpas would have started the big cooker, but they had not. They had left it out in the snow, and it took me an hour to get it working, having had to refill it too. This last was an exasperating job always, with the morning frost shadow still on us, the breeze tickling through the trousers. Having filled it I must light it. At each move out for snow from my kneeling position I risked up-setting the tottering masses around: the top-heavy cooker itself, films, boots, packets of Knäckerbrot surmounted by tubes of gluey milk dripping at the neck, my books and diary —all resting on clothes, sleeping-bags, half-deflated Li-Los.

Mike went out to examine the Sherpas. For Da Namgyal and Balu the prescription was "Go down lower." The frost-bite would be well in a fortnight, and Da Namgyal, still very sorry for himself, looked reassured. A stiff breeze rattled on, but at long last a very slow rope of four disappeared over the edge, and we settled to work. There were only two jobs, but they took the remainder of the morning. Mike and I had attended the same preparatory school, St. Edmund's, at Hindhead, and I was obstinately determined to write a letter-card announcing that we had had the highest dinner held by associates of that school on record; even if the menu was no more than soup and Ryvita smeared with condensed milk. Our next job was the alveolar test which was the prime excuse for our being here.

From his sack Mike drew out a series of glass tubes and globules which he handled with all the reverent care of an expert in Dresden china. These were accompanied by rub-ber piping and business-like forceps. The plan appeared to be to catch the air at the bottom of the lungs unaware, so to speak. One must breathe out normally, without effort; then suddenly, with immense force, puff out down a tube. Here the forceps came in, for before the air had time to retreat, the poor thing was caught in the glass at the end of the tube, trapped and sealed off all ready to be borne back to London and analysed. I did one successful puff, Mike two. I felt that I had at last worthily served the cause of science.

At one we warmed lemonade and ate biscuits. Should we stay on? There was not much to eat up here, hardly enough for the others when they returned. We packed up slowly. It seemed harder and harder to leave, therefore we delayed the moment by wandering in turn up the serac side to view the upper slopes. Suddenly Mike gave a cry. Four small figures were descending below the Spur, very slowly and sitting down frequently. Thank Heaven, we had an excuse for staying to receive them! We unpacked. I think neither of us realised at the time (the effect of height) that had we not seen them, it would have been still more important to stay.

We sat fiddling in the tent. At what time should we get tea going? Every now and then we peeped out, straining after the sound of voices. At three I put on snow for water, but it was after four before they appeared, labouring like yesterday's party across the slope above. I left Mike at the stove and walked slowly along the level to the crevasse bridge fifty yards to the right. They were coming down the couloir, now the bulky leading figure turned towards me over the bridge. It was John. He was soon across the downward sloping bridge, and Tom followed. I was shaking hands with John. Suddenly, over his right shoulder, a blue flash streaked downward against the grey curtain of ice beyond. It was the third of the four figures, apparently taking a header straight into the crevasse that they were crossing! And indeed a header he was taking. Exhausted, Ang Temba had put his foot carelessly into a step and thrown his weight over it, stumbled and gone head over heels. Charles, last on the rope, held him. It had been the reaction of a skilful mountaineer to hold him so, and then hitch the rope round his axe. But he could do no more. Ang Temba was safe. Safe but helpless. John and Tom, the first two, looked. They were more than tired, Tom breathing heavily into the oxygen apparatus that had got him down from the Col.

I looked at the lumpy wedge of snow forming the bridge. It was broad and soft, and Ang Temba was upside down against the side of the parapet, as it were, not dangled in space. If I could scramble out beyond the others I might reach him. I crawled out past them, and I cannot at all remember whether I tied on to their rope or not. I think not. I remember only, in my diary's words, "a strenuous little struggle over space. Charles holds from back, I fish with axe, and heave. Ripped his sack off and carried to camp. They going very slowly. Tea for them in tent." In fact, it was fortunate that the side of the bridge was shelving and not quite vertical. Ang Temba is a very small man, though broad, and his load hung below his head. Thus a good pull at the load —and his braces—righted him, and I could get hold of his arm. He could help himself very little, and I have never seen anybody more tired; putting one foot before the other, on the fifty yards to camp, only because he was so used to doing so that the movement was automatic.

The first assault party had returned.

4

In the tent, over the tea that Mike poured out, we heard between gasps an account of yesterday. Ang Temba had flattened out in the pyramid to himself; Tom was on his back in the tent adjoining the original tent of Camp VII, now end-on to make a two-some. The remaining four of us squatted in and out of our tent. We heard how John and Da Namgyal, with Open-Circuit oxygen, had carried their loads to 27,350 feet. It was an effort astonishing all the more for a man of forty-two, and with the burden of a leader's responsibilities. Tom and Charles, you will remember, were to make direct from the Col for the South Summit, and if it looked easy, the summit itself, using the Closed-Circuit. With their higher concentration of oxygen they had steamed past, at a rate of nearly 1,000 feet an hour, till poor snow slowed them down, then the steep and rotten snow slope below the South Summit. This they took very cautiously. They had stood, at 28,700 feet, higher than man had ever stood before, and looked for the first time along the summit ridge. In the snow-laden mist that half-veiled it that day, the cornices overhanging the Kangshung Glacier (12,000 feet below) had looked very formidable indeed. Charles thought it might take three hours or more. They were late on the South Summit, after 1:00 P.M., because they had started late. Charles had had freezing trouble with his set. They would not have had enough oxygen to go on and come back, partly because, Tom thought, they had changed the soda-lime canister too early. There had already been evidence on the expedition that wearing Closed-Circuit oxygen for many hours had a "de-climatising" effect. That is to say, if their set had given out suddenly on the summit ridge, they would certainly not have got back. They had lost contact with the outer air. They had returned, after a climb "historic" indeed, if that misused word can be applied to any mountain exploit. The descent had been desperately slow, for then they realised how tired they were. Both had slipped, one after the other; the slips of exhaustion. The third windy night had not helped that tiredness.

Balu had done badly from the start. It is almost impossible to tell, with Sherpas, which have the courage to rise above high-altitude weakness. Balu had been exhausted by the climb to the Col, and lost his nerve with the wind. This made Da Namgyal's effort specially stout, the more since he had not very long ago been still at Lobuje with bronchial cough. As for John, he joined Odell in the ranks of those who defy the forty-years age limit.

Even on the Col John's mind had been busy with plans. Would I go up with Sherpas to support or reinforce the second party, stepping into the breach if one had fallen out? This he had intended to ask me at IV, thinking that I would be there, and to bring up the necessary food and kerosene. I asked nothing better, but as I was already at VII, it seemed a pity to descend in order to collect my Sherpas and come up the next day. Could Mike and Ang Temba take the order? But Ang Temba was incapable of movement, he would have difficulty getting down tomorrow, and tomorrow food and oxygen must come up on three men's backs for me. It was looking as if I would have to go myself after all, when the slow voice of Charles joined the conversation. Perhaps he could manage the journey down with Mike. The situation, for me, was saved.

They left soon after five, and the next three hours I found busy ones. I wanted to look after John and Tom, who were "out" in the next tent. But if only I were not so *slow!* I had meant to blow up their Li-Los, but an hour's lapse still found me struggling with the big Primus and its defective pricker. Only the small one was slowly, very slowly, melting snow for soup. It seemed a confession of failure to ask Tom, whom I was trying to tend, but pride swallowed itself. "What's that?" A grunt, some panting, and Tom was on his side. A good deal of grunting on my side as I pushed the Primus in, dirty mess that it was. Tom was sitting up now, breathing heavily. For ten minutes he fiddled. I lit the Meta, and before the Primus roared up Tom was on his back again, apparently as dead as before. I admired nothing on the expedition more than this little feat.

I went out to take water and pills to Ang Temba, who refused even tea. Then back, alone in my tent, I could spread the cooker over one side and get on with the depressing business of melting water simply to wash the mugs. There followed soup, porridge, biscuits and lemonade, all that we now had at this camp, with the oddments of cheese, raisins, condensed milk in a tube. Passing food into the next tent (whose funnel had been connected with my funnel) was made doubly awkward by a tube of milk which had leaked itself over the connecting passage, demanding a special combination of caution and skill. Yet I never had the strength of mind to wipe away the débris.

At last, at 8:00 P.M., I had offered the final cigarette, joy and culmination of the day, to the others, but they were already dozing off. Even here I enjoyed the nightcap cigarette as much as ever, far more than I enjoy cigarettes in the plains. My pipe I had abandoned at IV, finding that it went out too much, the drawing was too strenuous. Now the fumbling of matches and the lighting up were safely passed. In the rings of smoke, the day's doings and news sorted themselves out, as mistily as happily; the day's doings, the thoughts and desires of tomorrow. Beyond tomorrow my mind never reached.

5

A slight snow fell in the night, and perhaps it was this which caused the tiresome wind to drop. Only an occasional slap on the fabric disturbed us, but what would that snow mean on the higher south-east ridge? At 6:45 I lit the Primus for tea, having water by me melted the night before. Though this required strength of will in the evening, it was well worth it when morning came, and with it the cheerless job of climbing out for snow. I took tea and codeine to Ang Temba, still prostrate and incapable of uttering more than the occasional groaning word. The Sherpa's morale descends with his physical state. I think John's opinion of the *élite* Sherpas had descended too, though it is probably a matter of education in facing unknowns. To the Sherpa physical exhaustion is itself terrifying, terrifying too the first experience of South Col wind. I could not help thinking, as I nudged the groaning figure, that Tom had every reason to be more exhausted. Yet he had mended the Primus.

We breakfasted, none of us very hungry, on Grape-Nuts, which John always liked in tea. Then the daily Ryvita, with cheese or jam upon it. I had taken a dislike to the expedition jam, a typical high-altitude fad, and condensed milk was too much trouble. While the others very slowly got themselves together, and in the intervals of seeing how they were getting on, I made ineffective show of washing-up. But when they had gone, with the day to myself, I returned to my Li-Lo and slept for two more hours. Then I lay and watched the ceiling. Any effort *can* be made if urgent. But if it is a job that can be done any time, like tidying or washing-up, then it is much easier to lie still, turning another page of *Nicholas Nickleby,* or quite simply to lie. What about poems? With all the weight of the world on my hands I opened the diary, wrote a line or two, then stopped. My head sank in a drowse. Then I started, wrote another line or two and again stopped.

In this way the morning passed. Inside the tent it had become blazing hot; I was reduced to flannel shirt over my string vest. But as soon as I opened the door chill squalls armed with ice splinters attacked me. I made some lemonade, and then, unquenched, some Nescafé. Biscuits and cheese forced their way down. There was nothing else, but I could have taken nothing else. What had seemed palatable up here before now lost its taste. The afternoon I passed in exactly similar idleness. Conscience told me that there was much I could do; beauty to be recorded, *tsampa* saucepans to be cleaned out. My body told me that both could wait.

At four I put on water in expectation of the Sherpas. At 4:30 voices sounded distantly below the bulge, and four figures, not three, slowly drew up. It was my Sherpas, Ang Dorji, Phu Dorji and Pasang Phutar, with Charles Wylie in person escorting them. The three carried loads of silver-papered Assault Ration, and kerosene. Charles plumped down on a packing-case, gasping tired, for they had come up fast. He told me he had come to accompany the Sherpas and avoid the monotony of Advance Base. He had received the news from Charles Evans and Mike last night (27th) and the order for supplies. The former had been very tired, but had talked and answered questions bravely.

Charles sat drinking tea on the packing-case, head down. I looked at the loads. They all seemed to be square, Assault Rations or kerosene. "Where's my oxygen, Charles?"

"Oxygen?"

"I mean what I asked for to get me up to the Col."

"Oh golly, you mean those cylinders!"

"Which cylinders?"

"Well, we did have a couple of cylinders. But we met John coming down, and he said they were extra weight and we'd better leave them. They're at the bottom of the Face."

I thought, what a funny effect of "anoxia." John knew last night that I needed the oxygen, particularly if I had to go far above the Col. His mind must have been fixed on the one purpose of saving weight, and now he had told my precious oxygen to sit below. Two days later I was to see it myself, reposing forlorn on the platform below the Face.

I looked up at the great tilt of slope edging the blue sky alongside the Geneva Spur. Tomorrow, without oxygen, I must get three laden Sherpas and myself, all on our second voyage, over that to the Col. And perhaps beyond.

A.J.VEILHAN

12

The Col and No Oxygen

May 28th and 29th

1

Charles flopped on to the Li-Lo in our tent. He looked very tired, with the foam of thirst about his mouth. Tea he wanted, just more tea. Then I hoisted myself out to see if there was anything in any of the cylinders, before the cold of sun-down. In the portly black variety there was nothing at all. But what of the set that Tom had been wearing when he came down? One light-alloy cylinder, bless its grey-green smoothness, seemed to have a pressure of 1400 p.s.i. It surprised me that I looked forward to those slopes so little without oxygen, when the British expeditions on the north side had been to well over 26,000 feet without it. I was spoilt. But I reasoned that the climbing on that side was very much easier than here; indeed for much of the way they did not rope. Besides, I might need to do rescue work higher still, repitch tents and certainly tend exhausted men on top of the day's climb. I wondered, nestling in over the soup and sausage, whether Ed and Tenzing had their tent safely pitched that night. There was no wind here; only the same faint boom over the Col tinged the silence. I was to learn next day that the conditions had been none too bad for them. By now they were ensconced in the small tent set at an angle against the snow, 27,900 feet up. Greg, George and Ang Nyima were back at the Col. Those two, the representatives of two different and yet friendly creeds, were by themselves. As I was thinking of them, they were making lemonade and eating sardines and biscuits with a matter-of-fact efficiency.

◄ *There were three figures coming down the slope towards me. George was waving his axe. . . . "They've done it!"*

Charles had earned my blessings by bringing *saucisson*, French sausage of the salami-tasting variety. Appetite returned at the thought of getting teeth into something meaty. Down in the valley I would never have expected to be so anxious for it, so indifferent to other delicacies. Several of us preferred the savoury to the sweet.

The evening was fine as I did the now well-worn tramp past the serac, to our *toilette* which was also our view-point. Only some golden bars, great ingots spanning the horizon and cut by Pumori as by a knife, had begun to look ominous. All else, the pointed peaks and the sky, was vivid with the evening's soft golden beauty that is not of this earth. At seven a strange creak and tremor sounded over the whole side of the mountain upon which we were. It seemed that Everest was alive, shrugging itself to the night's sleep.

In the Himalaya pains feared are often not as bad as fear has painted them. So it was the next day, May 29th. We started with the humdrum round of tea, brought by Phu Dorji and enlivened by us with Grape-Nuts. Then "getting up." If a god had ever appeared upon the mountain I would have asked him not to transport me to the summit but to bear me in a flash past that dreary hour and a half which separates the first push back of the sleeping-bag from the last flick of the rope as I set off. Today a large worry would be the packing. I had worked it out neatly in my head, but as for minutes of physical time—that was another matter. My personal kit would be divided between myself and one Sherpa, Pasang Phutar, who would also have his own. The other two could carry the high-altitude rations and precious kerosene for the Col. They would be coming down the same day, therefore would need nothing of their own. I must now pack up my own things and complete my dressing. Not knowing that I would be going higher, I had come up in the neater, general-purpose Lawrie boots, for comfort on the lower Face. But they would not be warm enough for the Col. Charles fortunately took the same size, and generously exchanged boots. A happy afterthought, I had packed my oxygen mask into the sack at IV, "just in case."

I had determined to keep my hour or so of oxygen for

higher up, when I would need it more. I would have, therefore, to carry the apparatus up the glacier section unused. Before nine we were away, with a wave of the axe (more jaunty than my feelings) as we crossed the slope above, overlooking the camp. To my surprise and pleasure, I seemed to have acclimatised. The Sherpas were not treading on my tail as I had feared for certain they would, and I was not panting unpleasantly. I was not enjoying the view either; but breathing seemed far more rhythmic to the pace than twelve days ago, and I was doing twenty to thirty steps without stopping. I was the more surprised, since I expected that demon "high-altitude deterioration" to have set about my throat. I did not realise that he rests below a certain level, as is evident from the case of George Lowe. George went up above the Col after nine days on the Face, an awesome feat even with oxygen. So I went on, having my eyes fixed upon the slope that had hardened greatly since the first visit. Only at rests I turned to the horizon. It seemed a fine day for the summit, and my thoughts were busy about the two above. The golden bars silvered to grey against the cloud-banks, but otherwise no veil misted the sky's blue. In the fixed-rope sections the rope was now secure, though the moves remained delicate in clumsy boots with a weight behind. We moved up to the more level ground of the glacier top.

I was about to jump over a crevasse when something about it caught my eye. This could not be . . . I looked again. It certainly *was* the crevasse, about which I had often thought since first crossing it with Anullu. The ledges were now flattened out and proved to be of solid ice supporting snow. They were scoured with the pricks of crampons. Very little fresh snow had fallen in the interval; each day the surface of the slopes had packed down further, the steps had filled with wind-driven pellets, which clotted to cream when the crampons left their signature. It was a curious experience; now I felt like a boaster adept at making mountains out of his molehills. But the surprise only proved the truism that a climb becomes progressively easier each time it is done. Why on earth had I been so ridiculously fussy about it?

Previous acquaintance had certainly increased the speed and ease of this part. Now, at 11:30, we sat and lunched where Anullu and I had eaten at 12:15. We had taken less time to do the journey without oxygen than I had needed on the first ascent with it. Before we started the traverse I switched on, hoping that Tom's cylinder at two litres a minute would take me as far as the Spur. We had caught sight of a party of three descending the higher slopes of the traverse: the support party. We pressed on.

It was a long time, in and out of unsuspected shelves and valleys of ice, with the feet pressed awkwardly against the bend of snow, before we met the returning party. It was Greg, with Pemba and Ang Nyima, all muffled and panting. Greg told me that Ed and Tenzing had been seen passing the South Summit at nine. Himself, George and Ang Nyima had done the carry yesterday, had left everything for the camp high on the ridge. The summit party had camped, and started out about 6:30 this morning. We stood loosely in the snow, each putting off the moment of going forward. Greg had been very tired, returning to the Col. "Tell George I'm going better today," he said as they moved off.

It was soon after this that I noticed Ang Dorji going very unsteadily. More frequent became the calls for *aram* (rest), the gestures of head down on axe. His eyes had the unseeing wildness of exhausted men; his mouth hung open with a scum about the lips. We divided part of his load, then bent forward again. I remember well the awkwardness of replacing my oxygen, after I had switched on. The weighty rucksack above the cylinder toppled me over as I swung it back. We were now going more and more slowly, it was more and more clear that the supply, an odd hour's worth at best, would get me very little farther. It was windier today, and colder. I was glad that I had Charles's boots, for nobody dislikes more than I standing about in powder snow, wriggling toes that have lost sensation.

Another halt. Ang Dorji's head dropped even before his body, his eyes had no sight in them. We stood in the snow, in the hope that rest would recover him, and I put on another sweater, another pair of gloves. It looked unlikely that he could go on; a few steps farther he was down again. He must clearly stay. At this point forgotten shafts of sunlight started playing upon the immense slope over which we were making our ant-track; warmth had penetrated our day. I looked up at the rounded skyline crest, seeming deceptively near. We could divide Ang Dorji's load, reach the Col and send Phu Dorji speeding down to accompany Ang Dorji to VII. Pasang Phutar and I would stay up, go higher if need be. I said, "Ang Dorji wait here." He looked vaguely grateful, lying in the snow, not caring about anything much except rest.

We made another division of loads and went on. But I had underestimated everything, our slowness, my cylinder's capacity, the distance to the Spur's top and the wind's force. It was very soon after we had once more started that my cylinder gave out, and I knew well what effect that would have on my going. We were not 200 yards from Ang Dorji, when the wind playing about my trouser bottoms hinted to me the danger of his lying there. I knew that I could not leave a man to the risk of that cold. The Spur looked farther than before, the pencilled shadow of the jutting rocks upon snow a more arduous climb. *Phu Dorji nicche jaega* (Phu Dorji will go down). Phu Dorji, tall and piratical of appearance, with orange balaclava and perpetually dirty face, was one of the most reliable. He was well set for the Col, and could have reached it easily. But he took the order without hesitation. A trained Sherpa, he was doing his job, obeying the sahib's instructions and going down. That, I think, is the attitude of these men. They have come to climbing through load-carrying. Load-carrying is the job and mountaineering a higher-paid carrying job than most. To be among mountains, yes. That is their life, their work. To be on their snow is a different matter, hard work and dangerous at times. Sherpas have been killed on Everest. Therefore Phu Dorji went down, and I do not think he regretted it, for I later gave him the recommendation of a man who had reached the South Col twice. With Tenzing it would have been different.

What of the loads? Phu Dorji had been carrying most of Ang Dorji's, which Pasang and I must split. My oxygen hour was over, leaving me at least freer to carry. I leaned the frame against a little rock. Even if I needed oxygen higher, I could not carry that plus a load; and at the moment a load seemed the more important. The event proved that the kerosene was precious indeed, for the South Col was quite without it. The Assault Rations so laboriously heaved and hoisted up remain, most of them, on the Col now. Perhaps they will be useful to somebody. But at the time they seemed most important, as of course they might have been. Pasang's infinite sack took much; mine would not fit all that I wanted, and I went on armed with two sacks, one uncomfortably over each shoulder. Pasang must have been carrying over 50 lb., myself something over 40.

Before we had taken a few steps Phu Dorji had rejoined his friend. The two were resting, then making off, slowly, down the dotted line which crossed the slope, towards the upper snout of glacier. The first few steps: that showed how slowly we were going. At very first my impression was, "Well, I've defeated it. Here I am chugging up all right." But that was only for a few steps. A dead weight, two long leaden arms, began dragging at my two shoulders. Curious things were beginning to happen to my breath, to my mind. As in a dream I was back at the end of the cross-country course at Charterhouse. I was spattered with mud, breathing hoarsely, exhausted. Now somebody was asking me to run the thing again. No, it was too much!

The good effect of stopping was almost instantaneous. Panting would continue, yes, but not that wild, end-of-the-tether panting, the feeling that this was timeless, endless, a purgatory *in perpetuum*. The little rock intrusion, perhaps a hundred feet in all, took a long time. Then snow-crust with the print of feet upon it. These prints led straight up beside the Spur, not out to its crest on the gangway of eight days ago. I knew that the others had followed the original line of the Swiss. It was easier to take to their steps, and I followed, too. But the prints were deceptive, clogged with rounded pellets that the wind had not allowed to feather but driven relentlessly from Heaven knows where, from Tibet across the West Shoulder and beyond. The foot would not rest flatly in them, sometimes it stayed ungainly on top, occasionally it floundered through and the breath jerked in unison. Three steps up and a pause. A twitch of the shoulders at the weight dragging my body down. A few gasps with my forehead rested upon the gloved hand clasping ice-axe head. Then on. To my own surprise I had no feeling that I must continue resting longer than the moments allotted for recovering breath. Certainly I could not have gone faster to save my own life, but I did not want to go slower, to stop altogether. I was consumed rather with an impatience to step on and on, till the fickle skyline of the Spur should be at last below me.

Looking up, I kept comparing my slope with the approach to a rock buttress of Tryfan in North Wales. Say it was five hundred feet to the top. That was just about the height of a Tryfan buttress, and here it was, snowed up. It would take, at good speed, quarter of an hour. Would I ever reach "a good speed" again? The idea of walking fast, ever, up a hill was ridiculous. Yet the top rocks looked near, very near. Suppose I tried a trick: cheat the breath by taking seven or eight steps at a time, then pause for longer if necessary. The breath I must check almost completely, just breathing in and out lightly on the top layer for the time, instead of trying to be deeply rhythmical with every step.[1] For a while this ruse against the body seemed to work. Pasang, surprised at the change of pace, changed his own manfully. But alas, my lungs perceived the deception and compelled me to revert to the old rhythm. Three . . . slow . . . steps . . . and a pause. Life held no more than that, for the time being.

It is usual with me, as I think with many climbers, to be two people at once on a climb, particularly when I am alone. Here I was in several senses alone. One half watches and criticises the fumblings of the incompetent other, and is itself removed and remote from the physical conflict. In high climbing this schizophrenic condition becomes more pronounced, as I noticed on Pauhunri in 1945. I believe that

[1] This device was tried independently by John Hunt, as he describes in *The Conquest of Everest*, E. P. Dutton & Co., New York, 1954.

such a state led to Smythe's strange act on Everest in 1933, when at 28,000 feet, alone, he broke a piece of mint cake and turned to give half to his supposed companion. On the Spur one half of me hovered airily above the slope, wondering why in the name of everything it was tied to this grinding, panting creature. Even, as we turned left towards the crest, it admired the hanging wonder of Everest's final pyramid, now clear of snow plume. The rest of me laboured painfully, gasped and groaned; abominated the horrible hole that the sacks seemed to be making in the small of my back; pleaded with the superior partner, "I can't, I can't go faster"; and yet felt a thrill of subcutaneous joy not to be going slower.

At longest last we were nearing the flatter top, on shelving, jumbled rock splinters. Suddenly a cry from behind. It was Pasang, pointing with his axe. I looked up, and in my condition of the moment it seemed by no means surprising, indeed commonplace, that two small figures should be blotting the white diamond slope below the South Summit of Everest. From the Geneva Spur the South Summit, hiding the main summit, is a most queenly mountain, a mountain in its own right. The left skyline descends in a curving plunge, to divide itself between west and south ridges. To the right, invisible from the Cwm, the south-east ridge of the pyramid swings in one graceful sweep, then bulge, down towards the right-hand edge of the Col, where it ends in an abrupt little rock tower. The steep slope immediately below the South Summit appears as a dazzling jewel of snow. Upon this, stepping down, the two black figures were venturing. They looked for all the world like climbers descending from Snowdon's top at Easter. So clear is the air, they seemed no smaller than such climbers on such a day from near the top of Snowdon's P-y-G track. And so bemused was I, that the dramatic suddenness of this sight, with all its possibilities, stirred only a very small layer of me. "That's good, they may have done it." And I pushed on for the next three steps.

All the same, the sight of them, with its presentiment of good, was a great goad to our dragging bodies. It still seemed another age before we were again treading snow, over 26,000 feet high on the bald crown of the Spur, and looking down at the "Uniformity of Barrenness," as Dr. Johnson would certainly have described the South Col plateau. This time, however, it was enlivened by standing tents beside the wind-torn tatters: the yellow pyramid, the little orange "blister" and a two-man Meade. From above we could see the fabric ballooning before the wind. All the way up we had met heavier gusts than last time, for conditions vary from day to day. And yet the ridge above looked far calmer, no longer shrouded by the blank streaming mists that had blotted out further views. This time the blue hills of Tibet danced with their coronets of snow against the brown back-cloth of plain to the right. They looked very distant, in another world from ours. My eye came back, to a figure moving slowly between the tents.

2

We crunched down to the level, swung rucksacks off and paused for a moment or two. Now to bend down, to face the wriggle through the funnel and into the flapping pyramid. A swimming motion with the arms and I was lying on the floor. But it was some moments before I sat up and looked around. I have never seen so chaotic an interior. The ground-sheet was ripped with great triangular cuts, and these showed the boulders among which the tent was pitched. Through a tear in one of the side walls—the wind's work, George said —the air entered sharply, pulling at the fabric to squeeze more of itself inside. All over the floor were littered the remains of high-altitude rations, fragments of cheese and frozen biscuits, mixed up with connecting tubes and oxygen masks, cylinder heads and the occasional carrying frame. Torn paper everywhere. I poked my head outside and pulled in the two rucksacks. For Pasang, I cannot remember whether he came too, or whether he retired at once to the "blister." Although some unimportant details from those two days have left me (the lapse in my diary from the 28th I made up as soon as we were back at IV), the main outline is as clear as any experience I ever had.

George Lowe, the figure I had seen, was in with me now.

225

"It looks as if they may have done it. I'm just going to meet them," he said.

"What's been happening, George?"

George sat there in his massive Robinson Crusoe beard, cross-legged and calm as if this had been Base Camp. But his eyes were red. He told me more of the tremendous effort and tiredness of Tom and Charles, of his own and Greg's carry yesterday to the highest camp ever pitched, 27,900 feet.

"And we were carrying a pretty fair lot from John's dump onwards. Reckoning bit by bit Ed must have been carrying over sixty, and the rest fifty or forty." Greg, dead tired, had taken ten minutes over the last hundred yards back and had been filmed, to his dismay. He had relapsed prone in the tent, only wakening from coma to call "soup *hai*" to Pemba, himself prostrate from the day before. Then there was John's decision, a reluctant but wise one, to go down with Tom and Charles on the 27th. By making it he left George free to do the carry for which he was fit, when only Ang Nyima of the three special Sherpas proved capable, on the 28th, of stirring out to join the four climbers. Ang Temba had already gone down with John's party.

"Well, I must be going. I'm getting some soup in the thermos. Would you like to settle down and make some tea? Come up after if you like."

"All right. . . . Where's the cooker?"

"In the Meade. We don't fancy this tent now."

It was not surprising. The wind, squeezing itself under the ground-sheet, lifted it like a living thing and shuffled the scraps of paper over the floor. George crawled warily out to see to the soup, and I started to open my rucksack. I had for some time been waiting an opportunity to put on my down trousers and coat. Under my wind-proofs only thick flannel pyjamas over cotton encased my lower limbs. I was greedy for the fluffy warmth of down. But it was a long business. First, boots to be taken off, a breathless stoop to untie them. Next, wind-proof trousers off; a vigorous wriggle of a body supported on one elbow. If only I could be suspended in space and could kick! Next, down trousers on.

The same wriggle in reverse direction. No need to worry about the braces, these can stay up of themselves. Then wind-proof trousers on. Now the blue wind-proof coat off, down coat on and zipped up the middle, then the wind-proof coat on once more. But first the outer braces must be fixed: simple, high-altitude braces, but any braces that mean fumbling in the small of the back up here will be a grunting, groaning affair. And the wind-proof coat, what a nuisance to have to struggle in from below, arms waving and head enveloped!

The whole passes in a few words of description, but takes a long time to perform. Half of me read the scraps of paper, looked at the ceiling, while something like the following dialogue took place:

"Wind-proof off. That's the next thing."

"Yes, but what's on the label. Wait a minute, I must read it."

"Come on, hurry up. George will be gone by now."

"Well, let him. Think what we've had to do today, coming up all that way without oxygen. And forty pounds. There's no reason why I should go up any more at all really."

"That's nothing. You know you want your down clothing on anyway. You've been feeling cold for quite a time. Even if you don't want to do the proper thing and go out to meet them . . ."

"Yes I do, of course I do, but I must rest a minute. I wonder what's the advertisement on the milk tube . . ."

This conversation between every move of my clothing change made it some time before I scrambled out, on all fours, to totter over to the Meade tent, just vacated by George. This, by contrast, looked most homely: two Li-Los side by side and sleeping-bags upon them; at the far end, away from the wind, a cooker. There was already water melted; I struck a match and lay on my side fiddling for the ingredients. How clever! I thought. But I now realise how slow I was. Powder milk I poured with the tea straight on top of the boiling water, reached for the thermos and poured the whole in, spilling some.

When I left the tent to go up too, George was some way

on the slope towards the south-east ridge. The two higher figures were hard to see against the black rock bordering the couloir. I plodded over the flat, icy surface of the Col, for no snow is allowed to rest here. Cutting the surface are boulders that are the bone of the mountain. Had that mountain been kind to Ed and Tenzing, towards whom I was heading? A silly question now. Everest was aloof, had no thought for us. Some have seen in the mountain a malignant enemy, interposing icy barriers between man and his desire, beating him with the weapon of wind. But to me, upon that slope, Everest was cold, impersonal as never before. This wind was not here to harry me. It had blown across the South Col long before there were men swarming upon this planet. The alternation of the seasons which allowed me to be here now, the hot with the cold, monsoon with the dominion of frost, these passed in a cycle immeasurably above our Lilliput conflicts. That queen of created masses, the summit, swept up there equally upon its glorious ridges, whether Ed and Tenzing had reached the highest point or no.

George had met them by now. They had stopped, rested, then there were three figures coming down the slope towards me. The afternoon mist hung and puffed across the lower reaches, now masking the hills of Tibet, now the stupendous fang of Makalu and its satellites across the way. The lower slopes still hovered gleaming through cloud windows.

I went on. Now they were very near. George was waving his axe.

"They've done it!" He pointed his ice-axe towards the top. But my reaction was disappointing. With the slowness of all motion, my brain refused to receive the impression. It takes time, at that height. The top. That meant Everest climbed, job done. Good—*wonderful*. Now we can go down. No more problems.

Somehow like this my thought went, if thought it can be described. At the back of my heart I knew that, had they failed, I would have been of the third party. But that mattered nothing now. I can certainly remember no disappointment for myself at all. Why should I? Slowly, I began to feel immensely happy, though I realised not a thousandth of the deed's implications. "We" had got up, had done what we came out to do, without accident. And now we could go down, be greeted by our friends, sleep in beds, have hot drinks and an appetite again; leave Everest to the choughs.

"Sorry I can't say much. Oxygen just given out," Ed panted out. He refused the tea, not liking tea and being full of George's soup. I felt childishly happy that Tenzing drank some, and seemed to like it. But I doubt if he did; he is very polite. Then we returned, down and across the plain to the tents. They moved steadily, without spring in the stride but always steadily. We had arrived.

There was an unhitching of oxygen sets, a fumbling between the tents. Tenzing joined Pasang Phutar in the "blister." Ed fell prone on his Li-Lo in the Meade. We fussed around, pulling rucksacks in, getting the cooker going again. The wind beat at the canvas.

Everest was climbed. The summit of the highest mountain in the world was reached, after thirty years of endeavour, on this day, May the 29th, 1953. The eyes of everybody in every country would soon be on us.

George, squatting over the cookery, asked, "Do you know what Ed said when I met him first? He said, 'Well, we knocked the bastard off.'"

A.J.VEILHAN

13

From the Twenty-ninth
to the Thirtieth

1

It always seems to me right to bring lectures to a close
soon, or not too long, after the summit. With its attainment,
ambition has been fulfilled, the deed done. Some would say
that a book's story should end here, too, at the climax of
the year's hope and dream. But does the *Iliad* end with the
victory of Achilles? Or any dramatic tale at the point of its
highest emotional excitement? After the climax the *détente*.
In the case of a personal narrative I would say that the most
important remains, for me viewing the ascent as an individual. This was partly because the question of Everest's "personality" entered my thought *after* the climb far more than
immediately before; partly for the childish reason that I
had always wondered, from a boy, what it would "be like"
after Everest had been climbed. Now I know.

Of course, at the time the whole achievement seemed
laughably small, measured by the standards of some months
later. We nestled into the tent, myself half-lying bulkily
near the entrance. The conversation was often not far from
the level of this:

"I bet old so-and-so will be bucked. He was pretty interested in the whole show from the start."

"Yes. The N.Z.A.C. and the Alpine Club ought to do us
well, too."

"Wonder if they'll give us a dinner."

Such we accounted it. But first there were other things to
think about. I left the Meade tent and wandered past Tenzing and Pasang Phutar in the "blister." I went on hap-

◀ *We laid down our bags, in T position
against the slope.*

hazard between these and the pyramid; wondered whether to unpack my rucksack; crawled in, very slowly, started and decided not to. All this time I was really trying to make up my mind whether to keep a promise to John. It had been my own suggestion, though it seemed now a silly one. All good expeditions that I had read of put out sleeping-bags to signal to those above or below. The classic case was the 1924 expedition, when they gave the news of Mallory and Irvine. Well, just below the top of the Geneva Spur there appeared to be a convenient snow-patch upon which to lay sleeping-bags so that they could be seen, through binoculars, from IV. I had suggested, therefore, that if they reached the top, I should put two out in the shape of a T; John added that if it was the South Summit, one should be alongside the other; if nothing at all, then one sleeping-bag.

By the time I had decided, it was 5:30, nearly two hours after the descent. I stooped at the Meade entrance and looked in. I tried to shout.

"I promised John I'd take two bags up and put them on a slope. So that they can see from below."

"Wouldn't bother. Probably won't see them, anyway. What's wrong with tomorrow?"

"I don't know. Perhaps I'd better though."

Collecting Pasang was a harder job. I called three times, going off between to do jobs that seemed very important at the time, but which I have completely forgotten. At last his broad face emerged at the "blister" door. Usually a gay face, it was not grinning now. Very reasonably, Pasang had assumed that after a day with a 60-lb. load the sahib would leave him alone. And why the sleeping-bag? He dragged off ahead up the crust.

I followed slowly behind, but at last we had arrived at the boulders. They seemed in their turn to go on for ever. As as excuse for stopping, I stooped and put some small fragments in my pocket. They would like them back in England, my son above all when he grew up. At last we were on snow. But meanwhile I was having uneasy doubts. As we topped the crest it seemed that there was cloud in the valley. Soon it could not be mistaken. Banks of afternoon mist hung over the floor of the Cwm. Above them the evening sun shone behind Nuptse, a dark paper silhouette traced against turquoise sky by the divinely delicate pencil of sun and wind. But in the Cwm, mist.

We stopped at the first good snow-patch. The gusts, very strong on the Col, had dwindled here to a stiff breeze. "Down," I said, and we laid down our bags, in T position against the slope. To keep them there we lay upon them, myself the upright, Pasang the cross of the T. What was the poor man thinking of me? Hard things, I doubted not, and probably with reason, in view of this mist. We lay for ten minutes, myself hoping forlornly that some providence might have opened a small gap, allowed John a vignette of the two suffering figures. But after ten minutes with the wind flapping at us we had suffered enough. The evening cold was creeping up, through down suit and sleeping-bag, into the bone of us. "We go down," I said, longing for warmth and ease. We picked up the sleeping-bags, and Pasang was making fast tracks for home almost before I had started. That was all; until I was told, many days later, that there is now a pleasing legend in the valley, of the very mad Englishman who once wanted to sleep out in the snow above the South Col of Everest.

At the crest I halted, watching Pasang's strong figure moving down the frozen crust between the rocks, expressive in its every jolt of the conviction that all sahibs are off their head. I fancy that most Sherpas believe the sahibs to be harmless lunatics with plenty of money. Behind him the Col, above and beyond lurked the presence of Everest. Once again I remember thinking: Did the mountain feel an emotion, anger at the thought of "conquest"? That impression I certainly did not carry down as I thought about it. Everest *is* a mountain, by definition an emotionless mass of rock, snow and ice. If mountains move "between the eternal mode and mine," in Geoffrey Winthrop Young's phrase, then they are indifferent, caring neither one way nor the other, to all our crawling. If there is any personification of Everest at all imaginable, it is for me in the impersonality of Swinburne's "Proserpine."

Pale, beyond porch and portal,
Crowned with calm leaves, she stands. . . .

It is our human presumption, or so I thought, to sentiment-alise the struggles that we endure upon these monstrous crea-tures into a struggle *against* them, rather than against our own feebleness which cannot face the magnitude of their ice cliffs and rock towers. In that huge loneliness of the Spur's top it seemed a miracle of his own nature that man the tiny had been allowed to tread so high.

Returning I bent down again before the tent funnel.

"Do you mind if I do come in?" It had been George's orig-inal generous suggestion, and I fancied the pyramid to my-self extremely little.

The two shifted to make space between, while I went over to collect my belongings. This simple operation took over twenty minutes, and meant two journeys across the fifty-odd feet separating the tents. In the little "blister" alongside ours, peace now seemed to reign. I looked in at the contented, re-cumbent forms of Tenzing and Pasang, to be cheered by the flashing smile. *"Ji hazur. Thik hai."* I crawled in, rammed belongings half-unpacked into the rucksack, climbed out and walked across, to put them in heaps outside the Meade door. It seemed a long time before I was sitting down, that being the easiest way, in bulky down clothing, of getting in through the Meade's sleeve entrance. A wriggle on the elbows, feet first, a hope that there was nothing precariously balanced just inside.

The far or windward door of the tent towards the Cwm was closed, the leeward door was not draughty. I could reach out to pull in rucksack, sleeping-bag and oddments, without endangering the Primus, in action at the other end. I found myself in a valley between two long New Zealand forms re-posing on Li-Los. The ideal, of course, would be to get the sleeping-bag under me, but that involved raising on one el-bow and wriggling it in by stages; a not easy feat up here. At last I was in a lying position, with sleeping-bag under or around me, reminiscent of the Romans (or was it the Car-thaginians?) in Livy *"Impedimentis obruti magis quam*

234

obtecti." Overwhelmed I was, rather than protected, for the bits that would not go underneath I piled on top. But it was warm, George had the Primus going nicely. I tried to tie up the funnel door, but found myself bulging out into it.

2

We were now all settled for a cosy, fuggy evening, in the last light that lingered genially up here. Each of us was praying doubtless that nothing would occur to force him outside during the next twelve hours. Fortunately nothing did. Some expert concocting had been going on; I remember lemon with plenty of sugar, far the most refreshing drink high up, soup and fragments of food. For me it was raisins, a little chocolate, and, best of all, the scraping of a pot of Swiss honey found here. That honey I could have eaten in large quantity.

Ed was now talkative, and told more of the climb which would soon be a classic of mountaineering history. I heard for the first time of the two-hour job of digging, or at least levelling a platform for the tent yesterday, at 27,900 feet after George's party had left the loads; how Ed had to sit against the slope, to keep things in position, trying not to roll on top of Tenzing, while Tenzing lay below, doubtless trying not to be rolled on by Ed. They seemed to have made a lot of lemonade in the night, Griff's teaching bearing fruit, and to have eaten biscuits and sardines, even tinned apricots. It was fortunate that Ed was enamoured of lemonade, for medical authority prescribed six pints a day of liquid. They had also had four hours' sleep on oxygen, in two batches, for when sleeping on oxygen, one woke as soon as the supply gave out and remained awake. At very first light they had looked out, over the sleeping black valleys that writhed like snakes among snow masses. In the east the dark sky lightened. They could pick out one patch, where must be the monastery of Thyangboche, far away and 16,000 feet below. Perhaps even then the monks were praying for our safety.

Tenzing was active very early with the cooker, and they started at 6:30, in comparatively windless conditions. Tenzing led the first stretch. The slope to the South Summit Ed did not like; it looked dangerous, nasty snow, a place to be left alone. But this was Everest, and others had been up before. He asked Tenzing, "What about it?" Tenzing, who is a perfect gentleman, replied, "As you wish," and they went on. The summit ridge from the South Summit looked formidable, a path narrow as virtue itself between the cornices on the right, overhanging the Kangshung Glacier 12,000 feet below, and the western precipice to the left. The snow was hard, steps could be chipped. At one point Tenzing had suffered. Something wrong. It was the ice blocking his outlet valve, easy to remove. But a nasty fright. So at last they had come to the forty-foot rock step in this final ridge. It must have been a fine piece of climbing at that height, a wriggle up the fissure between rock and snow, back against snow, hands against rock. We had looked at it time and again through glasses, a tiny vertical nick in the ridge, but it has been said that you cannot tell what a rock is going to be like till you have rubbed your nose on it. The whole climb from the South Summit took two and a half hours. (The rise in vertical height is, of course, no more than 400 feet.) "A good climb by New Zealand Alpine standards," thought Ed, who had been leading, and the top a perfect top, with a ridge dropping away in each direction. The blackness, bareness from snow, of the north side seemed to impress him specially, and the steep drop there looked to be after the first few feet, down on to the route which so many earlier parties had attempted. It is very easy, looking down, to misjudge the steepness of a ridge, for the eye leaps lightly to flatter ground beyond. But it looks certainly as if this north side, on the final pyramid, is steep indeed. For ten minutes Ed had his oxygen off, while he photographed in all directions. He felt no ill effects, but "I was quite glad to get it on again."

They had turned after a quarter of an hour, anxious about the descent and whether the oxygen would hold till they reached cylinders left by Tom and Charles. Ed had been doing mental arithmetic half the way up, and calculated they should just make it. Where we saw them descending from the South Summit they had been extremely uncomfortable. The slope was steep, descent is always more nerve-wracking, and

THE SOUTH COL – Looking south: The South Col and Lhotse from the South East Ridge. The route passes over the top of the Geneva Spur (the long gentle snow ridge on the right) to the South Col Camp (near the centre, extreme bottom).

THE SOUTH COL – Looking west: Down Cwm from top of the Spur, showing where the sleeping bags were placed (foreground). Camp IV is smudge to the right of glacier, near cloud in centre (about 2 miles away).

THE SOUTH COL – Looking north: The final pyramid from the South Col.

THE SOUTH COL – Looking east to M

nd Kangchenjunga (left) in distance.

THE SOUTH SUMMIT
May 26th. Bourdill
photographed by Eva
on the South Summ
looking at the final ridg

THE SOUTH COL – M
26th. Exhausted! Char
Evans and Tom Bo
dillon after their clin

THE SUMMIT – 11.30 a.m. on May 29th, 1953.

The Devil Dancers of Thyangboche. Stobart on right, filming.

Goodbye to Everest.

they looked straight down on to the Kangshung. The snow was rotten. It was a huge relief to be down, at the bottles left by Tom and Charles. Then back along the ridge, to the ridge tent which a modest wind had half-torn from its moorings. They had stopped here, to rest over the Primus and make drink. They came on down, very tired, not conscious of the greatness of the achievement. We knew the rest.

Even from that first, fragmentary account, full of mountaineering understatement, it was easy to judge that it had been a superb climb, by two companions worthy of it and climbing as a rope of two should. After this the conversation wandered a good deal, to scenes like that of Tom trying to get back, on his knees, up the Geneva Spur on the 27th. Sometimes he needed help. Greg had been all in, too, returning from the carry. Next day he had wanted oxygen for the Spur, but there had not been enough to spare. Both Ed and George generously said that it was now bad luck on me not to have the chance of a third shot, but I cannot recall any feeling of disappointment at all at the idea; nor later, when I wrote in my diary next day, "Ed and George very generous on me, say bad luck I can't do third assault and fittest to go high. But after it all I think my feeling is of great relief, the thing is done and I have had a good run." At the time all I knew about the third party was that I believed I would be on it. Only afterwards John confided his secret hope that he and I might make that last attempt.

The top layers of my mind were probably dormant up there, but it is very true that we all felt strongly that the team got to the top rather than the individuals, while the individuals chosen were worthy representatives of the team. Others had worked as hard. (George Lowe's performance, nine days' work on the Lhotse Face, the ridge carry and four nights on the South Col, was as remarkable as any on the expedition.) This was the opinion expressed time and again, particularly since the ascent, by John, and one secret of his leadership; his too the conviction that the "team" included those who had gone before, over whose shoulders we climbed to the top. Ed said, suddenly and apropos of nothing (though he will have forgotten it), "Wouldn't Mallory be pleased if he knew

about this?" Mallory forfeited his life on Everest, and I think
we all felt the same: we were part of a greater company. Now,
the summit was reached, therefore all was well.

"Disappointment may creep in later," I wrote. Later, perhaps, I would feel, "Well, I was very fit. Given the oxygen I
think I might have made it. A pity it wasn't me." No climber
would be human if he went to Everest without the secret
hope that he might be the man to find himself, those few
minutes, on top. He would probably be the worse mountaineer if he did not allow that hope to promenade his day-
dreams. But if his fears are often dupes, hopes may be and
are liars; he would be no mountaineer at all if he did not
have a far wider hope for the wider unit involved in climbing
the mountain. "Conquest" in connection with Everest suggests to me nothing but the conquest of rebellious bits of myself. Often on that mountain I must face and admit to my
limitations, always curb the extravagance of desire.

We talked of Tenzing. What a good thing he had made of
it. Good to have a Sherpa on top. John sent him, in the first
place, because he had proved his fitness with Lambert, and
this year too was "going like a bomb," in climbing parlance,
with Ed. But he was sent also, a far more important reason
as it seemed to me, as a Sherpa to represent all the Sherpas
who had worked, and in some cases died, upon Everest. Without the Sherpas the mountain could not have been climbed.
Therefore it was fitting that one of the small, brown and
smiling tribe should stand upon the top with a representative
of ourselves: Tenzing, who had taken a leading part in the
climb of last year, and before that carried a Sherpa load upon
the northern flank. "Good for Tenzing," expressed the feelings of those that talked that night.

3

It was a curious night, when we finally settled for sleep.
The valley between the two Li-Los proved to be on the short
side, which meant for me the posture of a Michelin Man
whose top half has been screwed sideways. My down hood
was up, my head hard against the rucksack which itself was

firmly against the now tied-up entrance. Half of me was at last in the sleeping-bag, but half, without violent movement of which I was incapable, I could not make enter. We had, however, achieved so rich an interior atmosphere that I hoped it would be thick enough to protect me. I had under my hip a good wad of sleeping-bag, but at some time in the night, with Ed's Li-Lo convenient against my buttock, I shifted my right hip on to it, and he, like a gentleman, moved over to make room. My toes were the greatest problem. They remained cold all night, despite bunching and stretching between sleeps. A very faint numbness lingered about them well after we were back home, and my toe-nails turned black.

The wind was with us all night, blustering across the level gap at the tents, pulling and pushing at the tent poles, squeezing in and then bellying out the fabric. There was no snow for the throwing, but occasional ice fragments tinkled against rocks or the poles. I must regret and apologise for being able to give no more dramatic wind scenes, but as I was not at the pitching of the tents on the 24th, undoubtedly our nastiest affair with wind, I can give no desperate descriptions to compare with those of the north side. I cannot remember wind being more than a very harassing nuisance, but nuisance it certainly was. It woke me at times, and I readjusted the buttock. But I must have slept, and soundly, for I heard only much later from Mike Ward that Ed and George had been sleeping on oxygen. I had not noticed, or did not remember, them putting it on. When the oxygen gave out at 3:00 A.M. they talked. I certainly did not hear them. I remember nothing until the sun, striking into the symphony of wind, set the whole tent on fire. I opened the sleeve and looked out, to the east, where it lit up the white wavelets of ice all over the Col; where, just within reach to my left, the little red "blister" lay snugly streamlined against the blast.

At 6:30 I stretched out a hand for the cooker, which we had left outside to make room. This I did at the request of Tenzing, whose face had appeared, rather cold-looking, in the windward entrance of the "blister." I was exceptionally well placed for doing things outside, he exceptionally badly. I reached over the cooker without either of us having to leave his tent, and waited. Nobody minded waiting a long time, before Tenzing's efficient hands produced tea, borne by a now broadly grinning Pasang Phutar. Poor Ed! He had never liked tea, even in the valleys, and had tested Thondup's resourcefulness by asking for coffee each time. However, we then went on to soup, at which we made some show but none of us a very good one. I took some raisins out of a sense of duty, some of our condensed milk (Lait Mont Blanc) and bits of *saucisson,* which, however, the others would not touch. Appetites were not now good. We had been above twenty thousand feet for just too long. It was an awkward business, the *saucisson;* cutting off a round, peeling it and cutting up pieces. But I got some swallowed and even enjoyed. I still think that if an omelette or a "nice bit of chicken" had appeared from a divine nowhere we could all have enjoyed it. I remembered Angtharkay's cooking, and was not Angtharkay reputed to have cooked a delicious three-course dinner at Camp VI on the north side of Everest?

The talk continued. I think we were now back with families and friends, how pleased they would be. My own thoughts were very vividly with my wife and family, and my year-old son who would know nothing at all about it. But how happy everybody else would be that this was safely, successfully over! The idea of an accident now occurred to none of us. It was all very pleasant, but at last the harsh time came when there could be no excuse for lying longer. It was my painful duty, as janitor of the door, to be the first to leave the easeful horizontal position, kneel up, reach for boots, put both slowly on and climb into the vertical. It had seemed to me, lying down, that the wind was none so bad. Standing up disillusioned me. I reeled over to the pyramid, bent down and entered. The interior was bleaker and less inviting, if that were possible, than before. I felt doubly grateful for my night with the others, one of the most happy, least comfortable nights with the best of companions that I have ever had. I sat and did up my laces, put on my puttees, then out again and back to the Meade.

They were taking some time getting quite dressed and adjusting oxygen sets for Ed and Tenzing to use on the descent. A clutter of pots and cooking gear lay blocking the door. It seemed a pity to leave all this valuable equipment. At any rate I ought to take *something*, now that our Assault Rations would be lying here useless. I went back to the pyramid. On the ground, inside and out, 6-oz. packets of sugar were strewn. Sugar—that was very important, I slowly thought, and I picked some up and put them in my sack.

4

Everest is climbed. At times the astonishing thought penetrated even the sloth of a high camp. Now we must go down, must keep that story for another day. In the east the sun was warming. Over there, if one walked across, Kangchenjunga's huge bulk (28,150 feet) dominated the morning. Pasang and I, not having oxygen to worry about, set off the first at 9:30. We climbed slowly up the wind-crust towards our Spur. It was gratifying to find the handrail still in position, even more so that it was useful. I was reminded of the bottle of Benzedrine tablets still in my pocket. John's concern about this slope was strong enough to make him feel that the stimulant might be helpful. Suppose the Sherpas reached the Col and then had not strength to return up the initial climb? There had been a good deal of discussion about Benzedrine; Griff recounted the extraordinary things that it made men do in the War, when they thought themselves dead-beat. I always had the timid feeling that it was unsporting, though why it should be any more so than oxygen I could not tell. It was decided to experiment with Sherpas in the icefall, and this Charles Wylie had done, with most strange results. One man had found that it was excellent stuff, it cured his cough. Another said that it made him sleep extremely well! The truth is, perhaps, that the Sherpas have a toughness of fibre little affected, except psychologically, by drugs. They knew that it must be meant to have *some* effect, so did their best for the sahibs' sake.

Going slowly, using the handrail, we had reached the snow crest; thence towards the rocks. I had some difficulty in finding the higher snow traverse into the wide snow gully, as it looks from here, that begins the Face of Lhotse. Crampons squeaked upon the flat stone as we cast about, found a doubtful line and descended ponderously. The wide, soft boots bent the unsupported ankle over at long steps down. At times feet slipped with a jolt through surface crust. Remember, there had been no serious snow for over a fortnight. Since then sun and wind had been playing with the remains. But I still blessed the warmth and comfort of the "H.A." boots. At the gully snow we halted, and I took off my down jacket. It was going to be hot, but I had not dared to take off anything on the Col. Here the other party, going strongly, caught us up. Ed and Tenzing were wearing their oxygen. The rock intrusions to which we now came were in fact two bands running across the Face, and at the lower of these Pasang had "crampon trouble." We suffered from this disease with the strapping of all three types of crampon. The strap had loosened, one crampon swung free from the ankle. While he was fastening it I went over to my oxygen set, still resting here from yesterday. With a delight pleasant at the time but which I regretted afterwards, for I would have liked the mask, I sent the whole thing sliding down towards the Cwm.

At the glacier top the others halted, and we sat with them in great heat. We took off remaining sweaters, but to take off down trousers, which meant removing boots, still demanded too iron a strength of purpose. This time there was almost a highway over the icefall: crampon marks, patches of dirt, silver paper reminiscent of the Tödi in a fine July. Over the topmost crevasse we jumped without a thought. Down the fixed ropes we swung and turned with ease, while George took out his ciné-camera for some shots. There was a holiday feeling about it all, as if this were the last day of term. The sun shone, the breathing came easier with descent, the down trousers grew hotter. Now we were on the last slope.

Nobody had suspected that there would be anyone at VII. Charles Wylie would have gone down with my two. Already my thoughts were wandering to the time it would take to heat a drink, or should we go on without? Perhaps we ought. All of a sudden we saw a figure walking out between the tents: Charles himself without a doubt. What joy! A final trudge along the flat, sticky and uncomfortable between the legs, and we were there. Here was Charles, stayed up to see that everything was well, appearing like the god in the story with great beakers of—lemonade! My first move was to get down into the shade of the tent which I had left, though it seemed quite incredible, yesterday morning. We drank and drank, sitting in the snow and pulling off down trousers. Charles, grinning hugely, heard the story and congratulated Ed and Tenzing. How good that he had stayed!

Ed's party was anxious to be away and down soon, to relieve John's anxieties and see once more the comfort of "civilised" life. Myself I was not sorry when Charles said he would have to stay and take the tents down, since all below the South Col were needed. I would have time, if I stayed with him, to cool out, collect my chattels, have another drink. My reaction from the excitement of yesterday was a feeling of happy relaxation. It did not matter, now, when we got down. Everything was settled, the weather looked fine, the golden ingots of the west had faded into a deep blue sky lightening at the horizon, above the frothy silver cloudlets of a Veronese canvas. Why hurry? Why not savour the last descent in its every detail, all the sensations evoked, at each step, by those words, "The last time. Everest has been climbed"? Even so, I might not have offered quite so gladly, had I known how much hard work would be awaiting us.

Ed, George and Tenzing were cramming their down clothing into rucksacks, roping up again, turning mugs upside down. They disappeared over the bend. We began to look at the tents. These had now been standing for nearly a fortnight. Each day the sun had melted the snow, then frozen it, melted and frozen, to rivet the pegs fast in ice and crease the tent floors into sagging hollows. Each peg we had laboriously to chip out with the ice-axe, with the help of Pasang Phutar and Phu Dorji, while Ang Dorji lay by the pyramid in the stupor of yesterday's weakness. It was a long job. Never had tents seemed to have so many pegs. Each hopeful pull at the canvas was frustrated by another, and the work started again. Outside, the whole scene was like a slovenly Bank Holiday. Now the tents were down, long stiff masses of them. They were being packed on to loads, smaller chattels were entering rucksacks. A last look round, for in a few weeks this place would be its clean, cold self again. Everest would have forgotten us.

Now we were ready to move. It was early afternoon, the sun blazed upon us unclouded, although mist rose from the witches' cauldron of the lower Cwm. As we at last prepared to step out, delaying the moment of fastening crampons, making the odd adjustment to sacks, it was clear that Ang Dorji would have a hard time. His face, handsome in the Sherpa way, was dulled with the unseeing listlessness that I had seen already on Ang Temba. He fumbled weakly at his straps. I suggested to Charles that I might take him on one rope, Charles the other two on another. We started off. After a very few steps both Ang Dorji's crampons came off, almost simultaneously. I leaned across in the steps to fasten them, but to do that service for another person is almost as hard as tying his bow-tie. He cannot sit down upon the slope, you cannot get right above him. I kept very close on the traverse, holding the rope tight. Then I let Charles's party through, saying that we would make our way, slowly. Ang Dorji moved on, like a sleep-walker. Often his foot caught and he stumbled, giving every indication that he was about to plunge into the Cwm. Once he stopped for some time, and I wondered why. He wanted to drink water from a dirty little puddle set in the pock-mark of a crevasse-edge. But he kept on, from sheer instinct.

Charles most thoughtfully waited at the empty ledge of Camp VI. Here we rested some time, watching the mist as it boiled up and reached webbed fingers between us and the sun. The slopes below, with their fixed ropes, went easily down to the last steep stretch some 250 feet below VI. Ang Dorji descended the last feet as a suspended lump. Before 3:00 P.M. we were down through the lower ins and outs, now muddied with that ice-cream-carton appearance that snow can have after a dry spell. We were at the roping-up platform, looking at three solemn black cylinders reposing in the snow. I now felt glad that they had not come up; it was satisfying to have managed without them. Here we took off crampons and prepared to carry them in our hands. But the Sherpas asked to rest; could we go on and they come after? We untied and left them a rope, for no harm could now come to them; two strong men could support Ang Dorji if he needed it. But he looked like one who would go on.

I shall not forget the walk back to IV. The afternoon mist, battling at the lower buttresses of Nuptse, interposed wreathing veils that thickened, and dispersed, and thickened again between ourselves and the burning sun, which burned none the less fiercely. We walked in shirt-sleeves, crampons in hand, with a weight upon our backs. We walked down upon a trail now beaten by many feet: one trail through a white loneliness, and that too would soon be covered up. We reached V, now desolate, and paused only to admire for a moment the great slanting ice plunges of the West Shoulder, with their metallic shine as if a myriad jet aeroplanes were speeding down to destruction. I have never asked Charles what he felt here, but I sensed that he too was tired with the thought that it was "over," with the weight on his back and the looseness of muscle in descent. Tiredness took strange forms. We were going on together for ever, through this loneliness, among magical personalities around. One of them was friendly. The shapes of the hills, half-hidden and magnified by mist, were present watching us. And the mist, a diaphanous green through my sun goggles, laughed in and out of them and played with the outline of their faces. Mingma Dorji might any moment step out from his grave, over there on the right, to greet us. The ghosts of Mallory and Irvine themselves were not far round the corner; it seemed even that the Swiss would climb up to meet us. *Would* anybody bother to come?

There, at last the smudge of tents showed over a bend. We were descending slowly towards it, but there seemed nobody there, only two figures making off down towards III. Perhaps ghosts were here, too. But there was John himself coming out and up to meet us. Even under the white smear of glacier cream, under a white hat and sun-glasses, it was clear that he was very moved. With the warmth of his pressed hand the spell of tiredness was broken.

14

Down to Thyangboche

May 30th—June 6th

1

I had always wondered what a return from Everest would be like, supposing the mountain were ever climbed. I think Charles Evans, before we went out, put the chances at thirty to one against, in any given year, because of the "unknowns" of weather and the party's fitness. Therefore we must all have been steeled a long time against failure, orientated that way in order not to be disappointed. Now the orientation must be changed: Everest had been climbed, the year's dream had come true. It was almost as much a bewildered as a joyful party that drank tea in the big tent, that afternoon of May 30th. But I know that one very strong feeling of all was relief, relief that we were safe and well, that we could go down now while still fit and even with the shreds of an appetite. The climb is in this one respect like a boat-race. The winning crew has something to spare, is on top of itself. The defeated break themselves in last desperate efforts to catch up. Hence that disastrous attempt in 1922, after the monsoon had set in, which lost the lives of seven Sherpas. Or listen to Ruttledge in 1936, "The avalanche was decisive; the climbers had pushed their attempts on the North Col to the very limit. . . . Shipton and Wyn Harris' courageous experiment probably saved the expedition from a major disaster, for had a large party tried to reach the North Col the next day, the entire slope might well have gone down. . . . The game was now up." (*Everest: The Unfinished Adventure*, pp. 122, 123.) It is as dangerous as it is exhausting to go on with the battle for too long.

But for the moment it was difficult to realise our luck, that

◄ *We return to Thyangboche.*

we had *not* to go on straining upward beyond the last ounce of strength. Nothing remained but to get ourselves down, safely, through the icefall. After tea John spoke briefly, with great emotion, of the success and of the spirit which had contributed, from each, to the total achievement. Then he went to his small tent, very unwell. The reaction was for the moment as unnerving as the strain. Since last October his every faculty had been stretched to this one end. Since March he had been physically on the stretch, too, besides now shouldering full responsibility for the party's welfare. He had climbed the icefall two days after a set-back of illness; had led the first party into the Cwm; had refused to rest at Lobuje, and instead accompanied the reconnaissance of the Face on the first part of its route; had carried 45 lb. to the dump above the South Col, and had clung to the Col until driven down by circumstance. I think most felt, at various times, that he was unlikely to stand his own pace. But he stood it. Nobody was really surprised next morning when once again, after a night on oxygen, John appeared fresh as ever and ready to go down.

The rest of us sat round at supper, in talk that flowed endlessly, easily, over rum. I heard for the first time of Tom Stobart's faintly guileful manœuvre to get a shot of the "reception." Tom had met the party above V; had told them to give no indication of the success until quite near, and then filmed the resultant, very un-British scene of hugs and embraces. "We so far forgot ourselves as to shake hands," Tilman said of the top of Nanda Devi. It was much worse here. I also learned that the two figures we had seen going down were Mike Westmacott and James Morris. James had chanced to choose this day of all days to come up and see if there was any news. He had hurried down to convey it. Then the talk went on: the climb, aspects of the climb, the summit, the climb again, the return march, the welcome. I crawled out into the starlight over Nuptse that was the same now as it had been a month ago. It would be the same thousands of years hence, when all our excitement was gone and buried. Then would be a time to talk of "conquest."

My sleep lasted over twelve hours. Then I lay and re-read letters. Particularly pleasing were those of my wife, which urged me generously to stay out if there should be a post-monsoon attempt. Now, there would be no need to worry her. How glad they would be, those that we wanted to be glad! Of the world in general we had hardly begun to think. That morning there was a great sorting of stores. What should go down? How many carries should there be? Nobody wanted to risk Sherpa lives in the icefall to bring down what was not necessary. And who should go down first? Most were anxious to be off. I chose to stay and "help" Charles Wylie, who was going to carry the main burden as usual. He would organise the loads up here. One body of Sherpas would descend now, with loads, right down to Base. They would come up to III tomorrow, to fetch loads which another party, working from IV, would take down today. All should be at Base on June 2nd.

I suspect we would have chosen different items out of the many to take down, given the same choice later and in our right minds. I now regret not taking down at least one of my high-altitude boots as a souvenir, but at the time there seemed every reason for leaving both behind. After the main party had gone, I at last copied out my article and some poems. The sun was hot, Charles had done his job most effectively without more than token assistance. Then I lay and finished *Nicholas Nickleby,* which had just lasted neatly through the Cwm—a pleasant and unexacting companion. Tomorrow back to *The Brothers Karamazov.* Meanwhile, Camp IV began to look more and more desolate, less and less attractive as a residence. Nearly all the tents had gone, leaving dirty craters. The remainder were finding great difficulty in standing upright, since pegs would not stay in the hard ice that our site had become. The tins, paper and rubbish from three weeks' cooking were being pecked and pushed by the choughs, the only ones who might be sorry to see us go.

The eighteenth full day above 21,000 feet. We sat that evening, Griff, Michael Ward, Tom Stobart, Charles and I, under the tarpaulin. A fine hash-up of rice and meat faced us, but we returned it almost untouched. We seemed to have passed the limit beyond which men do not stay high and keep an appetite.

2

I shall not forget the descent of June 1st, in company with Mike Ward and Tom Stobart. It was a strange journey. Tom moved very slowly, giving opportunity to admire the scene. Mist crept up on us, and once it snowed slightly, but the sun shone through the flakes. The crevasses were caricatures of themselves; wide still, their lips had fallen in and they gaped a muddy grey. The little plods up-hill were slow indeed; altogether we took two and three-quarter hours down to III. There we sat and basked in the hot sunshine of the moment, while the mist parted to unveil Pumori, its old self again, in the most elegant of cloud shawls, a dream recollection of earlier days.

Tom was very tired. He had climbed most courageously up the icefall very shortly after pneumonia; now, the prolonged stay at IV began to tell; not that Mike and I would have moved at high speed without him. The time of four and a half hours from III to Base is comment on our progress. Mike went ahead to find the route, I last on the rope. The icefall was a nightmare of itself, dirty as only snow dust-smothered can be, grinning and gaping with a myriad chasms that had never been there before. But no, on second thoughts these were the same, the old friends that had been turned by the alchemist into ugly sisters of their past beauty. This crevasse we had once jumped, we must now go round; that tower had threatened, it had been half-tumbled down a long time. For it was the blocks and towers that had changed most. Every flake of snow covering them had been fried away, so that sun and wind worked upon the remainder to carve a shrivelled gargoyle. No more the creamy waves, the sudden cool, blue plunges. Now, a jagged, jumbled succession of muddy block upon muddy block, indeterminate and fussy in outline. For James Morris's classic comparison to a "squashed meringue" only holds if you reckon the meringue to have been squashed by a garden boot. The colour of the icefall had changed to a light brown; the dust of Tibet had wafted over the Lho La and lay uncovered by fresh snow.

The going too was very different, for we had come up last in the heaviest snow of all. Now we were stumbling on blocks and cracks of unabashed ice. The Nutcracker meant an awkward swing into the crevice; the crevasse between II and III had widened, but had been more securely bridged with two lengths of log added to the duralumin sections. This had been the work of Michael Westmacott, whose presence we felt over the whole scene. Not much had been heard of him, apart from vague talk in the tent of work with the Sherpas in the icefall. In fact he had been saving the party; because of him we returned without fearing the Sword of Damocles which the Swiss told us they had felt the icefall to be, all the time that they were up in the Cwm. Without his patience, not to say engineering skill, the party would hardly have got down in safety, since the bridges would have fallen in and it would have taken days to find alternative routes. Below the site of II, where the seracs had indeed crashed and covered, as far as I could judge, the ground where the tents had stood, we found an entirely new route; no longer across and down the H. M. Bateman valley, but straight down and then over to join it at its bottom, across a mass of fallen ruins resembling the Baths of Caracalla metamorphosed into ice.

We were very slow, and Tom in some straits. Down, always down into this new, brown, mist-ridden world. The surfaces made easier walking in many places than before, yet the line was harder to follow, since crampon points left little mark and we dared not take off our glasses. Sometimes we seemed lost; yet no, there was a grinning old ice-man with icicles hanging from his nose; just the one who, with ermine snow mantle, had looked three weeks before a full-cheeked babe.

At last we were on the flat above the fixed rope of Hillary's Horror. The others took the rope in turn and swung down out of sight to the easy slope fifteen feet below. As last man I put my feet into the steps of the edge and grasped the rope. The next that I knew, I was sitting on my bottom in the soft snow beside them. The shaft used day after day for six weeks had worked loose. I had added the last straw. I must have turned in the air and landed, fortunately, in exactly the right position. The shaft still rested out of sight above; I tugged it angrily down lest it deceive parties the next day. Everest had had the last laugh after all, and on me! Thank Heaven a harmless laugh, a little smack on the behind rather than a serious shaking.

We went on. As we approached the level troughs, the ground became more and more difficult to recognise. Where the little silent valleys had run enclosed among færy pinnacles, now clean torrents poured between slag-heaps. Instead of taking to the stream-bed and walking on it, we climbed these heaps that slithered and disintegrated at every push of the boot. From each top, in darkening dusk, we could see the broad mount of first Base as far away as ever. It was after seven when we trailed in, crampons in the hand, just in time for supper.

Once more we were crowded into the big tent, to be comforted by the parties of yesterday. They also had found descent a heart-breaking labour. "Horrible," Ed described it. James Morris, with Mike, had reached Base from IV on the 30th, a fine performance for anybody, let alone a novice to ice-work. Though tired, he had set off next day with the news. There was some speculation as to when it would reach England. Most thought (and hoped) two days or so after the Coronation.

Anullu, bless him, had secured a tent for Tom and me. Tom had hardly eaten even now. We had had only a bar of chocolate and some mint cake since the morning, but none of us felt really hungry yet. We needed sleep; and very soon we slept.

3

June 2nd. Coronation Day. A day of toothache.

For some there was still work to do. Mike Westmacott was going up himself with Sherpas, who were to bring the last loads down from III, with Charles's party. Now came the business of ordering coolies from the Sherpa villages for the journey back, as far as Thyangboche first of all. How many loads of climbing equipment would there be? At one the Sherpas from the last carry returned, very early; we looked up at the icefall, even at this distance almost brown between its retaining walls, with the happy thought that nobody would go up there again. Charles Wylie was down, too, but having paid for devotion to duty with sun-stroke and a temperature of over 100. Sun-stroke on Everest, a strange thought! Charles retired to bed with pills.

At four George Band succeeded in getting the Coronation Service on our wireless: a not undramatic moment, but the music came through fitfully. Later, on All-India Radio, we were astonished to hear already that Mount Everest had been climbed—by ourselves. We had hardly dared to believe it. With an official announcement to the same effect from the B.B.C., far earlier than we had expected, something seemed to have happened. Everest, the mountain I knew, had begun to assume two personalities: first, the cold calm mass that lay there still above the South Col, as indifferent to our struggles as it had ever been throughout the centuries; and now another Everest which we were seeing for the first time, Everest symbol of Coronation Year, Everest climbed by a British party, Everest laid at the feet of our Queen for her Coronation Day, Everest whose top had first been trodden by Hillary or Tenzing—which? This new Everest was as unreal to me as the other had been until these very months.

I had said to Tom Stobart in the morning, How lucky we are to have had no trouble with teeth. By divine judgment I was stricken now with excruciating pains, perhaps the result of a difference of pressure lower down, for they were gone in two days. Therefore I could not in good faith say that I enjoyed the supper, or celebrations. These were preceded by a discussion of "Tenzing on top." Would it spoil him? Was it best that he had been chosen, when there were three or four sahibs and Sherpas, like Anullu, who could have taken his place? Tenzing had not, through no fault of his own, played so prominent a part as others lower down. Charles Evans reasoned that Tenzing was there not as Tenzing, but representing all the Sherpas who had endured hardship and even lost lives on the mountain. Without them it could not have been climbed. John said he had feared this problem, but had chosen Tenzing as obviously the right person to choose, for his record and fitness as well as for Charles's reasons. There the problem resolved itself, for the time.

After supper the toasts. We had heard that messages of congratulation were coming from the Queen and the Prime Ministers of Britain and New Zealand. Healths were proposed therefore to the Queen, the Duke of Edinburgh, patron of the Expedition, the Prime Ministers, Eric Shipton, who should have been here, and finally George Lowe gave John himself, a toast drunk with deep feeling. The rum circulated, the quality of the stories degenerated, but I crawled off to bed to nurse the toothache with Mike's codeine. I was roused only occasionally to "the sound of revelry by night" from the Sherpa tents. Charles Wylie had explained the Coronation to them, and they were celebrating in earnest after their own fashion.

4

At 7:30 of a sunny summer morning, June 3rd, the "coolies" arrived, well before the celebrators had thought of packing up. These temporary carriers were a strange assembly from the nearest villages: old and shrivelled men in brown rags, tough Sherpa males including once again the reconciled Pemba Norbu, toothless grandmothers, mothers with a baby on top of the pack, pretty Sherpani girls and minute boys. Our stores for the return would demand over a hundred carriers. All tried to secure loads before they were ready, and spent the intervals "tidying" the camp site. Very soon Tom Bourdillon was bemoaning the loss of a piton hammer, Ed that of some spanners, while I was quite certain I had seen much more nylon rope coming down the mountain.

By 10:30 all was moderately packed, and I left Base for the last time with John amid an incongruous crowd: a tough-looking Tibetan type wearing light upper garment and dark kilt, underneath which European lady's boots: a ragged boy girt at the waist with rubber tubing, Griff's cast-off; and an ancient hag clutching an airmail copy of *The Times* as if her life depended on it. The real fun began later, when these coolies were paid off, for then they came up for their pay in pairs, to the infinite amusement of the onlookers when a hulking fellow appeared beside a grandmother, or a wizened wild old man beside a strapping maiden.

The Khumbu had not changed greatly. The change was to come lower, in the grassy valley above Lobuje. Primulas of a beautiful mauve, *Primula Sikkimensis,* John said, were nodding from every bend and boulder, vying for place with a small vetch and budding dwarf azalea. Flowers often give joy; to none more than those who descend from snow. When we arrived at Lobuje the majority were stretched luxuriously on grass, looking up at the blue sky. The tents were pitched —on grass. The weeds still waved their invitation from the stream; the bank beside it now offered an even richer couch. I was chiefly occupied in nursing the toothache, for a man with toothache can look at the loveliest scene without emotion. Only the flowers spoke to me.

It remained to dispose of the mortar bombs, which had been reposing ungallantly all this while at Base Camp. Tom Bourdillon advanced first on the mortar, pointed it across the Khumbu, dropped a bomb in and off it went, to the immense delight of the Sherpas, for it was fun guessing whereabouts on the moraine opposite the bomb would fall. Others tried their hand, until all twelve bombs were exploded. Altogether a good *feu de joie,* though possibly not worth the £5 paid to the coolie who had carried them up. But a love of fireworks is one of the pardonable peccadilloes of military men.

In the evening, on the wireless, we heard a special message from Sir Edwin Herbert, President of the Himalayan Committee, and a brief message to John from his wife. Into an ensuing conference about the chances of flying home there burst the sound of chanting. It was the Sherpas. Before a fire, dimly seen, a row of them, interlocked and with Sherpanis at one end, were swaying in an attitude reminiscent of the Palais Glide. Some wore expedition blue wind-proof; with some the round Mongolian faces and narrow eyes were set off in the half-light by the freer Tibetan clothes. It was a dance which in England would seem as clumsy as primitive. There, at 15,000 feet, under Nuptse and the stars, its regular, endless rhythm was moving. What do the Sherpas think of Everest? To us it is a thing different, utterly apart from everyday life, beautiful and awesome. To them it is Cho-molungma, Goddess Mother of the Snows, as much and as little a part of life as those snows themselves, and the gods believed to inhabit them. I think they have little idea of mountain beauty. As for getting to the top, I have said that this is no common ambition. But that these men and women dancing under the stars should find it natural and proper to be on Everest's sides, that seemed to me plain obvious. Everest was in their home. Everest was their work, as are the fields and pastures; and perhaps its beauty creeps into them with the air they breathe.

In the intervals, not to be outdone entirely as entertainers, we performed Ilkla' Moor, Widdicombe Fair, and the very few other songs of which we all knew some words. There was a polite, not I think enthusiastic, silence. The mad sahibs at it again! Then Charles Wylie was brave enough, or weak-minded enough, to be caught up in the line of dancers, to find the swing of the leg right, then left, not so easy as it looked. At any rate the sight of them completed the cure of my toothache. Yes, it must have been the change of altitude.

If there is a joy in climbing high peaks more vivid than any other, it is the joy of contrast: to lie upon grass rather than snow or rock; to wake to a bird's song, not the creak of ice; to look out at a flower, not at endless whiteness. My memory of June 4th is indeed of flowers. The day started with a crossing for some of us (on the wrong route) of the Lobuje Khola, now swollen and sharp to the legs. This made the walk afterwards, down the grass-covered banks to Pha-long Karpo valley bed, a still purer delight. Everywhere the primulas, some blooms unknown to us, and loveliest of all, as we came down to 14,000 feet, the pink of dwarf azaleas and the white of anemones carpeted the flat. Green grassy couches would allow no man to pass without lying and ad-miring these, with their background of Ama Dablam, a tremendous spire as we saw it once again to the east. It was impossible that we had been higher than that! Clear streams simply asked to be drunk, yaks to be admired, cloud shadows to be photographed. We wandered on in lazy ones and twos and threes, not caring for anything but the beauty of the present. From Phalong Karpo we should have seen up the friendly Chola Khola, but mist veiled Pointed Peak.

At the junction of the streams from Phalong Karpo and Dingboche, a peaceful gathering slept a while in the sun. Legs, long draped and invisible on the mountain, were un-covered for the first time and declared by their owners to be thinner. In fact most had lost about a stone in weight, Tom Bourdillon much more. There was a warmth even in the lightest breeze such as we had not tasted for two months. A pipe smoked sweetly. It was hard to get up and go on, not to remain a lotus-eater for ever, but on we at last went, down the valley, now watching the dark skirts of rising mist sweep the hillside and just tip Thyangboche monastery itself.

We crossed the river below Pangboche. At this village, later in the year, Charles Evans was shown the "scalp" of a Snowman or *yeti*. It was, he said, a remarkable object, conical and leathery, covered with reddish hairs of which he brought two home. Finally, at 12:45 (we had started very early) we reached a meadow just before the last wooded slope. This time, because of lack of water at the monastery, we were camping below. We waited for Thondup, tents and Sherpas, and we waited some time. There had been cele-bration already in the villages; Dawa Thondup and Da Ten-sing were solemn with intoxication. Dawa staggered round the tents, very slowly hitting in unnecessary tent-pegs. He seldom struck the mark. In the intervals the two of them wagged portentous fingers at each other. It was therefore 2:15 before there at last appeared from Thondup's kitchen the lunch which became of all the most popular: a great pan full of the small local potatoes, in their skins, along with pepper, salt and butter. The custom was to sit round and eat as many as possible before everybody else had eaten them.

There appeared here the first breath of our new life: a reporter. Peter Jackson of Reuter's had established himself in a room in the monastery buildings, and came down to prowl round us. He was invited to share the potatoes. Ed in particular faced up to the first of many interviews, "Did you have a great feeling of accomplishment at the top?" and the rest. Jackson earned our gratitude by expressing no rancour at James Morris's neat side-step. James had hurried down, evidently with *some* news but declaring chattily how nice the weather was; finally hastening on to Namche and the wireless.

The lamas had earlier promised a Devil Dance for Tom's filming. It was staged for this very afternoon. Most of us finally dragged ourselves from the unpacking and sorting, climbed the hill to its cloudy ridge and entered the monastery. A Devil Dance: that would be a fitting finale, would let us glimpse some of those unseen forces which we seemed, sometimes, to have met upon the mountain.

5

Perhaps with thoughts of Marco Pallis's enthusiasm, not unmixed with hopeful recollections of the Abbot in *The Ascent of F6,* I climbed the hill to this performance with eagerness. Some of us, on the boat out, had read Madame David-Neel's book on mystics and magicians in Tibet. Devils are very real to the Buddhist. Here, under Everest itself, with ghosts at every turn of the path, spirits upon every spire, I hoped to have that sense of communion in a religion that I have had, say, at a Quaker Meeting.

We were afraid that we would be late. But as we passed into the wood-balconied courtyard before the main temple, it was very clear that we were too early. We climbed a staircase on to the balcony, passed before the Deputy Abbot's throne and were seated on thick carpets immediately opposite the graceful pagoda top of the temple, or *gompa.* John presented 500 rupees for the roof to the elderly Deputy Abbot, after a little speech in Nepali from Charles Wylie. Between us the monks passed to and fro; their robes yellow and *very* dirty. The Deputy Abbot asked how far we had climbed. John said, to the top. That, it appeared, was impossible. The gods live there. But because of the monastery's prayers

on our behalf we had been allowed to tread very *near,* and
to come back safely.

In the centre of the court, by a prayer-flag pole, there was
a table, tapestry-covered. Flags were displayed, including the
expedition flag which John had presented, prominently
placed. On the table were maize and water to be sprinkled
in some of the dances. We remained seated, rising to shake
hands with the Sugi Lama, the most dignified and truly
thoughtful of the lamas, as I thought. His position seemed
to be that of Emeritus Professor, with no official responsibilities in the monastery but a very high standing. A red
robe, black beard, benevolent eyes. The monks had a more
Chinese appearance than the ordinary Sherpas: slightly
drooping eyes and high cheek-bones.

We had arrived at 4:30. After nearly an hour the dignitaries took their seats. Tea (English style) appeared for us.
Then there were brought out long horns, conches, cymbals,
short trumpets. More tea. The swarthy music master took
his stand. All ready. The music, a rhythmical time rather
than tune, started as a yellow-helmeted procession filed
round. A deafening din, one small boy beating a drum hard
in the gallery. Meanwhile, a yellow-helmeted dance, pos-
tured and rhythmical. An interval. The Sherpas in their
shorts wandered in, climbed up, bowed before the Deputy
Abbot who sat with towel over his head.

The long trumpets now appeared in the gallery. They
could be telescoped out to ten feet, and at full length looked
like the Swiss Alpenhorn. Their sound was a low, monotonous plaint, and the dances that succeeded were slow,
heavy, with the figures joining and separating in postures
that must have had symbolic significance. The costumes
were sometimes of Chinese brocade, and the elaborate,
painted wooden masks would be terrifying if they were not
comic. Once I thought I nearly understood a *danse à quatre.*
Two lively skeleton masks danced against two sedate human
masks: Life against Death? But the dance ended disappointingly in friendly embrace. Again, three "men" danced
against three devils. Symbolic of Man versus Devil? But
the "men" went off first, apparently happy.

In an interval a yak that had found its way in raised a lugubrious moo that exactly chimed with the mournful trumpets. . . . No, I could make nothing of it. It was not beautiful, and seemed to have no religious sense. It made me think of D. H. Lawrence's opinion of Buddhism: "Affects me like a mud pool that has no bottom to it." I had seen no fish swimming, no fair shells in the depths. But I was prepared to agree that this was no pure Buddhism.

We returned in the dark. But two days later some of us came back again, so that Tom could film in better light. A novelty this time was a frankly comic dancer, with black hair over a smiling human mask. He danced a begging dance, "Baksheesh dega," asking for alms at all the corners. But religion? Maybe the Thyangboche lama would be as disappointed at the lack of religious feeling in a "Te Deum" sung in Westminster Abbey. But I think not. There was no awe here, that I could see; no awe in the sense in which Everest is awesome. "Superstition" is a word easy to pronounce but not to be uttered, certainly not to be generalised into a judgment of all Buddhist ceremonies. I would say rather, a difference of outlook which I can only recognise.

6

That night, the 4th, was our last together as an expedition. Charles Evans had planned, before we left England, to stay out and explore before and after the monsoon. Being a strong-minded person, he saw no reason why the ascent of Everest should change his plan. He kept with him Anullu, Da Tensing and Changjiu. Meanwhile John was to go on with Greg and Tom Bourdillon as advance party, accompanied by four Sherpas. Rum and stories therefore again celebrated the last night, after a supper of eggs, spinach and an enormous rice pudding.

The main party spent the 5th at Thyangboche, John's party set off at 9:30. We must wait for "long distance" coolies, since those who had carried from Base now departed to their fields. Tenzing returned from the festivities of Tami. He had been teetotal before, but to resist now would have been inhuman. It was a pleasant, easy time; I did not share the impatience to be off. All too soon we would be back in the whirl and heat of Kathmandu, of India. It was still a joy to walk a few yards and sit on grass, among primulas, by the clearest water; to lie at night on turf; to find Himalayan poppies; and to eat hugely. Our appetites had returned in force, in greater force than local resources allowed. We had finished the Compo; eggs were difficult to buy in quantity and the villagers so poor that a sheep, their total wealth, they would not part with. *Dal* and rice, potatoes and *dahi,* or yoghourt, had become the substratum of all meals.

We were the centre of admiring throngs. Nuns with cropped heads came shyly to look at us. The lamas from the monastery came to beg of us. John had given them kerosene; they wanted more. They wanted anything they could get. One elderly lama I found making off with a large wooden box that I was hoping to use for crampons. It seemed irreverent to lay hands on a dignitary of the Church, and I was in some difficulty. Da Namgyal, however, had no such scruples, seized the poor man by the shoulders and pushed him without ceremony out of the camp. But much of the day we spent indoors, reading, for after a fine dawn, rain spoiled the scene. It was the pleasantest reading, just for the sake of reading, as reading after the ascent of a mountain always is. Then to bed, on *chang* brought up by Mrs. Da Tensing; a *chang* soporific but not intoxicant, or very mildly.

The 6th we spent also here, for the coolies had still not arrived that morning. Disquieting messages were coming back from John, who had been held up at Namche four hours by the intoxication of his Sherpas. Only Dawa Thondup, who drank as much as any, had been able to stagger on. Nimmi was sent back in disgrace, though not penitent to look at. Could Charles Wylie send a reliable man as sirdar? Our Sherpa team was dwindling, for six more wanted to stay in Sola Khumbu, and Charles paid them off, sending Pemba and Ang Tsering down for John.

A smaller, quieter party supped on the evening of the 6th. Everything was ready for the return.

A.J.VEILHAN

15

Honour and Hunger

June 7th—June 20th

1

June 7th. The first day's march. Ed started very early numbering loads. Most of us crept out more prudently at 6:45, then felt cold in shorts, the morning being for once misty. We still had to wait some time for our coolies, who arrived in driblets. Most were robustly female, promising well for persevering past the *chang*-pots. At 9:20 we said good-bye to Charles Evans and his faithful Da Tensing.

After the damp, clinging mist of the top ridge, we descended into a world of warmth. It was pleasant to tread downward the long slanting path to the Imja, up which I for one had panted desperately in March. Near the bottom I met Anullu, making back fast to rejoin Charles. He brought out an Army water-bottle. "Sahib drink."

I sipped a little. It was the methylated-spirits *rakshi*.

"Sahib drink more."

There was no refusing; out of courtesy I drank.

"Sahib has not drunk much. Sahib drink more."

This time I tried putting it to my lips without taking any in.

"More, sahib."

The game looked like going on for ever. I broke it off on the plea that after all this *rakshi* I could never reach Namche Bazar. After a tender farewell, I went on down, and Anullu went up. We climbed the long slope on the other side, towards the Namche hillside. Sun and cloudlets played on the bluffs opposite, where the shadows rested purple as on Cumbrian hills, no longer green on ice. Just before the

◄ *We leave the land of Everest.*

"*chang*-place" of the outward march, charming dells of silver birch conducted the path in and out of a fell-side hollow, among monumental blocks, fascinating boulder problems to the rock experts. Arrived at a grassy bluff, just before the path cuts horizontally across ribs of mountain to Namche, I found a large assembly halted. The sahibs were with admirable calm eating chocolate, around them the villagers from the nearby village of Khumjung were gathered in an excited group. They had come to greet and rejoice with friends and relatives, and to do honour to Tenzing, for the bush-telegraphy system of these valleys had given the news long ago. Standing in the crowd a small old woman with shrivelled face was pointed out as the famous Angtharkay's mother. I tried without success to win an answer from her, to say that I had climbed with her son. All around were urchins who would one day be the Tenzings and Angtharkays. Already they had acquired certain skills, but of a rather different character. Within a comparatively few minutes three boxes of Assault Ration had disappeared by magic from before our eyes. We searched and searched, in vain. As sleight of hand the feat would have roused the admiration of any English schoolboy.

We went on, across the hillside ribs. We passed the old Namche camp site and were looking down into the brown amphitheatre round which are ranged box-like stone houses in their rows, wooden roofs weighted with stones; a regular pattern but without the grace which the splendid site might inspire. I found myself with George Band, who was being invited by Kancha, his personal Sherpa, into a nearby house. My new orderly, Ang Dawa II, did not live here, and had no relatives. Therefore I was invited, too. This was a humble house of only one storey, one main room in which the whole family was assembled, and, as far as one could see, lived. The mother, a straight-backed Sherpani with fine features, served milky *chang* which tasted to thirsty lips extremely good. Whenever it approached emptiness the standing cup would be filled. Weavers sat at two looms—one for rugs, one for cloth. George bought two yards of the Sherpani apron cloth for ten rupees.

Kancha, a big boy, as he seemed, of eighteen years, told us that his mother was not allowing him to accompany us to Kathmandu. The mother smiled and shook her head. It was clear that she ruled the family, and she did not want him, I understood her to say, to be spoilt. Then we went out into the sleepy sunshine, down past a square building which proved to be the Indian wireless station, the same which had transmitted our news. An Indian representative of the *Daily Telegraph* greeted us, but at this point, with Tom Stobart, I was invited by little Gyaljen into his house. We looked for our companions. All around sahibs and Sherpas seemed to be disappearing in and out of houses. Namche was quietly *en fête* in our honour; it looked unlikely that we should go far beyond today, and as if the town was using its persuasive powers to keep us here. But why worry? Better to bask in a simple hospitality such as we might never taste again.

Gyaljen's house was more sumptuous, on the regular Sherpa lines. The ground floor was used as a store, in the upper big hall the family lived. We sat on rugs by an open window, looking out over the *chorten* towards the Dudh Kosi Valley and the blue hills beyond. This time we drank *jañr*, a refinement on *chang* with the colour and something of the taste of draught cider. Sherpa wares were displayed. Tom Stobart, with a thirst for acquisition not quenched by purchases at Thyangboche, added a wooden *chang*-container, a tea-mixer and two china cups with silver covers. I abstained, not seeing how to transport such treasures home. From our conversation over the prices it appeared that Gyaljen too was not being allowed to accompany us. This time it was his wife. The Sherpas are something of a matriarchal society, one symptom being that it is very common to marry a boy to a girl perhaps ten years his senior. There is also some polyandry. Marriage includes various stages: first the boy brings presents, then comes to live in his wife's parents' house, finally the marriage is consummated. It is easy to see how the woman comes to dominate the home.

Charles Wylie joined us and reported the revelry going on elsewhere. He told how he had found Pemba, sent down on a horse with Ang Tsering, in answer to John's urgent request, nursing a sprained ankle in a croft. In the road a prostrate figure lay, apparently asleep. This was Ang Tsering, who stirred and fumbled in a pocket. He brought out a dirty piece of paper which he handed bleary-eyed to Charles. It was Charles's own message to John, saying that he was sending down two absolutely reliable men. "It's important, sahib," Ang Tsering had said.

The afternoon was passing too quickly. We kept looking out of the window for signs of the others, but Mrs. Gyaljen pressed us to stay. It was not difficult to linger in this tidy room, with the pots and pans brightly rubbed, the couches laid for sleeping near the open fire. What would Gyaljen do if he did not accompany us? In a few days he would do a "carry" into Tibet, for a vigorous commerce goes on between the two countries. Nowadays many Tibetans are coming with their families over the 19,000-foot Nangpa La, to escape the present régime.

2

When we at last removed ourselves from the hospitality of Namche, Gyaljen came with us to the end of the houses and we shook hands. We turned at last down the steep forest track, down to the gorge flooded with late afternoon light, down to the darkened bed of the Dudh Kosi 2,000 feet below. This we followed through the twilight, wondering whether we had missed the camp or whether the others were behind, whether they had even passed Namche. We were walking through a small cluster of houses when the head of George Lowe appeared at an upper window. The party had established itself, in the top storey of a newly built Sherpa house. Thondup was busy with the slaughtering and cooking of chickens, meanwhile there was tea and company. There are no hotels in the land of Sherpas; the custom seems to be that all assemble in the largest house available. This building was rectangular and solid, the door-posts and lintels being massive wood blocks. As usual, the lower storey was not used for living and the large upper hall extremely crowded.

Meanwhile our tents were pitched by the river a quarter of a mile farther on.

We ate in a cramped semi-circle round the only two chickens in the village, with rice and vegetable. Some deplored the advance party, which would surely be eating all the chickens that the country held. The Namche celebrations, rich in drink, had given us very little food, and we were ravenously making up for lost weight. Then at last to sleep, on the grass flat by the booming Dudh Kosi. Over the black walls of the ravine enclosing us stars shone, recalling a high world which we had left. Tomorrow we would be leaving the home of our Sherpas, the land of Everest.

I can remember nothing more until the clatter of pots woke me the next morning. We breakfasted first, just where we had breakfasted on the march in; the loads were packed and all prepared to move off. Suddenly there appeared in the early light a Mænad form—Mrs. Da Tensing, an angular, ageing Sherpani. Her son Mingma had by agreement with the father, as all thought, been allowed to accompany his sahib Griff down to Kathmandu. Now here was Mama. "They have taken my husband, now they are taking my son." Mingma stood irresolute, but not for long. Charles was soon paying his money to Mother, who led a most disappointed fourteen-year-old back to Namche. We knew later in the year that Mingma had entered the first stage of marriage. Mama again, I suspect.

There were others being paid off, fourteen local coolies who had decided not to come farther after all. The coolies were the daily problem of Charles, who never knew how many were going to drop off each morning. At long last we were thinking of moving on, when two figures in Tibetan costume clattered down the track. These, on closer view and looking much taller in their new dress, were Gyaljen and friend Nimmi. Gyaljen wore the high Tibetan hat and a toga-like garment, though still pyjama trousers and expedition boots. They wanted money to pay the new coolies engaged by Tenzing, for Tenzing had stayed behind at the Thyangboche camp site to bring on the loads left there unclaimed. Soon he appeared himself, in happy mood from the celebrations, accompanied by Ang Tsering bearing a carpet. This, it appeared later, was a subterfuge. Ang Tsering also had been forbidden by his mother to accompany the expedition, for fear that he might be corrupted by the glittering pleasures of the wicked capital. But she yielded so far as to allow him to carry for Tenzing the first stage. Arriving at Tate that night Ang Tsering said, "Bother her," and came the whole way. Arriving at Kathmandu, and perhaps fearing the maternal rod, he decided to accompany his companions to Darjeeling, where he now is.

On the bridge there was much rushing to and fro. The load-carriers filed heavily over, among them Ang Namgyal's wife (or sweetheart, nobody was ever sure which), a pretty Sherpani entrusted with a precious tin box of money. The coolie contractor, a young man from a neighbouring village, scraped rice with his fingers off the plate as he counted. Gompu rushed hither and thither bearing further plates piled high with rice. Charles watched from a strategic position. Now we were saying good-bye for the last time to the faithful Gyaljen and a most affectionate Nimmi, who alternated tears with his prayers that we should come back soon. John's very justified rebukes had had no effect on his loyalty, or he had not understood them. It was sad to be leaving the simple, happy welcome of the Sherpas for more complicated and exhausting demonstrations. I stood some time at a bend of the path, to watch Nimmi and Gyaljen, still waving.

3

Along the riverside next day purple orchids mingled with wild rose and thistle among woods of silver birch and fir. Three of our Sherpanis sitting by the pathside offered me as I passed bits of dry, crumbly curd, very tasty. They were an attractive group as I looked back: brown round faces with almond eyes that narrowed in a smile showing whitest teeth and full lips; jet-black, straight hair carefully plaited and coiffed with a towel or shawl to take the load; silver bracelets and jewel necklaces that showed off the brightness of the Sherpani apron. These aprons they would not abandon in

SUNSET OVER LHOTSE

the hottest valleys. The most that they would allow was a rolled-up sleeve. A number of our Sherpanis, like Ang Namgyal's wife, were accompanying their menfolk. Thus in the summer months both can earn money; if there is a baby, it rides atop the mother's load.

We supped in the largest house of Tate, above the right bank of the Dudh Kosi, this time off six chickens. Our ideal and ambition now was to have one chicken each at a meal, sharing with nobody. Though the chickens were not enormous, one between two with bits to spare seemed a fair second best. When I came out of the stuffy smoke the cloud had cleared. A peak of the Kangtega range showed white in the starlight across the valley, draped with one sleepy cloudlet about its shoulders. Far below in the blackness a single light shone. I wondered, why does it move me almost to tears, the light in blackness under the white mountain? It is surely by the contrast of tiny habitation, which still radiates human life, with cold snow. Certainly the same mountain would not move me in the same way under the Antarctic sky.

We were keeping to the right bank in order to avoid the valley. The bridge, by which we had earlier crossed, would now be down. This meant a climb up and across two long arms of mountain, the second leading down to the ridge above Taksindhu. Next day therefore started steeply. On the paths a few leeches were beginning the quest for blood. Excellent, Griff Pugh said. Since we had too much, they would help to thin it out for us. Then a descent through forest and lunch by a stream before the next up-hill. This, Tenzing said, would take four hours, and his estimate was not far wrong. It was the weariest grind that I have ever suffered. The path started in zigzag, then gave it up and took the line direct, straight up on great slabs placed staircase-fashion one on the other. After two thousand feet I felt that the top must be near, I would do better to go all out. But another thousand, and the mist had closed down, it was raining drearily, and the rise obviously had no intention of stopping at all, ever. Very well then, I would not stop either, I would go on till I died. This continued another half-hour until I simply must stop; to give relief to the utter monotony, a hitch to the rucksack. We put the height of that hillside at 4,500 feet, if you can imagine climbing a kitchen staircase of that footage, with no relief at all. At the top was a prayer wall and a slushy, level track. Suddenly, behold a boulder built into the hill, but no, it was a tremendous block slit underneath! Smoke was issuing and a ragged party huddled round a Thondup fire. It was a smoky paradise, a blessed rest and warmth after the weariness of rain. "Let's have potatoes," Ed said, or rather *alu*. When these appeared the whole party always indulged an infinite greed. Ed's plaintive query *"alu hai?"* must still linger in echo through the valleys of Nepal. But however many he ate, he grew no fatter. He used to feel his legs reflectively and say that he was very thin.

Next day we traversed, in thick mist, high ground exactly reminiscent of the Welsh hills. We must have been at between fourteen and fifteen thousand feet, and here, last year, the Swiss had lost two coolies from exposure in a snow-storm. Then down, past forests that dropped immeasurable thousands of feet, through clearing mist to rivers uncharted and unnamed. Down, chattily with Mike Ward, to the grass slopes of the ridge west of Taksindhu. We were on the flank of the next valley, and it was a richer valley. That meant that there might be a sheep. The camp pitched, one unfortunate of fair proportions was led in by a small boy of perhaps eleven years. He prepared to behead it in the traditional Nepali way. With legs apart, kukri grasped firmly in both hands, he brought the blade down sharply. The sheep's head leaped one way, body the other. All who had held back now eagerly joined in the distributing.

One focal point of each day's march was the arrival of mails. Each day, walking along the track, you would be sure to come across a prostrate crowd absorbed in letters, telegrams, newspaper articles. Telegrams were appearing in sheaves. Some of those to the expedition John kept, but sufficient flooded in to make us realise that the interest aroused by the ascent was far greater than we had ever anticipated. Telegrams from the Queen, the Duke of Edinburgh, the Prime Ministers and many other personages; telegrams from

Everesters such as Shipton, Tilman, Somervell, Norton; a touching telegram from the Swiss, who had splendidly helped us, and a most generous telegram from Maurice Herzog, who would have led the French expedition to Everest next year. Besides these the happy personal telegrams, some of them from people entirely unknown, or else to my embarrassment forgotten, but truly appreciated. Then the letters, also embarrassing now because written by those anxiously wondering what was happening to us, in the month of May. Newspaper reports had led them to believe that the "assault" would certainly start on May 15th, preceded, as one paper had it, "by a bombardment from the 2-in. mortar." Then the newspapers themselves, with their reports of how the news had "hit" the world on the morning of the Queen's Coronation; of how the crowds waiting in Trafalgar Square and all along the procession's route had been livened through a rainy summer dawn by the news: "Everest's been climbed"; how it had passed from a murmur to a roar of acclamation; how it had been taken, not unnaturally, as a symbol of glorious augury to the new reign, the new era. "The Crowning Glory," "All this and Everest too." In such vein the headlines ran on.

This was certainly the other Everest, an object presentable on a platter; a very pleasant Everest, though it was difficult at times to adjust focus to the two. At one such meeting with the daily dak runner a note arrived in John's handwriting addressed to "Sir Edmund Hillary, K.B.E." Ed spluttered, thought it was a joke, but it was true. "You go and have a good time on a mountain and then this happens to you. How on earth am I going into the grocer back home now in my old trousers to ask him for pots for my honey?" At this a certain mild chaffing ensued, including a proposition from someone that the expedition should syndicate Sir Edmund and draw profits, to be shared equally by all, from the highest bidder in the matrimonial stakes, since he was certain to (and later did) receive proposals of marriage. But on that subject Ed must have already made up his mind. He remained a dark horse until he announced his engagement in August.

4

Thus we advanced westward; and particularly after we had crossed the Chyangma ridge and passed quite out of the Sherpa country, Everest receded. It remained a pleasing thought that Charles Evans was still in touch with it. You will say: "That first Everest has never been very clear as a picture of a personality. First a plan and a hope, then a mass of rock and snow across which the winds play, now a sort of captive Frankenstein." Very true, and that is exactly the impression that it has been giving me. Mountains have always appeared in the colours that the eye of the beholder wishes them to take: to Rousseau a noble refuge, to Wordsworth an argument for Universal Good, to Leslie Stephen a peg for agnosticism, to Achille Ratti (Pope Pius XI) a manifestation of Divine Love. Just so Everest is what we want it to be. To the Buddhist or Hindu it is the home of the god and goddess Shiva and Parvati, "and any invasion of the privacy of it would be a sacrilege fraught with disastrous consequences to the Hindu country and its people." [1] To our predecessors upon the northern side it was a giant which flogged its assailants with the wind and unnerved them with the rarity of its higher air. It was an enemy. "We had the weather and a good opportunity for a fight with our adversary. There is nothing to complain of. . . . We have been beaten in fair fight." So Howard Somervell wrote in 1924. Or Smythe again, after 1933: "Everest had been hostile towards us, and we felt that there was something almost personal behind this hostility, in the bitter cold and sudden, smiting storms." To me, when I stood on it and viewed it from its sides and surroundings, Everest was aloof and impersonal, as impersonal as the thought of death and as testing. We in our braver moments make of it a challenge and an adventure, splendid whatever its character. In our everyday we conceive it as a climbing problem, a grease-pole as Ruskin would have it, about whose smallest intricacies we fuss and bother as if they were the most important things on earth. We finish by regarding it as

[1] Letter from the Maharajah of Nepal, 1924.

a friendly old thing, just as we have come to feel friendly with "Cloggy," the awesome cliff of Clogwyn du'r Arddu in North Wales. Now, as the climbers come back, those who know nothing of mountains are talking of "conquest" over a fallen adversary. But they, the climbers, are thanking the mountain, the weather, their luck, which were friendly enough to allow them so high upon a hill which tested but did not repulse.

Therefore you are right, or at any rate agree with me and I hope you are right, if you are saying by now: "This is really rather absurd. There is no personality to Everest at all. What does Everest care about them? Its cliffs and cols are now being lashed by winds such as no human could ever endure. What difference does all this little summertime fuss make to it?" For that calm, inscrutable hugeness was my picture of Everest too, as we started the descent, and that impression only receded as the blaze of publicity began to light up the second, different Everest with the light of our action. This imagined Everest, however vivid in book and picture and headline, could not be the great impassive mass that still towers behind us.

5

The way home was lovely with flowers; orchids beside the path before Junbezi, and in the meadows of Tapka beyond, where we camped, mauve irises nodded their fragrance. Food—sun—rain—tiredness—beauty; these are my recollections of the march. At Tapka mutton and champagne (the last generously sent by the Ambassador), a real feed for the New Zealand two who were perhaps more accustomed to meat than the rationed British. Our hunger knew no bounds. It was here that Ed ordered himself rice pudding, after a large shoulder and leg of mutton, plus jam pancakes. The conversational topic that beat all others was food. The attraction of civilised life was bread, fruit, meat.

Sun. On the Lamjura Banjang Pass at 12,000 feet I lay sun-drenched and read *The Brothers Karamazov*, stock favourite of Himalayan climbers. Often these mornings were fine and sunny, then cloud descended and thunder boomed, making it unlikely that this was monsoon. The soft, misty sun disappeared behind vaporous veils. The rain poured down hot and oozy, then cleared, usually, in the evening. As we drew westward over the lower ridges, it made the path slippery with yellow mud. I blessed my boots, which I wore all the way back. The behinds of some of the gym-shoe wearers ended the day as splodgy patches of ochre. Then out came the sun again to dry us, and towards the end of the march the rain cleared to the sultriness of the tropical greenhouse. The first bathe for most was in the stream at the far side of the Lamjura Banjang, from which we had dropped in the heat some six thousand feet. In and out of the cold mountain water we washed off the dirt of months, and yet, considering the months, the dirt was surprisingly light. We lay on grass by the sparkling pools with the luxury of letters from home to hand. Gompu's father, a shaven lama of learned appearance, had come to greet us from his mountain home up in the wooded hills. It seemed strange that the scholar's son should have been disporting himself on Everest. Gompu himself, like Mr. Pickwick, had grown in stature from a round and laughable character as you came to know him. He had over other Sherpas the great advantage of being able to read and write. This gave him, as he scuttled up and down on the self-appointed task of checking coolies, the air of an earnest sergeant. I remember the meeting for the sticky heat of the valley that evening, as we sat round trying to drink an undrinkable brand of *rakshi,* the present of Gompu *père.*

We were leaving Sherpaland; for at Chyangma the next day we were stared at by girls wearing the Indian, sari-type dress, leaving the stomach bare, and men with the Nepali carpenter hat. Here Thondup bought chickens, to be carried over the Chyangma La and down into the Those valley, where they would join more chickens and make our supper. Here I am back at food! It remains the strongest memory. In order to satisfy our greed, it was necessary to plunder villages all along the way, specially as we feared that John would have foraged before us. That night we had seven chickens, but most declared this to be not enough. Only one night did we achieve our one chicken each, but it was a very satisfactory occasion. When there were less, we shared one between two. Then, usually, those who had finished first got on to the remainder. It did sometimes happen that a finisher-first got on to his neighbour's scrapings by mistake. Then the puddings. The most filling was rice, and we once tried to use rice also with the chicken. But there ensued an argument of the Big-Endians against the Little-Endians; that is of those who favoured fried pilau with the bits of chicken intermingled, and the separatists who could not bear fried rice, and wanted their chicken cooked separately and the rice plain boiled. As always the negatives won, since the pilau enthusiasts had to admit that they were not *averse* to plain boiled rice. Meanwhile there would be a conference on how to supplement the meagre morsel which the Assault Ration gave us for the midday. Most had eaten their biscuit lunch by 10:30, and were racing to reach the camp site in the hope of *alu*. Could we not carry cold *alu?* It all seemed very important at the time, more important than Everest.

Tiredness. It must be confessed that the legs do not face a slope with the same zest, after they have been doing nothing for three months but climb similar slopes. So three of us thought, plodding in afternoon heat up from the flooded rice-fields to the ridge beyond which Yarsa lay. The body is possibly doing its job as efficiently, but the old eagerness is gone. One step on a mudbank after another, a bend in the path and hope of easing, more uphill still round the corner, a sigh, wriggle of the rucksack to greater comfort, then on again. There is no joy here. The worst plod brought us from the river beyond Kirantechap up to the high ridge, over 7,000 feet, of Manga Deorali. Now Kirantechap of the pipuls is no more than 4,500 feet. The night had been sticky, I had been diagnosing dysentery in myself and taking Sulphaguanadine. We dropped early to the river and fell before the temptation of its cold waters. We bathed and dried and bathed again. Ang Dawa II, my orderly, washed my socks, since I was much too lazy to wash them myself. Even some of the Sherpas were tempted into the luxury of muddy water. Now to bathe is delicious. To climb 4,000 feet immediately after a bathe under tropical sky is not. It was a weary climb indeed up pinewood slopes, through rice-fields, past villages, through more fields, always up. It must have been gruelling for John, whose party, on June 13th, had already arrived at Kathmandu. They took only eight days from Thyangboche. Thondup alone was ahead of me as we crossed the ridge and descended several hundred yards, to my increased fury at every step. Not until the two "Aunties" had arrived and tea was cooking did I feel peace. I must present these ladies again. They were both Sherpanis *d'un certain âge,* one of them Ang Norbu's solid sister. In the morning they were always helping Thondup over the breakfast, and among the last to leave; in the afternoon they were always first at the next camp site, collecting wood and fetching water. They were always smiling, true jewels of their sex, and at a camp site the fairest objects on the landscape.

Several of us suffered from a weakening dysentery against which we waged on the whole successful war. Poor Griff suffered very badly. But I look back at the stages before the dysentery, before the heat, among the Sherpas, as the happiest days of the expedition. The work was done, Everest seemed a friend, there were no problems immediate beyond the next meal. Now, as we advanced into the hot valleys, the nervous excitement of anticipation began to weigh, as the physical conditions became more unpleasant. Tenzing would come into camp red with *holi* dust and garlanded from some local celebration, to lie in his tent and be ministered to by his two nieces. The interior of this tent reminded the visitor more of an Eastern potentate's than of a Sherpa dwelling: a handsome rug on the floor, tea vessels, two women busily in and out. By contrast the other Sherpas looked as if nothing had ever happened to them; Ang Namgyal and his wife quiet as ever; Ang Nyima lame from a leg infection which he only showed at Chyaubas; Da Namgyal always attentive on the march, carrying his six-year-old son who had been brought up to Sola Khumbu to meet father; Pemba Norbu always first in and always with Griff's tent, to the great annoyance of everybody else.

Our last day of liberty was June 19th. We left a rainy camp at Chyaubas and descended in bright early sunshine the long slope to Dolalghat on the Sun Kosi. Far to the west a silver tooth which I took to be Gosainthan, over 26,000 feet, stood up above cloud. The village of Dolalghat was in festal attire with painted triumphal arches and flower-stewn paths. Reporters from Indian newspapers had come out from Kathmandu. As we bathed in the sunny river, Ed in particular became "the admired of all photographers"; he was snapped once cleaning his teeth, once washing his buttocks. Besides the reporters there were some politically-minded gentlemen anxious to see Tenzing before anybody else did. I was struck with what might be the world's general knowledge of Everest, when a reporter said to me, "When I come along those terrible paths and think that Everest must be even worse than that . . ." Finally Tenzing appeared, almost unrecognisable under huge wreaths.

The long valley up towards Hukse was very hot after our bathes and breakfast, but enlivened by the great grey langur monkeys swinging in and out of the jungle above. At the top of its little col Hukse too was *en fête*. Here we camped, in company with John, who had walked out energetically as ever with Joy, who had flown out. The reporters of one or two British newspapers joined us, having set out from Banepa to meet us with no very definite ideas for the night. It was a strange evening, full of talk, plans, programmes, uncertainties, the need to stave off controversy, friendly reminiscence at ease on the grass. I walked along a little path and sat looking at the darkened hills and woods.

> *Über allen Gipfeln*
> *Ist Ruh,*
> *In allen Wipfeln*
> *Spürest du*
> *Kaum einen Hauch; . . .*

Here there was peace in the moonlight, peace broken by the ceaseless chirruping that is part of night in the Himalayan foothills. It would be the last sleep on the ground under these stars; and while I rejoiced at the thought of a bed, and the return to home, one part of me was sad at the ending of an adventure with comrades who would be different in future,

even as I myself would be different. We returned to the un-
guessed excitements of limelight. I felt a great longing to
jump straight off that hillbrow into the arms of my family,
with no fuss intervening.

6

John and Joy had told us something of the festivities brewing at Kathmandu and of the reception committee that
would be meeting the party at Banepa; I started a feeling of
uneasiness as we neared the little crest on the other side of
which that village lies. We were a hot and motley caravan,
for already a crowd, many of them school-children, had come
out to greet the national hero of Nepal. Tenzing therefore
was some way behind. A few days before he had chatted of
the delights of our homes and family welcome; I wondered
now what the poor man was thinking, whelmed under garlands and deafened by the chant of "Tenzing Zindabad,"
"Viva Tenzing Viva Tenzing," which rang along the paths.

At the pass we were met by Colonel Proud of the British
Embassy, and two smooth young gentlemen recognised with
difficulty as Mike Ward and Charles Wylie. They had gone
ahead from Kirantechap. Most of us were now very hirsute.
George Lowe particularly fine in his Robinson Crusoe,
George Band in an orange Dr. Livingstone set off by his
spectacles and panama. Colonel Proud regaled us—there is
no other word—with beer, plums and cake, three delicacies
luxurious beyond belief. Tenzing, John and Ed came in for
the garlands and *holi;* scores of white-robed figures chanted,
pressed, cheered around. The procession continued slowly,
down the path of our first day's march, on to the knoll above
Banepa. Where we had camped by the half-built school, a
platform was now erected for the principals. For the rest of
the party no provision had been made over the twelve-mile
journey back to the capital, and I must confess to a sharp relief, particularly when George Lowe and I were received by
the architect of the Embassy and his wife, Mr. and Mrs. Mac-
millan, into a hospitable jeep provided with sandwiches and
cake. We had taken a few looks at John, Ed and Tenzing be-

ing pushed into position, prepared as they were to give tongue. We escaped gladly.

As we jolted along the twelve-mile track lorries bursting with men and women came bumping and swaying past us. They stopped with a cry: "Where is Tenzing?" and rushed on when we pointed back. As it is difficult to transport motors into Nepal, the available resources are stretched to bursting. Instead of twenty in a lorry there will be fifty. At last we were driving through the picturesque streets with their carved fronts and wooden balconies, we were at the Embassy drive and in at the Macmillans' bungalow. An arm-chair. Tea in a cup with a saucer. Biscuits and cake. Bliss. It would have been most easy to dawdle the rest of the afternoon away, for it was by now after four, but the shreds of a conscience drove us out to join the procession, which, of course, had been very slow and would only now be arriving. The Macmillans' jeep bore us back on to the route. We found ourselves among an immense crowd, white-robed and pyjamaed. All were waiting excitedly, and we waited too.

At last it came, a state coach invisible under flowers and drawn by four horses with liveried horsemen. As outriders there rode four dark damsels dressed in white. Seated high in the centre of the coach, facing forward, was Tenzing, flower-wreathed and looking bewildered, but at the same time exalted. Below him his wife and daughters. It was some time before we spotted John and Ed, who faced to the rear and sat in a sort of pit below Tenzing. The crowd nearest to the coach was thickest, and we must wait some time before we could join in the procession, which must by now have included every motor vehicle in Nepal. All were full; the chant of "Tenzing Zindabad" rose from every bumping car. That just behind us was the most vociferous, in English for our benefit. "Hail Tenzing, first man to conquer the Everest! Hail Tenzing, first man to conquer the Everest!" The chant repeated itself, on and on and on. The chanters never grew hoarse.

The procession was now slower still, for we wound through every street. I took the opportunity to scribble down the inscriptions on the walls, those that were in English. "Welcome

279

Tenzing, first man to conquer Everest!" "Hail Tenzing, star of the World!" "THE UNPRECEDENTED (the letters enlarged towards the end of the word) HERO TENZING." "Poor Mount Everest!" "Smiling Nepal welcomes Tenzing"; and so on. Over a number of streets painted triumphal arches displayed their welcome. Tenzing stood on top of an Everest unknown to us, waving an ice-axe. Sometimes Ed was present, in the bottom right-hand corner, and then in some doubt as to whether he would need a pull on the rope. Sometimes he was even being hauled up. And meanwhile I noticed, almost with terror, that the chanting swelled, the crowd pressed closer. Hymns were being sung to a god, not to a mortal man.

We were now at the town hall, a porticoed modern building facing a five-storey pagoda. Loudspeakers blared music, the crowd swayed, many had climbed to every storey of the pagoda; others draped themselves over the huge lion statues. The three figures, as smeared with red *holi* as any Cairo boys, appeared on the balcony between the pillars. Ed and John swung a foot over and sat with legs dangling. They caught sight of our jeep, sea-washed in the crowd with George Lowe reclining on the roof, and grinned hugely. Then the speeches of welcome began. Tenzing spoke. John made an excellent and dignified little speech in Urdu, Ed spoke briefly and to the point in English. The crowd cheered wildly, flowers were thrown, the whole open space and the buildings decked with people seemed to stir and sway with a life of their own. I felt as if we would be here forever, jammed in a shouting, gesticulating mob.

We were off at last, a wild rout with the men singing, women and children smiling and sprinkling flowers from every balcony. I waved to James Morris in the car behind us. He smiled and shrugged his shoulders. We made our way past the parade-ground, finally to enter the big gates of the royal palace. Here the crowd lessened as we drove through the gardens, though a fair number pushed their way across the lawns. We drew up before a large building, having porticoes on a first floor, to which wide stone steps led. By the time we arrived it was late, perhaps 7:00 P.M. Were we to go up, dirty, unshaven, in our shorts? Uniformed Nepalis seemed to be expecting us; up we went. We were in a lofty hall with decorated roof and chandeliers on the pattern of the Victorian 1850's. Men and women in a variety of costumes were taking their seats along the sides; we did likewise, finding ourselves opposite the Ministers in their black frock-coats and tight white trousers. I was near Griff, who still wore the now very grey pyjamas in which he always walked, because the sun on his legs burned him, he said. His spectacles surveyed the scene with interest: the first time surely that an investiture has been attended, or a king had his hand shaken, by a man clad in pyajmas.

All at last took their places. The three red-smeared figures, looking even less reputable than before, were seated in the centre of the left-hand wall. They now seemed very weary; they had in fact had no food or drink since the meeting with Colonel Proud at eleven that morning. Tenzing was conducted to the King at the end of the hall and decorated with the Star of Nepal, first class. John and Ed received very portly medals. Finally the whole assembly moved back to the fresh air under the pillars. The King shook hands with each of us, and the whole expedition was photographed, with the Ministers beside. This greeting was pleasantly unceremonious, the King being dressed in simple Nepali costume and wearing the national hat; Griff, of course, in pyjamas.

After 7:30 in the evening a group of very tired men with grateful hearts was conveyed to the British Embassy; to food, to a bath, to sleep between the sheets of a bed.

A.J.VEILHAN

16

Limelight

From the 20th of June

1

"A useless toil, why endure it? Then I thought, with an inward grin, what a fuss there would be if we reached the summit. We would have to endure long adulatory speeches, our digestions would be ruined by innumerable dinners, we would be pestered by autograph hunters. Here on Everest, at least, there was peace." The words are Frank Smythe's, written about the climb over the northern slabs of Everest in 1933. He ends his book on the plateau of Tibet. But it must be that in an *ascent* of Everest the innumerable dinners and the autograph hunters are part of the total experience. As soon as the climbers return, the total act is seen as a much wider whole than just a climb on a mountain; it is a pool rippling away from the stone thrown into it. Therefore I am not going to give a description, but an impression to round the picture. In what way was this event different from the ascent of any mountain?

The festivities began as I have described them. It was clear at once that Nepal was wild—uncontrollably wild—with excitement, not for the mountain, about which nothing was known or cared, but for the foot or two of snow upon which the hero of the nation, Tenzing, was remembered to have stood. On the day after our arrival an enormous crowd gathered on the grass *maidan,* in the centre of which a platform was erected under an awning. Some fifty addresses were read and presented, many of them framed and mounted under glass. Most were in Nepali, but of those in English one, delivered by a yellow-robed member of the Buddhist fraternity, struck me specially. It drew attention to two men great

◀ *Home-coming.*

in the history of Nepal: one was Gautama Buddha, the other Tenzing. The Active and the Contemplative Life? No wonder Tenzing looked a good deal puzzled. As I thought of the last carefree stages of our walk through Nepal, a link seemed to have snapped. A man of simple life, but of determination and ambition, a friend and happy companion, was borne suddenly into this world strange to him as the planet Mars. A passing reality was restored when the other Sherpas, who had been watching wide-eyed, were "introduced" to him. They wore their old clothes, or expedition wind-proof and gym shoes. Ang Nyima, celebrating the recovery of his leg, was half-seas over. The vigour of his handshake knocked every wreath awry, and was as restorative as fresh air in an Indian summer. There was still the simpler comradeship.

In any achievement that becomes "news" the world over, there will be some opportunism, political, social, and also in matters of money. But if the core of the enterprise remains hard, it is safe to snap a cautious finger at any outside disrupting force. My impression is that we have been lucky. In our days at Kathmandu there was far too much to be done for time to allow worry about unnecessaries. First the packing. George Lowe and I were chiefly concerned with this, while everybody came to pack his own department. In the sheds of the new Embassy we spent hot hours, greatly heartened by the help and tea-time hospitality of the Macmillans. It was a strenuous, sweat-laden job, to sort everything into crates. Moreover, as we were going back with so much less equipment than we had taken in through India, somebody must sign certificates convincing a number of authorities that we had not sold a number of articles at vast profit during our passage. At every turn Colonel Proud came to our aid; at every exhausting difficulty the Ambassador, Christopher Summerhayes, stood ready to help us. The moments of rest allowed at the Embassy and the Prouds' house were the pleasures we had dreamed of for our return throughout the march back.

On June 26th, after as many receptions and dinners as could be fitted in, John and Ed, Greg and Tenzing flew to

Calcutta to be fêted there. The remainder joined up at Delhi. India was honouring the occasion royally, though not at the easiest season climatically. The temperature stood at over 100 degrees, the monsoon had not yet arrived, dust-clouds masked the sun in stifling coils that made our posture upon platforms a trying as well as ungainly one. We were most nobly received by the President of India, who gave decorations and shields, and by Mr. Nehru, the Prime Minister. There were lectures and attendant dinners. On July 3rd the whole party, with Tenzing's wife and daughters on board too, took wing for England.

2

"Lui, naguère si beau, qu'il est comique et laid." So Baudelaire sang of the albatross, glorious creature winging its way in stately swings and swoops through the blue sky. When it is trapped on deck it waddles about trailing its long wings, absurd object of ridicule. So he might have sung of successful Everest climbers, who seem, to the general public at any rate and on the authority of the newspapers, intrepid heroes slashing a path to victory up hazardous ridges. When they come down, when they are seen to be mortal creatures with hands and feet and stomachs like the rest of us, stomachs perhaps more capacious than most, then the sense of disillusion will come. They eat and drink, indeed are capable of doing both in excess. They can be ill-dressed, ill-featured, altogether exasperatingly disappointing. They can suffer from coughs and colds and sneezes, they can shiver with the best and be inefficient with the humblest. When they go back to their jobs, let us say to teaching modern youth French and German, the idol may be found to have feet of drabbest clay. How much better if he could have stayed remote on his mountain top!

This is a sad thought but inevitable. At the time when my book is written, the honeymoon has not yet quite ended. Not one member of the party can have anticipated one-tenth of the excitement which the ascent caused. It would be an amusing task, perhaps that of a cynic, to picture the news had the forty-foot rock step proved just that fraction harder. The happy coincidence of the announcement that was made on Coronation Day itself, the feeling that in this year especially Britons can do it after all, the correlated feeling that British prestige abroad would be enhanced: all these factors contributed to the aureole now thrown around the ascent of Everest. The Himalayan Committee met the party at the airport and a first lecture programme was planned. But the public demand for lectures far exceeded the restricted audiences of those who knew something about mountains. Manchester, for instance, insisted on seven public lectures instead of the one originally planned. This was good in that the message, to use so badly flogged a word, of Everest's comradeship and leadership reached a wider set of ears. Youth clubs with their adventure trophies, colleges with their holiday travel funds, Boy Scout associations with their "Climber" and "Venturer" badges, all profited in a worthy cause. The Everest Trust was founded to assist exploration. Schools, institutions, legions up and down the country profited too. Many other countries demanded lectures. At the same time, of course, the wider the audience, the greater must be the misapprehensions; which misapprehensions matter not twopence, if only the main story is straight.[1]

The misapprehensions were largely cleared by John's official book, which appeared in November 1953 and became a classic as well as a best-seller straight away. Cleared, that is, for those sufficiently interested to read, and who do not think that, if they have seen the film, they have "done" Everest. For the film, magnificent as photography, can give only one picture, the outside of an Everest which dominated the thoughts of many men through many months. Even the lectures can give no more than a picture of the surface happenings. The gala lecture at the Royal Festival Hall in September gave a queer sense of that stranger ghost, the

[1] Sometimes indeed they are very diverting. At one school a very small boy with a pink face got up at the back. "Excuse me, sir, did you find any dead people on the mountain? *Bodies* or anything?"

second Everest, at whose altar we smart young men in tail-coats and white ties were parading. We stood on a stage and were introduced in the kindest terms by Sir Edwin Herbert, President of the Himalayan Committee. There was a clap for each. Some of us bowed, as it seemed the only thing to do. After this those not engaged in giving the lecture walked to the bar, or we peered at ourselves on the screen over the attendants' shoulders. The applause was most genuine and gratifying, and yet the applauders were clapping something that was not us, but a faintly celluloid representation of a more Hollywood us. We would have been disappointed, doubtless, if they had not clapped.

For when all is said, the joy and enthusiasm with which the lectures were received were *good*. The adventure was inspiring to further adventure. The poetry of it suggested to some "those other Everests of the mind." The pushing out of the human spirit into fields beyond and above ordinary life (though the climbers themselves are very ordinary people) interpreted itself to men and women, above all to boys and girls, who had never seen a mountain. This is not to say that the tales of other mountain ventures have not been as moving in exactly the same way. But the circumstance of the highest summit in the world has meant a wider range of appeal, quite disproportionate but understandable. Many are being introduced to the Everest story who might otherwise have had no thought for it; and through Everest to other mountains. The spontaneous, unrestrained "Coo" of amazement at the pictures, which will rise from the front rows of a girls' school, is a tribute to utterly new worlds being opened to new eyes.

And the dinners and the honours? At the time of writing no stomachs seem to have been seriously affected, though they may have been enlarged. The honours are a demonstration of interest by those in a position to give them, who see in the expedition something more than a private venture. The informal pleasure of an afternoon visit to the Music Room of Buckingham Palace will remain a "green thought" to us and to Tenzing, as well as to our families.

3

And the future? It is common after lectures for a questioner to ask whether the ascent of Everest means the end of interest in Himalayan or any other mountaineering. The best reply is perhaps by another question. Did the ascent of Mont Blanc in 1786 kill the interest in Alpine mountaineering? Everest is not one of the hardest, technically, of the many huge peaks over 25,000 feet. By continuing their climbs, men will explore further the limits of themselves, and the relation of these large creatures to their small spirits; until the day when we have either blown ourselves up or further planets have claimed us. For I have said that the medium of some men is paint or stone or boats, or a schoolroom or engines or paper and ink; that of a few is rocks and snow and the uphill movement of limbs. This is the only answer I know to the very reasonable query: "Was it after all worth the labour? Was it worth the anxiety to others, the expense and effort of many people on your behalf?" However peculiar and apparently profitless the talents, these mountaineers would be as foolish as the man in the parable if they buried them in the ground. If they did that, they would remain incomplete as the persons their temper intended them to be. And they will not, but will go on climbing.

That is why I am writing this book, indeed being forced by those "peculiar talents" parts of myself to write it. I like paper and ink as I like rock and snow. Moreover, I believe, as I have said, that a great literary work remains in the Himalaya; first of all concerning the relation of the human animal to the slope that he climbs. Here Griff Pugh will come in, for physiology and the other sciences are increasingly helping men to accustom themselves to the oddities of high altitudes. Their discoveries are increasingly important. On this ground writer, explorer and scientist meet, the one acknowledges his debt to the other; and I was struck, upon Everest, with the thought that here was I, a thoroughly unscientific person, enjoying sensations which could only come to me because my body was plastered with the aids of modern science and technology. Above the South Col I was breathing and appreciating and even feeling a certain inspiration—because I was wearing an oxygen mask and my feet were encased in special boots. Without the mask, away goes the enjoyment, indeed any æsthetic sensation at all. I was feeling well, partly because I had been told by a doctor to drink some six pints of liquid a day. And so on. Thus Western man depends for his explorations and even meditations upon artifices which are the fruits of his own powers. This dependence is a miniature of the dependence of all, painters and poets too, on the sisterhood of the sciences.

When this has been said, the physiologist and his brethren will admit that the dependence goes so far, but no farther. Here is the saving clause rescuing us from a mechanical Moloch. In the last resort a man goes beyond his physical body, on resources of the spirit which may be further explored but which will never, I hope, be accurately charted. That is why no physical test is able to tell who, on his medical qualifications, will climb well high up. The little extra of spirit, the individual and inalienable concern of each, remains unpredictable by any known test. Everest was not climbed by limbs and oxygen, but with the help of these. Something else climbed it:

> *Something else surpassing that,*
> *Something of mine which, mixed up with the mass,*
> *Made it bear hammer and be firm to file.*

That "something" that Browning intended, which each has and shows to his friends on a mountain, is the kernel, surely, of personality. It can be only very superficially demonstrated by cinematograph or pictures or even the spoken word, for these simplify. It may be impossible to demonstrate it at all. It may be an embarrassing process. Men come nearest to the demonstration when they take paper and pen and write what they have seen and felt, out there under the stars.

The Poems

A PRAYER FOR EVEREST

Written before the Mountain

That I may endure,
And love of friends confirm me;
That I lend my ear
Kindest to those who vex me;
That I may be strong,
My will guide the faint footsteps;
That heart and lung
May learn, rhythm is conquest;
That in the storm
My hand may stretch to help,
Not cringe in the glove to warm;
That courage of mine
Bring to friends courage too,
As I am brought by them;
That in the lottery
(My last, my worthiest prayer)
No envy bleed,
When, as I know my heart,
Others succeed.
Here be content, the thought:
I have done my part.

NEPALESE VILLAGE

Written at Bhimpedi

The beauty of evening. Curtained the valley mist,
Orange skirt frilled, at last has coolly kissed
The darkening ridges. A hushed good-bye is said
With rain libation softening the dusty tread,
Planting quick seeds of coolness underfoot,
Painting spring's colour across the emblazoned shoot.

Carriers have laid their loads; this day is done.
Miles of blind path, the scraping foot on stone,
Sweat of the cheek, plumb weight's tug at the head,
The slow step in the naked stream bed,

290

All for a day are done. On the far hill
A glow, then a flash, a brighter light still
Than the first stars written over a paling sky,
Like the eyes of an old man defying death to die . . .

Fire: it is food. The metallic overtone
Drops with the earth's light. The hungry day is done.

WALKING TO EVEREST

Here on the green grass lawn,—
Pine-tree and primula rare,—
Here I would rest and be done,
By my one self this one,
    But I do not dare.

Beyond, the hill climbs away
From forest to grass, from grass
White to where snow-tops sway,
Rock-tower cloud-capped grey
    By mists that pass.

Man made to suffer, to stray,
Why must you go beyond?
Fountains your thirst allay,
Torrents their sweetest play
    Here, the still pond.

Sadly the answering heart:
World, you were never mine.
Tiger and snake have art,
Gorged, to sleep out their part
    Of Time's tortured line.

Lost among these comes one
Who cannot once be still.
Sleeping he dreams with moan,
Waking he will not be done
    Until done his will.

Wandering he must know
The first grey peak and the last;
Sunset and polar snow,
Tropic to desert glow,
    Present with past.

And if he suffer for these,
That is his voyage too:
Dim-wrapped in doubts that tease,
Half-lord of doubtful ease,
    He must pass through.

Knowing death is his end,
Death he weighs in his hand.
Where the ice ridges bend,
Where the feat's pride is his friend,
    Straight let him stand.

EVEREST FROM THE WEST

Camp Below Pointed Peak

Everest: terror and love:
No veil is upon you, no cloud
Doubts the huge hump, mighty monument set on earth,
Harp of the wind, snow-song and avalanche tears,
And tinier tale of men. But men are so proud,
Their mole-story is hill-high. Glorious their one wish absurd
To stand on that cone, one moment enough. Aloud
They recite the story: Changtse, North Col, the tilt
Of slab swinging sky-bound; yellow band thrust in black
And the wicked steps; here, perhaps here they fell,
Those two. And the others went on, gasped and loathed.
The cone still taunts them; storm and the years fret on,
Terror and love remain. Again the men come
Drawn from soft home, comfort and ease, to endure
One spell and be done: suffer, and win a crown,
Memory's store for life. Look then, the south,
An easier slant, one tiny point, and between
Our glasses grip in hot fingers of hope; there, there,

That is our ridge; down still to South Col, joy gone
In the sting of wind on a cheek. Now it is calm,
Now beckons to hope in the afternoon's serene.
The heart-break breath, dim of the eyes, the swing
Of axe upon ice are hard to disravel from beauty's dream,
Dream of a summit, ten thousand feet up, all seen,
And not known.

Everest: terror and love.
We fear and are drawn, love your infinite sides
And loathe our Lilliput crawling. Men we descend,
Conquerors never. So soon has the ant-marked trace
Of our step disappeared. Again quiet reigns,
And the choughs wheel in a world dead once again.
Terror and love are done.

THE CHOUGH

Base Camp in April

Beautifully black, with frilly ruff,
Pecking at the snow is the immortal chough.
Solitude's inhabitant, over the dead
Glacier he wings to lonely bed;
Yet sociable by nature, a friendly bird,
Gracing our company with cries absurd,
Foraging the scum of tea-leaves, abased
To fatten on muck no other will taste.
Are the worms scarce? Or do you prefer
Company of humans as a higher sphere?
Unasked you encourage us; mocking our pain
Fly to twenty thousand and back again
Before we are started; and higher as we climb
You laugh from Pumori at our laggard time,
And again are back—just right for tea,
Cheerful, untired, still fancy-free,
Ready for a bite of whatever may clatter
Down from our tent-site: gobble, gobble, chatter!
You accompanied Norton to heights hard won;
Mallory, perhaps, you saw dragged down,

293

And Herzog dropping the fateful glove.
But here you are, back, as if we were your love!
No story for us of the immortal dead,
Only one vast, oceanic greed.
Such is the chough . . .

ICEFALL

Written at Camp II

Silent stream:
Once a god took note of you,
Struck with his rod, ordered you guardian of treasuries.
Then your voices were stilled, your babble, your slithering
Cool between walls' primeval dream of the valley bed.
Slowly your level rush broke, the great pits
Yawned as your deep waves toppled to motionless,
Yawned as the waters crunched to icy, to cavernous,
Yawned as your lower rush foamy, cascading,
Halted and tangled and stayed. The little waves creamed up
Frothed to a fall. But so slow! Silence and night's shade,
Only these mark the change.
                              Wavelets are pinnacles
Pressed by the silent stream from above to oblivion.
Built for a day, a week, they fall, and confusion
Gapes in the spray of blocks that have once been
Reared with the hugeness of marble, ghost city ruined
At the day's shaft.
                              Still the river creeps onward,
Still in each fringed crevasse the wind of silence
Echoes the trump that once froze. Mortal man pressing
Sees astonished the rift; as once, land-faring,
The Israelites stared, dumb at the parting of waters.

AT CAMP IV, 24,000 FEET

One two three four
Five six seven eight
Steps and my head
Falls a plumb weight.
One breath and two, the picture again
Is a silvered back-cloth
To release from pain.
As breath to the legs,
So ease to the mind,
So joy in the scene
For a cause undefined.
Below, the white table
Of glacier plain,
The toy dot of tents
A human stain.
Above, the steel curve
Of greyest ice,
The blue and black gulf
Of hungry crevasse.
And leaning over
One rocky spire
Bending to watch me—
The world's highest spire.

BREATHLESS

Written at 21,200 feet on May 23rd

Heart aches,
Lungs pant
The dry air
Sorry, scant.
Legs lift
And why at all?
Loose drift,
Heavy fall.
Prod the snow
Its easiest way;
A flat step
Is holiday.
Look up,
The far stone
Is many miles
Far and alone.
Grind the breath
Once more and on;
Don't look up
Till journey's done.
Must look up,
Glasses are dim.
Wrench of hand
Is breathless limb.
Pause one step,
Breath swings back;
Swallow once,
Dry throat is slack.
Then on
To the far stone;
Don't look up,
Count the steps done.
One step,
One heart-beat,
Stone no nearer

Dragging feet.
Heart aches,
Lungs pant
The dry air
Sorry, scant.

THE SOUTH COL

In Retrospect from the Plains

Great hill above
And cloud below;
Reckless of love
The fast winds blow.
But all between
Is space beyond dead;
Spirits unseen
Here make their bed
In blackened rock-rift
And ice rubbed bare,
Crusted snow-drift
That blizzards tear.
Long ago
These were the same,
Never small, never slow,
Never soft, never tame.

What are men here?
What have they done?
A heap of rags here,
Yellow and brown.

Index

INDEX